Six Cultures Series: Volume II

Nyansongo:
A Gusii Community
in Kenya

Six Cultures ✳ Studies of Child Rearing Series

Editor:
Beatrice B. Whiting, *Harvard University*

Senior Investigators
Irwin L. Child, *Yale University*
William W. Lambert, *Cornell University*
John W. M. Whiting, *Harvard University*

VOLUME I

Field Guide for a Study of Socialization

VOLUME II

Nyansongo: A Gusii Community in Kenya
By Robert A. LeVine and Barbara B. LeVine

VOLUME III

The Rājpūts of Khalapur, India
By Leigh Minturn and John T. Hitchcock

VOLUME IV

The Mixtecans of Juxtlahuaca, Mexico
By Kimball Romney and Romaine Romney

VOLUME V

The New Englanders of Orchard Town, U.S.A.
By John L. Fischer and Ann Fischer

VOLUME VI

Tarong: An Ilocos Barrio in the Philippines
By William F. Nydegger and Corinne Nydegger

VOLUME VII

Taira: An Okinawan Village
By Thomas W. Maretzki and Hatsumi Maretzki

Six Cultures Series ❋ Volume II

Nyansongo:
A Gusii Community
in Kenya

Robert A. LeVine
Barbara B. LeVine

John Wiley and Sons, Inc.

New York · London · Sydney

Library of Congress Catalog Card Number: 66-18786
Printed in the United States of America

Introduction

The six monographs in this series report research undertaken in 1954 by a group of social scientists from Harvard, Yale, and Cornell universities. In its broadest conception, the research aimed at exploring cross-culturally the relation between different patterns of child rearing and subsequent differences in personality. The overall research was designed to study the degree to which the experiences of a child in the first years of life determine his behavior and in adult life influence his perception of the world, his philosophy, religion, and code of ethics.

Theories of the relationship between specific types of treatment in early childhood and subsequent personality differences have been advanced by psychologists and anthropologists. This project was established with the hope of being able to test some of these hypotheses using material collected in a standard manner in six parts of the world where families have divergent ways of life and theories and methods of training young children.

The intellectual history of this project begins with the work of Margaret Mead, Ruth Benedict, Edward Sapir, Ralph Linton, Abram Kardiner, John Dollard, and other pioneers in the field of culture and personality whose work formed the foundation of this study. To detail the contribution of these pioneers would demand an essay on the entire new discipline that grew out of the integration of anthropological and psychological theory, an undertaking not practical in this introduction. A brief historical summary by John Whiting appears in the preface to Volume I of this series.

Specifically, the impetus for the present study came from the cross-cultural work on socialization done by two of the senior investigators, John W. M. Whiting and Irvin L. Child, while they were colleagues at the Institute of Human Relations at Yale University. The results of this research were published in *Child Training and Personality* (1953). Using theories of disease as measures of adult personality, the authors attempted to test certain psychological theories relating the treatment of the basic behavior systems in infancy and childhood to adult personality characteristics.

The data on the 75 societies used in these studies were taken from published ethnographies which varied greatly in detail and areas of coverage. The dream of the investigators was to send field teams out to get comparable detailed material on 100 societies. As a first step in accomplishing this aim, the present study was planned.

In 1953 the Committee on Social Behavior of the Social Science Research Council sponsored a seminar* and a conference† to discuss cross-cultural work on socialization. As a result, the *Field Manual for the Cross-Cultural Study of Child Rearing* was prepared (Whiting et al., 1953), and Whiting and Child persuaded William W. Lambert of Cornell University to join them in seeking funds to conduct a comparative study of child rearing. A generous grant from the Behavioral Science Division of the Ford Foundation made it possible to carry out these plans. The fieldwork and part of the analysis and writing of five of the six reports in this volume were financed by this grant. Later analysis and editing were supported by a grant from the United States Public Health Service.

Intensive planning for the study was carried on at Cornell, Harvard, and Yale during the following year under the direction of the senior investigators, William W. Lambert, Irvin L. Child, and John W. M. Whiting. As part of the over-all research plan, further cross-cultural studies were undertaken at Cornell, Harvard, and Yale. Irvin Child, with the assistance of Margaret Bacon and Herbert Barry, investigated the consequences of various types of training on nurturance, responsibility, obedience, self-reliance, and achievement using ethnographic accounts for cross-cultural comparison (Bacon, Child, and Barry, 1963; Barry, Bacon, and Child, 1957; Barry, Child, and Bacon, 1959). William Lambert and Leigh Minturn did further cross-cultural work on aggres-

---

* The contributing members of the seminar were Barbara Chartier Ayers, Hildreth Geertz, George Goethals, Charles Holzinger, Edgar Lowell, Eleanor E. Maccoby, A. Kimball Romney, Richard Salisbury, William Steward, and John W. Thibaut.

† Attending the conference were Robert R. Sears (Chairman), A. L. Baldwin, R. A. Bauer, Irvin L. Child, L. S. Cottrell, Jr., Leon Festinger, J. G. Gewirtz, A. Inkeles, Harry Levin, Gardner Lindzey, Eleanor E. Maccoby, Carson McGuire, G. P. Murdock, B. Paul, John M. Roberts, R. R. Sarbin, Pauline S. Sears, M. Brewster Smith, R. L. Solomon, John W. Thibaut, and John W. M. Whiting.

sion (Lambert, Triandis, and Wolf, 1959; Triandis and Lambert, 1961), and John Whiting worked on measures of guilt and other mechanisms of internalized controls (Burton and Whiting, 1961).

During June and July of 1954, a Social Science Research Council Summer Conference was held at the Laboratory of Human Development at Harvard. All the research personnel, with the aid of David Aberle of Michigan, Alfred Baldwin and James J. Gibson of Cornell, and Robert Sears of Stanford, wrote the *Field Guide for a Study of Socialization in Five Societies.** This guide appears as Volume 1 of the six culture series. It presents in detail the research plan, the hypotheses to be tested, and the research instruments agreed on by the field teams and the senior investigators. The reader should study this volume in order to understand the content and organization of the monographs and the methods employed in data collection. The theoretical background and the intellectual history of the project are presented in the preface by John W. M. Whiting.†

The five original field teams started work in the fall of 1954 and spent from 6 to 14 months in the field. Although the original design of the study called for a sample of societies whose culture had already been studied by ethnologists, the temperament and motivation of young anthropologists were such that they tended to choose groups who are relatively unknown and who, often from some personal reason, appealed to their interests. The actual groups chosen represent a compromise between the advantages of previous coverage and these personal interests, and also provide the great range of differences desired by the project planners.

Thomas and Hatsumi Maretzki chose the village of Taira on the northeast coast of Okinawa, the largest of the Ryukyu Islands in the Pacific. At the time, Thomas Maretzki was an advanced graduate student in the Anthropology Department at Yale University. Hatsumi Maretzki, a graduate of the University of Hawaii, was on the staff of the Gesell Institute Nursery School. Thomas Maretzki is now an associate professor of anthropology at the University of Hawaii.

Leigh Minturn worked with a group of families of the Rājpūt caste in the town of Khalapur in Uttar Pradesh in northern India. Unmarried at the time of the study, she used the facilities of Morris Opler's Cornell field station in Khalapur which then was directed by John Hitchcock, who collaborated with her in the study. Leigh Min-

---

* Published in mimeographed form by the Laboratory of Human Development, Harvard University, 1954.

† See also, Lambert, W. W., 1960.

turn received her doctorate from the Social Relations Department of Radcliffe College and Harvard University, and was, at the time of the study, a research associate at Cornell University. She is now an associate professor of psychology at the University of Illinois. John Hitchcock received his doctorate in anthropology from Cornell University and is at present an associate professor of anthropology at University of California, Los Angeles.

William and Corinne Nydegger chose a group of Ilocano-speaking families living in hamlets in northern Luzon in the Philippines. At the time of the study, William Nydegger was an advanced graduate student at Cornell University. His wife had done graduate work in anthropology at the University of Wisconsin. William Nydegger is now an associate professor of anthropology at Pennsylvania State University.

A. Kimball and Romaine Romney chose a group of families in the Mixtecan barrio of Santo Domingo in the town of Juxtlahuaca in Oaxaca State, Mexico. At the time of the study, A. Kimball Romney was an advanced graduate student at Harvard University. His wife attended the University of Colorado. A. Kimball Romney is now an associate professor of anthropology at Stanford University.

John and Ann Fischer agreed to take on the task of establishing bench marks for comparison by studying a group of mothers in the United States. They moved into a neighborhood in Orchard Town in New England. John Fischer, who has a doctorate in social relations from Harvard University, was at the time of the study an assistant professor at Harvard and his wife Ann was an advanced graduate student in anthropology. John Fischer is at present a professor of anthropology at Tulane University and his wife is an associate professor of anthropology at the same university. When they undertook the study, the Fischers had just returned from three years in the Caroline Islands in the Pacific where John Fischer had served as district anthropologist and as native affairs officer on the islands of Truk and Ponape in Micronesia. During this time, Ann Fischer was gathering material on child rearing in Truk; on the basis of this work she received her doctorate from Harvard.

In 1955 a sixth team, Robert and Barbara LeVine, left for Kenya, Africa where they studied a group of homesteads in the Kisii Highlands of South Nyanza District. They were financed by a Ford Foundation fellowship and a National Science Foundation predoctoral fellowship. At the time of the study Robert LeVine was an advanced graduate student in the department of social relations at Harvard University. Barbara LeVine was a graduate student of psychology at

Boston University. She subsequently received a doctorate in social psychology from Northwestern University. Now Barbara Lloyd, she is a lecturer in social psychology at the University of Birmingham in England. Robert LeVine is at present an associate professor of anthropology in the Committee on Human Development, University of Chicago.

To help insure comparability of data, a central clearing house was set up at the Laboratory of Human Development under the supervision of Beatrice B. Whiting, a Yale-trained anthropologist who was a research associate at the Laboratory of Human Development at Harvard. Field notes were mailed in periodically and field problems were discussed by correspondence.

The research design, agreed on by all the field teams, was set up to measure as accurately as possible the child-training practices and the hypothesized individual and cultural differences in personality, especially in the areas of aggression, dependency, and the internalization of various mechanisms of behavior control—areas of special theoretical interest to the senior investigators at Cornell, Yale, and Harvard universities, respectively. Previous research had been done in these areas at the Institute of Human Relations at Yale, at the Iowa Child Welfare Station under the direction of Robert Sears, and subsequently at the Laboratory of Human Development at Harvard University. The research conducted at Iowa and Harvard focused on a study of individual differences among groups of mothers and children in Iowa, Massachusetts, and in three different cultural groups in the Southwest (Sears, Whiting, Nowlis, and Sears, 1953; Whiting, Chasdi, Antonovsky, and Ayres, in press).

In designing the field research reported in this volume, an attempt has been made to assess individual as well as cultural differences. This is one of the unique aspects of the design. The hope was to test hypotheses about the relations of child-rearing practices and consequent personality, both intraculturally and cross-culturally. In the first instance, 24 mothers in each society were studied as individuals in their relationship to one of their children, and each of the 24 children (ages 3 to 10) was observed and interviewed in a standard manner in the hope of detecting behavioral and personality differences. (The mother interviews, child interviews, child T.A.T.'s, and the description of the observations of the children used in the study can be found in Chapter 5 of the *Field Guide for the Study of Socialization*.) The cross-cultural measures included material on child-training practices and also religious beliefs, theories of disease, recreational activities, and so on, collected by standard ethnographic techniques. The outlines for studying these are to be found in Chapter 2 of the *Field Guide for the Study of Socialization*.

A word should be said here about the nature of the social unit each field team chose to study. It was decided to choose a group large enough to yield an adequate sample of individual families. For our design this meant that a group of at least 50 families would be needed to draw our sample of 24, since at least half the families would have grown-up children, children under 3, or no children at all. On the other hand, we wanted a group who knew each other and shared beliefs, values, and practices so that it would be possible to use ethnographic techniques in collecting data and in describing certain aspects of the daily life in cultural terms. The techniques used to locate the Primary Social Unit (P.S.U.) are described in detail in the *Field Guide for the Study of Socialization,* Chapter 6.

In Taira, Okinawa, the Maretzkis visited 63 households in the central part of town and recorded the relationships among the occupants and their kin. The census included about 330 individuals, 83 of which were children under the age of 11.

In Khalapur, India, Leigh Minturn gathered census material in 38 courtyards; all were owned by members of the Rājpūt caste who constitute 40% of the total population of 5000. The courtyards are in a neighborhood inhabited exclusively by members of the Rājpūt caste; the area is bounded on two sides by a river and fields and is separated from the rest of the town on the third side by a temple, school, and meeting house and by a street occupied by another caste group, and on the fourth by a patti division line. (Khalapur is divided into seven political units or pattis.)

In Juxtlahuaca, a town of 3600, the Romneys made a census of 31 courtyards in the Mixtecan barrio of Santo Domingo. This section is separated from the rest of the town, which is inhabited by Spanish-speaking ladinos, by a deep barranca. The census of 31 courtyards included 90 children under 11 years of age.

In Orchard Town, population 5000, a census was made of 42 households, most of them on three adjoining streets in North Village, which has a population of 1000 and is one of the three centers of the town. The families participated together in P.T.A., school functions, women's clubs, and church, as well as in local politics. There were 83 children under 11 in the sample.

In the barrio of Tarong, Luzon, it was necessary to make a census of six adjacent hamlets before a sample of 24 children of the right age could be drawn. The barrio encompasses an area of about two square miles of land crosscut by steep ridges and valleys. The hamlets consisted of from 3 to 17 families. The sample was drawn from 58 families who had 76 children under 11 years of age. The genealogical material collected by the Nydeggers indicates that all but six of the 61 families in the barrio were descended from seven families who settled the area around 1860 (Minturn and Lambert, 1964, p. 18).

In Nyansongo, 18 contiguous homesteads were visited. The families in these homesteads all belong to one clan, and neighboring homesteads often belong to the same patrilineage. The census from which the sample was drawn included 208 individuals of whom 92 were children under 11.

In each of the six societies all the families knew each other and associated at certain times during the year and presumably met our criterion of sharing basic cultural values. If I were to judge the societies on the degree of intimacy of the mothers of the total P.S.U., I would rank the families in Taira as most intimate and those in Juxtlahuaca second. In the other societies there is intimacy in subgroups but not in the entire P.S.U. Although the Khalapur families live close to one another, the women are confined to courtyards, and most of their everyday contacts are limited to women in the same block who can be visited by crossing roof tops.

Women in groups of homesteads in Nyansongo are members of cooperative work teams and hence are on intimate terms with one another. There were three such work groups in the sample. The members of each belonged to the same subclan. Hamlet groups in Tarong are very intimate, especially when families face on the same yard. Visiting, kin ties, and a central school all unite the members of the P.S.U.

The Orchard Town mothers seem to be the least intimate in the sample, although they knew one another by name and knew the names of one another's children.

The P.S.U. groups are defined and selected to maximize the homogeneity which is essential for the use of standard ethnographic techniques. In gathering the background material and much of the material on socialization, the field teams used informants and participant observation. In areas that were not covered by standardized instruments, the data presented in the ethnographies is often based on a combination of discussion with from four to eight informants checked by observation of the daily life of the group. All the field teams lived in the communities they studied for the better part of a year or longer. Three of the field teams had children who played with the sample children. All the ethnographers visited the houses daily, participated in community activities, and became socialized in the habits of the group.

For the individual measures, 24 children were selected from the census material sent in by the field teams according to the following criteria: the sample consisted of four sex-age groups, six boys and six girls from 3-to-5 years of age and an equal number from 7-to-10 years of age.* To maximize the independence of cases, no more than one child was selected from each family. The sample mothers were interviewed and the children interviewed and observed in a standard manner for 12 five-minute periods.

Implicit in the research design is a general concept of the relation of personality to culture, which may be presented as follows: the ecology of an area determines the maintenance systems, which include basic economy and the most elementary variables of social structure. In other words, the type of crops grown, the presence or absence of herding, fishing, and so on, depend on the nature of the terrain, the temperature and amount of rainfall, and the location of the area *vis-à-vis* centers of invention and diffusion. These basic conditions partly determine the arrangement of people in space, the type of houses, and household composition. These in turn set the limits for child-rearing practices. The basic innate needs of both children and parents must be met within this framework.

It is obvious that ecology does no more than determine gross limits for the social structure. Within these limits the nature of the composition of households, neighborhoods, and other social groups will lead to variance in child training. Whether or not a grandmother lives in the house, or whether other relatives are close at hand, will influence a mother's behavior toward her child.

We assume that different patterns of child rearing will lead to differences in the personality of children and thus to differences in adult personality. Since personality may only be inferred, the problem of measurement is difficult on both the individual and the cultural levels. Individual children may be given tests of various kinds, interviewed, or observed. On a cultural level, we may analyze the patterning of child or adult behavior, for example, the games and recreational activity, the rituals or ceremonial life, or we may assess beliefs about the supernatural, theories of disease, or popular folk tales in terms of personality dimensions.

---

* The LeVines' sample was aberrant. They studied six sex-age groups consisting of four children each. They included a group 10-to-14 years of age since they wanted to follow the children through initiation. The Romneys' sample of older children was limited to five girls and five boys 7-to-10 years old.

Chart I indicates this conceptual system in a simple manner. To summarize the conceptual background in another way, the researchers viewed ecology, economics, and social and political organization as largely determining the behavior of the agents of child rearing. They viewed child behavior as an index of child personality and saw adult behavior, beliefs, and values as indices of adult personality. The causal relationships implied in this scheme are open to discussion. Such discussions, with the knowledge available at present, ultimately end with a problem similar to that of the priority of the chicken or the egg.

A word should be said about the type of ecology and economy represented in the sample. Five of the six cultures are agricultural. There are no fishing or hunting and gathering economies, nor are there pastoral people. With the exception of Orchard Town, most of the men in the six societies are farmers. In Tarong, Philippines and in Taira, Okinawa, the most important staple crop is wet rice. In Juxtlahuaca, Mexico and in Nyansongo, Kenya, corn is the important staple. In the latter, eleusine, a grain, is also important. In Khalapur, wheat and other grains are the main food crops.

Chart I   The Relation of Personality to Culture

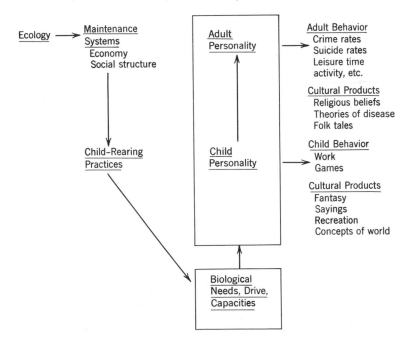

The ecology of the areas, however, makes the farming techniques different: in Taira and Tarong, men and women work together in the fields; in Khalapur and Juxtlahuaca only men work in the fields; in Nyansongo, with the exception of ploughing and building fences, all the agricultural work is done by women. An important variable in determining the amount of agricultural work women do is the distance of the gardens and fields from the dwellings. The gardens are closest in Nyansongo and Tarong, furthest away in Juxtlahuaca and Khalapur. Every Nyansongo woman has gardens close to her house, and she and a group of women who are members of her cooperative work group are responsible for all the gardening. In Tarong the fields and paddies lie directly below the houses which are built on the ridges. The town Juxtlahuaca is situated in a long, narrow river valley. Most of the cornfields near the town and in the valley belong to the ladinos in the Mexican part of town. The Mixtecans' main fields are usually a half-hour walk from home on the slopes of the mountains which follow the river valley. Women do not work in the fields in Juxtlahuaca. Clearing the mountain gardens is done by cutting the trees and undergrowth and burning it off, a technique called slash and burn agriculture. Khalapur is surrounded by fields that are a 15-to-20-minute walk from the courtyards. As in Juxtlahuaca, the Rājpūt women do not work in the fields; however, their enforced seclusion as married women would make such work impossible even if the fields were closer by. In Taira the rice paddies are also on the outskirts of the town. They are closer at hand, however, than are the fields in Khalapur and Juxtlahuaca, although not so close as are the paddies in Tarong. Both the Tarong and Taira women help in the fields, although it is my impression that the Taira women spend more time working in the gardens than the Tarong women do. It is interesting to note that, in the five agricultural societies, the women do more gardening work when the gardens are nearby. It also appears that in rice cultures women are especially good at transplanting the young shoots, a backbreaking and fussy job which requires manual dexterity and patience. Women do not work when slash and burn techniques are use. In all the five societies, men do whatever plowing is done. Buffaloes are used as draft animals in Khalapur, India, the carabao in Tarong, Philippines, and oxen in Juxtlahuaca, Mexico and in Nyansongo, Africa. In Taira, Okinawa there are few large animals. Because Nyansongo families cannot afford to hire ploughs, the women prepare the soil with hoes.

If the model of the influence of the maintenance systems on child rearing is correct, the amount of time and effort women exert in agricultural work is one of the several ecological and economic variables which influence their child-training techniques. The amount of time the fathers spend in the agricultural work and the distance of the fields from the house will influence the amount of time men spend around the house and the amount of time the children see them. The majority of the families in Nyansongo in Kenya, in Tarong in the Philippines, and in Khalapur, India have large animals which must be watered and pastured. There are no adequate fences in any of these three societies, so humans must see that the cattle do not get into crops. This is done either by tethering the animals, the technique employed by the Tarongans, or by employing a herd boy when the cows are in pasture, the technique used by the Nyansongo and by the Rājpūts of Khalapur. The latter keep the cattle in pens adjoining the courtyards for much of the day and bring fodder into town. The Nyansongo shut the cattle up only at night. During the day, young boys or occasionally younger girls tend the herds. Where the herding technique is used, children are important in the economy and their negligence may ruin the crops essential for the food supply. As a consequence, training in responsibility is early and irresponsibility is severely punished.* Although there are sheep, goats, and burros in Juxtlahuaca, only a few of the families in the sample owned these animals. Here also herdboys are used.

Besides doing whatever agricultural work is expected, some of the women are involved in other economic pursuits. Most of the sample mothers in Taira helped their husbands in lumbering, carrying faggots down from the mountains and bundling them for sale. Some of the Juxtlahuacan mothers cooked for the markets. Some of the Tarongan and Nyansongo women occasionally sold surplus vegetables in the markets. In Orchard Town some women worked outside the home at wage-earning jobs. Only the Rājpūt women had no possible way of earning money.

In sum, the amount of work, excluding child care and housework, required of women varies with the economy and ecology. The Nyansongo women have the heaviest work load, the Orchard Town and Rājpūt mothers the lightest. The Taira and Tarong women seem to rank second and third in economic work load, the Juxtlahuaca fourth. The burden of housework and child care also varies. Here comparisons are difficult, and there are several factors that should be considered. Technological development in the processing of food and in the procurement of water and fuel is one of the determinants of the number

---

* See Barry, Child, and Bacon, 1959 for a discussion of responsibility training in economies having large animals. The authors interpret the relationship in terms of the amount of property accumulated and owned by members of a society.

of hours a woman spends in cooking and cleaning. For example, the women in Tarong, Philippines, must pound their own rice whereas the women in Taira take theirs to a mill to be processed. Both the Rājpūt women of Khalapur and the Juxtlahuacan women spend long hours preparing grain for cooking. The Orchard Town mother certainly has the easiest lot in this domain; furthermore, she alone has water and fuel readily available in her kitchen.

A second factor that must be considered is the availability of help. As will be described later, in the kin-based hamlet groups in Tarong, Philippines, in the extended family courtyards in Juxtlahuaca, Mexico, and in Khalapur, India, and in the stem family households in Taira, Okinawa, other adult women are available to help with the daily routine of living. In the Nyansongo homestead, there may be co-wives and mothers-in-law within shouting distance. It should be noted, however, that the degree to which women help each other when they live close by and are related varies. In our sample, the closest cooperation between women occurs in Tarong, Philippines; here the kin group is often bilateral and a woman has her own relatives as well as her husband's close at hand. Similarly, in Juxtlahuaca a woman may have her own relatives nearby to help. Affinal relatives seem to be less predictably helpful. In Khalapur the mothers report that they receive little or no help from their sisters- and mothers-in-law, although these relatives are at hand in emergencies.*

In Nyansongo homesteads the cooperation between co-wives varies with the personality, with the difference in age of the wives, and with the executive ability of the husband. It appears that when the second wife is considerably younger than the senior wife, there is more likely to be cooperation. Most Nyansongo mothers, however, use children, usually siblings or cousins, between the ages of 5 and 8 to take over the care of their infants, and these children are the constant companions of their little charges until they can walk and travel with the rest of the children. The Taira mother who is lucky enough to have a mother-in-law or her own mother living in the house receives help with the daily care of her infant. The Orchard Town mother, in contrast to the mothers in the other five societies, has the least help. She can hire baby-sitters, but in general she seldom does so. Even when her own mother or her husband's mother lives in the same town, or even next door, she is not in the habit of asking them to do more than occasional baby-sitting.

---

* It should be noted that the Rājpūt mothers have outside help from sweepers, washers, and water carriers who do some of the daily housework.

Even in child care, however, it should be noted that technological development is important. In our sample, for example, only the Orchard Town mother has a baby carriage. In all the other societies infants must be carried, and children are used in lieu of carriages. Similarly, there are no playpens or high chairs to confine the infant safely while the mother works.

Still a further dimension of comparison is the degree of loneliness of mothers. It is here that the Orchard Town mother is unique: she spends most of her day in the company of her children, isolated from other adults. This is especially true in winter, when it is an effort to bundle up the family and go on a visit.

Associated with loneliness is boredom, and here the Orchard Town mother is similar to the Rājpūt mother in Khalapur who is confined to the courtyard day after day. Both enjoy seeing and talking to someone new and look forward to any breaks in the monotony of the daily routine. Although the Rājpūt mothers usually have adult companionship, they cannot wander downtown or break the monotony either by watching people interact on television or by reading about them in books.

As suggested earlier, the climate influences daily living routine and arrangements in many ways. Children react to excessive heat and cold and grow restive if continuous rains confine them to the dwelling. In all the societies there are days when the temperature is uncomfortably cool (see Chart II). During November through March children may feel cold in the early morning in Juxtlahuaca, Mexico. In June, July, August, and September the nights may be uncomfortably cool in Nyansongo, Kenya. In both of these societies and in Khalapur, India, winter nights probably seem colder than they actually are because of the diurnal variation which averages over 25 degrees. Orchard Town, U.S.A., has by far the most prolonged period of cold and the most days with temperatures that drop below freezing. However, it has insulated buildings and central heating; the children have special winter clothes and hence probably suffer less from the cold than any of the other children in the sample. On the other hand, the Orchard Town mother has to struggle with snowsuits and boots and would often rather stay home than face the task of dressing and undressing children and walking or driving through the snow and ice. She is afraid to leave her children at home alone, even for short periods of time, lest faulty heating equipment set fire to the house. During the winter months the radio broadcasts almost daily the names of small children who have burned to death in their homes. The seasonal contrast in the routine of living is greater in Orchard Town than in any of the other societies.

Chart II *Climatic Conditions for the Six Societies*[a]

SOCIETY	NYANSONGO	JUXTLA-HUACA	KHALAPUR	ORCHARD TOWN	TARONG	TAIRA
Weather Station	Eldoret	Mexico City	New Delhi	Boston	Aparri	Naha
Observed Period	1930–1945	not given	1866–1943	1870–1949	1928–1937	1891–1935
Temperature						
Hottest month	March	April	June	July	April	July
Absolute high	85°	90°	115°	104°	101°	96°
Daily Range	79–50°	77–51°	102–83°	80–63°	90–73°	89–77°
Coldest month	December	January	January	February	December	February
Absolute low	37°	27°	31°	−18°	59°	41°
Daily Range	76–49°	66–42°	70–44°	37–21°	81–70°	67–55°
Precipitation						
Average yearly fall	40.5 in.	29.4 in.	25.2 in.	40.8 in.	89.5 in.	82.8 in.
Number of months with more than 14 days of rain	3	5	0	0	3	0
Number of months with fewer than 7 days of rain	5	4	10	0	2	0

[a] The material for this table is taken from a report of the Meteorological Office of the British Air Ministry, 1960. The weather stations with the nearest latitude and altitude to the field site were selected.

The sharpest contrast in the weather occurs in Khalapur, where the long periods of heat and drought make the rains in June, July, and August dramatic. Although the actual number of rainy days, even during these months is few (average eight days), the winds that accompany the rains and the intense heat which precedes them in April and May make the seasonal variation striking.

In the other societies it rains frequently throughout the year. But a rainy day ordinarily confines children to their houses only in Orchard Town where precipitation during two-thirds of the year may be accompanied by cold weather. Orchard Town children tend to associate rain with being forced to stay indoors. The rainy season in Juxtlahuaca, which lasts from June through September, can be cold and unpleasant. It rains over 20 days in each of these months and 27 days in two of them (July and August), and the temperature during the same period often falls below 50 degrees. The rainfall, however, is usually a drizzle and does not seem to upset the daily routine so much as the infrequent downpours in Khalapur.

Ecology and economy affect the life of children and their parents in another important way—they partly determine the arrangement of dwellings. The number of people who live in a household, the number of generations which interact daily, the distance between households, and the nature and amount of shared work and play space are factors that influence both the training of a child and his daily experiences.

Chart III shows the composition of households in the six societies. It can be seen that half of the households in Taira, Okinawa include at least one grandparent. It is customary for one son, preferably the oldest, to stay on after his marriage to care for his parents. In Khalapur, India, the majority of the households consist of a man and a woman and their married sons and children or married brothers and their children. In Nyansongo, Kenya, half of the men are polygynists and their wives have separate huts.

Chart III also indicates the average number of adult males, females, and children per household, the extended courtyards in Khalapur having the most people, Orchard Town the fewest. Note that the houses in Nyansongo may have only a woman if her husband is a polygynist who rotates between the huts of his wives. The households have, however, on an average as many children as the extended families in Khalapur. In sum, Nyansongo women have more children than any of the other women in the sample.

Chart IV gives the frequency of the groups whose houses face on an area which the occupants use in common. For the Nyansongo it indicates the people who share a homestead (the people included in these

Chart III *Household Composition*

	TAIRA	TARONG	KHALAPUR	JUXTLAHUACA	ORCHARD TOWN	NYANSONGO
Nuclear Husband, wife and child. May include siblings of husband or wife	11	19	8	18	23	6
Stem Nuclear family plus 1 or 2 parents of husband or wife	12	3	3	3	1	0
Stem plus Married Brother or married cousins. May include parents' siblings	0	0	7	0	0	0
Extended Lineal Nuclear family plus married children and/or married brothers and/or cousins and their children	1	2	6	0	0	0
Polygynous One wife and her children per house	0	0	0	0	0	8
Other	0	0	0	1	0	2
Average number of adult males	1.3	1.4	2.6	1.3	1.0	.87
Average number of adult females	1.8	1.7	2.4	1.2	1.0	1.0
Average number of children	3.5	3.5	5.7	4.0	2.8	5.8

Chart IV Courtyard Composition of Groups Larger than the Household Sharing Intimate Space

	TAIRA	TARONG	KHALAPUR	JUXTLAHUACA	ORCHARD TOWN	NYANSONGO
Households Do not share a yard with another household	23	5	21	5	21	4[a]
Stem Share a yard with one or both parents of husband or wife (who have their own house)	1	3	0	3	3	0
Extended Share a yard with parents of husband or wife and/or aunt or uncle plus married brothers and/or sisters and/or married cousins of husband or wife	0	12	0	6	0	1
Collateral Share a yard with brothers and/or sisters of husband or wife	0	3	0	6	0	0
Collateral Extended Share a yard with married brothers and/or sisters and married children and/or married nephews and nieces of husband and/or wife	0	0	3[b]	2	0	0
Non-kin Share a yard with non-kin	0	1	0	0	0	0
Polygynous Co-wives share a yard	0	0	0	0	0	6
Extended Polygynous Share a yard with married brothers of husband plus husband's parents and/or husband's mothers co-wives and married half brothers	0	0	0	0	0	5
Average number of adult males	1.4	3.2	2.9	2.9	1.1	2.1
Average number of adult females	1.8	4.3	2.6	3.0	1.2	3.2
Average number of children	3.9	7.9	5.9	6.7	2.8	7.1
Total	7.1	15.4	11.4	12.6	5.1	12.4

[a] Includes one polygynous homestead where huts of two wives are far apart and there is tension between the wives.
[b] Includes married first cousins and their children.

units interact daily in an intimate fashion). In Juxtlahuaca the houses face on a private courtyard; in Tarong they surround a yard. Tarong has the greatest number of people who interact on this level of intimacy, and Juxtlahuaca and Nyansongo units are similar in size. Taira and Orchard Town have, on an average, two fewer adults per unit.

As mentioned earlier, the household and dwelling units partly determine the amount of adult help a mother has in raising her children. Our theoretical paradigm suggests, then, that the combined factors of a mother's economic role and the people with whom she lives influence her patterns of child rearing. The first test of hypotheses related to this paradigm are presented in *Mothers of Six Cultures* by Leigh Minturn and William Lambert (1964). Further tests of the hypotheses will appear in a forthcoming volume on the behavior of the children.

The salience of the father in infancy and childhood is another variable that affects the personality development of the society. For a discussion of the relative salience of the father and hypothesized consequent effects on aggressive behavior, see Beatrice Whiting's "Sex Identity and Crimes of Violence: a Comparative study."

Six of the volumes in this series are monographs of each of the six societies. The outline for each is organized around the conceptual system just presented. There are two main parts: one, a description of the adult world into which the child is born—*the ethnographic background*; the second, an account of how the child is trained—*child training*. In Part I, each account starts with a description of the environment and the local setting, including the village plan, the houses, and their interior arrangements. Then the daily routine of living and the economic pursuits of men and women are described. A chapter on social structure follows. In other words, these chapters describe the maintenance system that set the stage for child rearing. The selection of material for the remainder of Part I is also theoretically determined and includes descriptions of either adult behavior or the cultural products that seem to be the best indices of adult personality.

To explain the selection of behavior and cultural products, we must return to the discussion of the dimensions of personality selected for study by the senior investigators. As noted, the hypotheses to be tested focused on aggression, dependency, and the internalization of various mechanisms of behavior control. William Lambert and the Cornell group, because of previous research, were most interested in aggression, Irvin Child in dependency, and John Whiting and the Laboratory of Human Development in the development of internal controls that have been variously labeled as guilt, conscience, and superego.

It was the conviction of the researchers that the areas of study had to be limited and clearly defined if standardized material was to be collected. Chapter 1 of the *Field Guide for the Study of Socialization* is a description of the "systems" of behavior which were chosen for study and the hypotheses which the investigators hoped to test. Although it is impossible to include a detailed description of the theory in this introduction, it is necessary to present at least a summary of the behavior systems and the nature of the hypotheses.*

The nine behavioral systems include succorance, nurturance, self-reliance, achievement, responsibility, obedience, dominance, sociability, and aggression. In the most general terms, succorance is defined as asking others for help; nurturance, as giving help or emotional support; self-reliance, as doing things for oneself; achievement, as striving to meet internal standards of excellence; responsibility, as performing one's expected role duties; obedience, as attempting to meet the demands of others; dominance, as attempting to change the behavior of others; sociability, as making friendly approaches to other individuals; aggression, as hurting others. It was assumed that each of these systems of behavior would exist in some recognizable form and degree in every society and could best be identified by people's responses to specific universal situations. For example, whether an individual who encountered difficulty asked for help or solved the problem himself would indicate the relative strength of his succorance or, in contrast, his self-reliance. A measure of nurturance would be the frequency of the spontaneous giving of help, the reaction to requests for help, or the perception that others need help.

Returning to the monographs, our descriptions of the adult culture of each society include material which we consider relevant to these nine behavior systems.

A chapter on social control is included in each monograph to give information about the frequency of brawls, fights, crimes, and other conflicts and to describe the techniques which the society has devised either for preventing such conflicts from occurring or for stopping existing conflict. This material gives comparative indices of the expressed aggression of the adults and the existence and type of internalized controls. It will be noted, for example, that the incidence of rape is high in Nyansongo, that litigation is frequent in Khalapur and Nyansongo, and that there are few cases of physical violence in either Taira or Juxtlahuaca.

* For a full discussion of behavior systems see Child (1954).

The chapter on medical practices and theories of disease is included because variations in such belief systems were found to be useful indices of personality in the cross-cultural study by Whiting and Child (1953) and in later studies by Whiting (1959). Similarly, the analysis of man's relation to the supernatural was fruitfully analyzed by Spiro and D'Andrade (1958), Whiting (1959), and Lambert, Triandis, and Wolf (1959). Mourning behavior and death ceremonies have also been studied cross-culturally (Friendly, 1956).

We hoped that an analysis of the use of leisure time might be made along dimensions relevant to the nine behavior systems. The man who prefers to be alone in his spare time would be rated less sociable than one who always seeks the company of others. The amount of teasing or playful wrestling in leisure settings, or even the amount of pleasure derived from cockfights, might be used to rate the degree of preoccupation with aggression. The amount of time spent practicing skills might indicate the need for achievement. Whether or not men seek the company of women, men and women, or only men is of interest in assessing personality. Similarly, we might rate a man's personality in terms of his preference for smoking, eating, talking, drinking, dancing, or playing games. The nature of popular games can be analyzed along lines suggested by Roberts, Bush, and Arth (1957).

Part II of the ethnographies is chronologically organized, beginning with pregnancy and childbirth and continuing through preadolescence. The time required to observe this age span made it impractical to systematically study the lives of the adolescent children. The only exception to this is the monograph on the Nyansongo group in Kenya. The LeVines were especially interested in the effect of initiation ceremonies on the Nyansongo boys and girls. For this reason, they selected three age groups for study: the 3-to-7-year-olds, the 7-to-10-year-olds, and the post-initiation boys and girls. The Nydeggers included a brief chapter on adolescence in their monograph on Tarong. The other field teams did not feel that they had enough knowledge to include such a description.

The age span covered in the individual chapters of the six descriptions of socialization differs; each division is made on the basis of the age groups and the transitions recognized by the members of the society. Thus in Khalapur, India, where socialization is not broken by clearly defined stages, there are only three chapters. In Taira, Okinawa, on the other hand, there are named stages and sharp transitions, and the Maretzkis have followed this pattern in describing socialization. Weaning from the breast and back is an abrupt change in an Okinawan child's life. The transition from kindergarten to school age is also clear and dramatic. Before reaching school age a child is "senseless" according to the mothers and cannot be properly trained.

Within these chapters an attempt has been made to cover the treatment of the nine behavior systems by the parent or parent surrogate and to study the child's response to socialization. Obviously, some of the behavior systems are not relevant in infancy. In general, the early chapters in the socialization section concentrate on the handling of succorance, the mother's early contact with the child, the number of other individuals who share in the early care of the child, and their responsiveness to the demands of the infant. Among the hypotheses advanced in the *Field Guide for the Study of Socialization,* several concern the consequence of indulgence in infancy. As stated: "Indulgence in infancy, a large number of nurturing agents, and mild transition from infantile indulgence into childhood will produce (1) a trustful attitude toward others, (2) general optimism, and (3) sociability." It is also stated that training with respect to succorance will tend to influence sociability.

We hope that, on the basis of the information presented in the chapters on infancy, the reader can compare the degree of indulgence in infancy and the number of nurturing agents. A comparison of weaning from the breast and from complete dependence on caretakers should make it possible to evaluate the severity of the transition. For the consequent measures, we may turn either to the description of the behavior of older children or to the behavior and belief systems of adults. Is it true that the Mixtecan child of Juxtlahuaca is comparatively more friendly and sociable in later life than the Nyansongan? In infancy, the Mixtecan is constantly held or carried close to the mother's body, and she responds relatively quickly to the infant's demands. The Nyansongon child is tended for periods of time by a less consistently responsive 5-to-8-year-old child. In adult life, are Mixtecans more optimistic and trustful than the Nyansongans?

With the onset of weaning, other behavior systems become important. Training for self-reliance and the associated punishment for succorance are universal problems, but the degree to which this new behavior is expected of 3-year-olds varies from one society to another. The Orchard Town 3-year-old is feeding and dressing himself, whereas the Khalapur Rājpūt child of the same age may still be dressed and fed by his mother. Similarly, as mentioned earlier, the abruptness of the shift in expected behavior varies. The handling of aggression against parents, siblings, and peers at this age-level is also a universal problem which all parents and socializers must face. Probably closely associated with this behavior system is training for obedience and respect.

The *Field Guide for the Study of Socialization* contains many hypotheses about the antecedents of aggressive behavior in children and adults and stresses the techniques used by parents in the handling of aggression as well as their behavior as models. Specifically, one hypothesis is that permissiveness on the part of parents for teasing behavior should be reflected in the increase of observable unprovoked aggressive behavior on the part of children and adults. Is it indeed true that the Tarongan child who is "playfully" teased by his parents and other adults from early childhood instigates aggressive behavior more frequently than a Rājpūt child whose parents do not "playfully" tease him?

A second hypothesis concerning the handling of aggression states that children will be less likely to retaliate against aggression if parents and socializing agents punish any expression of anger. Again, the Khalapur Rājpūt child whose mother dislikes all expression of emotion, even excessive joy, and the Mixtecan child of Juxtlahuaca who is taught that he will become sick and die if he eats while he is angry should be less aggressive when provoked than the children of Orchard Town.* It will be noted that a distinction is made between unprovoked and provoked aggression. A further distinction is made for instrumental aggression, when a person tends to select aggressive means for attaining his goals. Comparisons between the handling of aggression in childhood may also be used to explore hypotheses about the conditions that lead to the displacement of aggression to others, the use of fantasy to express anger, or the projection of one's own desires to hurt others. For an understanding of consequent measures, the reader may turn to theories of diseases and the nature of the supernatural. Theory predicts that the societies which punish aggression most severely project their anger into the supernatural world and believe in dangerous and malevolent beings or attribute superhuman evil capacity to humans and believe in sorcery or witchcraft. To date, the best socialization variable for predicting the belief in witches and sorcerers is a combination of polygyny and the severe punishment for sex and aggression (Whiting, 1959). Among our societies, the Nyansongans are the most ridden with belief in superhuman individuals. Their treatment of aggression is therefore of particular interest. It is also of interest to

---

* For further discussion of the hypotheses regarding aggression, see the *Field Guide for the Study of Socialization*, Chapter 1.

speculate whether there is some relation between the Tarongan parents' treatment of aggression and teasing behavior and their belief in whimsical spirits who must be avoided and not annoyed.

Each monograph on socialization also includes an extended section on techniques used by the socializing agent. Our theory stresses the importance of rewards and punishments for the specific types of acts included in the nine behavioral systems. We are interested in the differential effect of various types of rewards and punishments and the conditions under which they are administered. Rewards may be material, such as food or money, or immaterial, as love and acceptance or praise and prestige. Privileges may also be given as rewards. All types of rewards may be given to commend good behavior or to incite desired behavior. Punishments depend on two types of sanctions, injury or abandonment; these may have as referents several types of agents—parents or authority figures, peers, the self, or supernatural agents.

These rewards and punishments may be given for different reasons. The locus of evaluation may be a specific response of the child, some consequence of his action, or the child himself as a person. In other words, a child may be praised because he does a chore well, because he has helped his mother by doing the chore, or because he is a good boy.

Rewards and punishments may also be intrinsic to the environment. For example, in a terrain where there are delicious wild berries, being able to locate, pick, and eat the berries without aid from adults may reward self-reliance. Herding large animals may reward dominance. Hot, humid weather may discourage physical exertion.

The nature and strength of internal controls—mechanisms which keep an individual from breaking the rules of a society—are thought to be related to techniques and agents of socialization as well as to the strength of a child's identification with both parents (Whiting and Child, 1953; Whiting, 1960; Burton and Whiting, 1961; Bacon, Child, and Barry, 1963). To determine the strength of these internal controls, we hoped to observe the differences in children's behavior in the presence and absence of socializing agents. On a societal level, we predicted that when a boy's identification with the same sex parent is weak, there will be a higher incidence of crime (see B. Whiting, in press).

We expected to find that authority figures would be important sanction agents in the adult culture when there was marked differentiation of authority within the nuclear family, when discipline was carried out by or in the name of the head of the house, and when responsibility and obedience training were emphasized. We expected peers to be important agents when there was little differentiation of authority within the family, when the right of discipline was not stressed, and when self-reliance training was emphasized. If these hypotheses are correct, we would expect consequent differences in the social control systems.

For most of the societies, the age period from 6 to 10 emphasizes responsibility training. A comparison of the chores assigned to boys and girls during this period, of the rewards and punishments for good or bad performance or omission, is an index of the training in this behavior system. The age at which different types of chores are assigned gives a clue to the age at which a society considers a child to have "sense," to be capable of reason, and it indicates the beliefs about the nature of the learning process. It will be observed, for example, that the Khalapur Rājpūts believe that children learn primarily by observing; hence there is little direct instruction. One type of responsibility is training children to care for younger siblings, cousins, and neighbors. This training may start very early, as in Taira and Nyansongo, or may be late and unimportant, as in Orchard Town.

The size and composition of play groups and the attitudes of parents about friendliness are described for each age level. It was hypothesized that sociability would be related both to training in nurturance and to the treatment of succorance, but initial comparisons of children's observed behavior indicate that nurturance is probably more closely related to training for responsibility and dominance than to friendliness.

In planning the research, the senior investigators were also interested in discovering age and sex differences in behavior which might be universal (Barry, Bacon, and Child, 1957). Is it true, in spite of radically different treatment in infancy and early childhood in the six societies, that boys and adult men are always more aggressive physically than girls and women and that girls and women are always more affectionate than men? Are there regularities in behavior that hold across cultures? Does succorance always decrease with age and dominance always increase? We have tested these and other hypotheses using the behavioral measures derived from the systematic observation of the sample children (see *Field Guide for the Study of Socialization*, Chapter 1). The results will be published in the forthcoming volume on the *Behavior of Children in Six Cultures*. Preliminary findings do reveal universal sex-age difference. Although these questions cannot be answered from a comparison of the six societies alone, consistent age and sex differences should be followed up by further research.

Mothers in Six Cultures by Leigh Minturn and William Lambert (1964) presents the first perusal of many of the hypotheses just given.

The authors based their analysis on factor scores derived from ratings made on the mothers' answers to the standard interview on child-training practices (see *Field Guide for the Study of Socialization,* Chapter 5). For example, the mother's economic responsibility outside the house, the amount of help she received in caring for her infants and children, and the number of other adult women and their kin relationship are studied in relation to her use of praise or physical punishment, to her concern with training her children to be responsible and to help with daily chores, and to her attitudes toward her child's expression of aggression toward other children and toward herself. The authors discuss the rank order of the societies on these variables and the rank order correlation between these and other variables. They also consider the effect of ecological and demographic variables on the mother's deviation from the norms of her group.

The reader will be aware that in spite of the research design, the data are not always comparable; in the different areas studied, some monographs have better coverage than others. These variations result not only from the personalities, interests, and training of the field-workers but also from the nature of the culture of the society they chose to study.

Although these monographs concentrate on the material that the researchers felt was theoretically relevant, it is hoped that readers with different conceptual systems and different hypotheses concerning human behavior will find it possible to peruse the data with relevant comparisons in mind. Those who were concerned with the project have developed new insights and new hypotheses. Some of these can be explored, but for many the relevant data are not detailed enough and further studies must be conducted. We believe that the need for further studies is inevitable in the social sciences and that progress comes from being willing to state hypotheses, test them, derive new theories, and plan new research to test these.

We believe that the detailed comparison of six societies is useful for generating hypotheses about human behavior. To test hypotheses adequately, the social scientist must study predicted variation among individuals within societies as well as across a larger sample of societies.

In conclusion, we should like to acknowledge our indebtedness to many people and institutions for their advice and help. The opportunity to do the study was provided by the generous support of the Social Science Research Council and of the Behaviorial Science Division of the Ford Foundation, and by a United States Public Health Grant, M-1096.

Various faculty members at the three universities helped in designing and planning the research. A list of these and other contributors will be found at the beginning of this chapter, but we wish to express special gratitude to Robert R. Sears, Pauline Sears, Eleanor E. Maccoby, and Alfred L. Baldwin, who have continued to give valuable advice to the project.

. While in the field, each of the teams was assisted by graduates of local universities and schools who acted not only as interpreters but also as informants and friends. The aid that these students gave was invaluable. We wish to thank Nariyuki Agarie, Gurdeep Jaspal, Simeon Nyaechae, John Okiamba, Felix Ombasa, Laurence Sagini, Sri Shyam Narain Singh, Taurino Singson, Muriel Eva Verbitsky Hunt, and Kiyoshi Yogi.

We are deeply grateful to all the staff and students of the Laboratory of Human Development of Harvard University who read and helped edit the monographs. Marilyn Johnson, Celia Kalberg, Dorothy Tao, and Susan Horton were particularly devoted assistants. We wish to express our appreciation to numerous other people for reading and commenting on some or all the monographs, especially Masanori Higa, Geraldine Kohlenberg, and Morris Opler.

We are especially indebted to the families in Nyansongo, Khalapur, Taira, Juxtlahuaca, Tarong, and Orchard Town, who were not only cooperative informants, but also helpful friends. We hope that the children we studied will become proud members of the adult world into which they were born and that these volumes will contribute to mutual understanding so that they may live in a friendlier world.

BEATRICE B. WHITING

Harvard University
September, 1965

BIBLIOGRAPHY

Air Ministry, Meteorological Office. *Tables of Temperature, Relative Humidity and Precipitation for the World.* London: Her Majesty's Stationery Office, 1960.

Bacon, Margaret K., Child, Irvin L., and Barry, Herbert III. A cross-cultural study of correlates of crime. *Journal of Abnormal and Social Psychology,* 1963, **66,** 291–300.

Barry, Herbert III, Bacon, Margaret K., and Child, Irvin L. A cross-cultural survey of some sex differences in socialization. *Journal of Abnormal and Social Psychology,* 1957, **55,** 327–332.

————, Child, Irvin L., and Bacon, Margaret K. Relation of child training to subsistence economy. *American Anthropologist,* 1959, **61,** 51–63.

Burton, Roger V. and Whiting, John W. M. The absent father and cross-sex identity. *Merrill-Palmer Quarterly,* 1961, **7,** 85–95.

Child, Irvin L. Socialization. In Gardner Lindzey (Ed.), *Handbook of Social Psychology*, vol. II. Cambridge, Mass.: Addison-Wesley, 1954.

Friendly, Joan P. A cross-cultural study of ascetic mourning behavior. Unpublished honors thesis, Radcliffe College, 1956.

Lambert, William W. Interpersonal Behavior. In P. H. Mussen (Ed.), *Handbook of Research Methods in Child Development*, Chapter 20, pp. 854–917. Wiley, New York: 1960.

————, Triandis, Leigh M., and Wolf, Margery. Some correlates of beliefs in the malevolence and benevolence of supernatural beings: a cross-cultural study. *Journal of Abnormal and Social Psychology*, 1959, **58**, 162–169.

Minturn, Leigh, Lambert, William W., et al., *Mothers of Six Cultures: antecedents of child rearing*. New York: Wiley, 1964.

Roberts, John M., Bush, R. R., and Arth, M. Dimensions of mastery in games. Stanford, Calif.: Ford Center for Advanced Study in the Behavioral Sciences, 1957 (mimeographed).

Sears, R. R., Whiting, John W. M., Nowlis, V., and Sears, P. S. Some child-rearing antocodents of aggroccion and dependency in young children *Genetic Psychology Monograph*, 1953, **47**, 135–234.

Spiro, Melford E. and D'Andrade, Roy G. A cross-cultural study of some supernatural beliefs. *American Anthropologist*, 1958, **60**, 456–466.

Triandis, L. M. and Lambert, W. W. Sources of frustration and targets of aggression: a cross-cultural study. *Journal of Abnormal and Social Psychology*, 1961, **62**, 3, 640–648.

Whiting, Beatrice B. Sex identity conflict and physical violence: a comparative study. *American Anthropologist*, in press.

Whiting, John W. M. Sorcery, sin and the superego: a cross-cultural study of some mechanisms of social control. In *Nebraska Symposium on Motivation*, pp. 174–195. Lincoln: University of Nebraska Press, 1959.

————, Resource mediation and learning by identification. In I. Iscoe and H. Stevenson (Eds.), *Personality Development in Children*. Austin: University of Texas Press, 1960.

————, and Child, Irvin L. *Child Training and Personality: a cross-cultural study*. New Haven, Conn.: Yale University Press, 1953.

————, Chasdi, Eleanor M., Antonovsky, Helen F., and Ayres, Barbara C. The learning of values. In E. Z. Vogt (Ed.), *The Peoples of Rimrock*, Cambridge, Mass.: Harvard University Press, in press.

————, et al. *Field Manual for the Cross-Cultural Study of Child Rearing*. Social Science Research Council, New York, 1953.

————, et al. *Field Guide for a Study of Socialization*. Six Cultures Series, vol. 1. New York: Wiley, 1966.

About the Authors

Robert and Barbara LeVine chose a Gusii community in Nyaribari in the hills of the South Nyanza District of Kenya. During their stay they lived in the official residence of the chief, who prefers to live in his own home. This house was at Keumbu, about a quarter of a mile from a community of scattered homesteads selected for the study. Robert Le Vine was an advanced graduate student in the Social Relations Department at Harvard and had been on the staff of the Laboratory of Human Development during the year when the other teams were in the field. He had assisted in checking the comparability of the material as it was mailed in and had the advantage of profiting from the experiences that the field teams reported in their journals and correspondence. Because he was interested in initiation ceremonies, he agreed to replicate the study, varying it to include a sample of older boys and girls whom he wished to observe and interview after initiation. Barbara LeVine was a graduate student of psychology at Boston University. She participated in the female initiation rites, observing, photographing, and dancing with the women in settings where men were not allowed or had to remain in the background. With the aid of an interpreter, she did the mother interviews.

The LeVines used four interpreters during their stay: Simeon Nyachae, the chief's son, and Lawrence Sagini (now Minister of Local Government in Kenya), a teacher's college graduate who was headmaster of a nearby school and contributed valuable information and help. These two men offered their services gratis because they lived nearby and were interested. Felix Ombasa, a health officer, worked with the LeVines from April to August 1956, and John Okiamba from October 1956 to May 1957. Both men were graduates of the Nyabururu Roman Catholic Intermediate School and spoke English.

Robert LeVine is at present associate professor of anthropology in the Committee on Human Development, University of Chicago. Barbara LeVine (now Barbara Lloyd) is now a lecturer on social psychology at the University of Birmingham, England.

Contents

Part I

The Ethnographic Background

✿
✿
✿
✿
✿
✿

Chapter 1

Introduction

On the eastern side of Africa, astride the Equator, lies a cool, fertile highland region with green hills and snow-capped volcanic peaks ranging up to 17,000 feet above sea level. Surrounded and bisected by semiarid plains and vast hot savannahs, the relatively small strip of well-watered highland in Kenya has attracted dense African populations and the largest European settlement in East Africa. The southwestern tip of the region, wedged in between the White (i.e., European) Highlands on the east and the arid Lake Victoria shore lowlands on the west, is the African reserve known as Kisii Highlands, home of the Gusii people. The Kisii Highlands (hereafter referred to as Gusiiland) are located (see map 1) in South Nyanza District, 50 miles south of the equator, 40 miles north of Tanganyika, and 30 miles east of Lake Victoria's Kavirondo Gulf, which is visible from its higher hills.

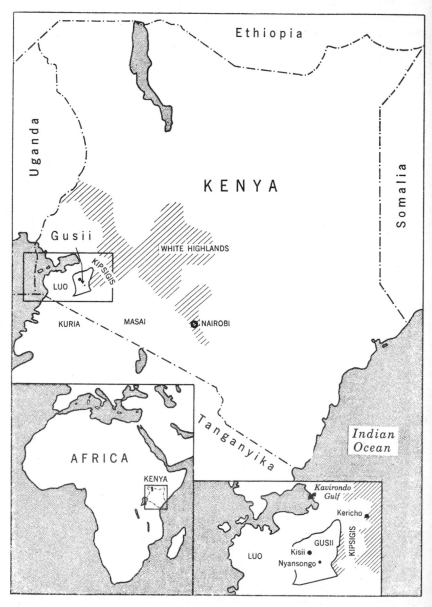

Map 1. Map of Kenya showing Gusiiland.

Gusiiland, situated at cool, 5000 to 7000 foot elevations above sea level, consists mainly of long, gently sloping hills and a smaller number of steep ridges and escarpments. Running between the green hills are swampy streams and rivers, fed by more than 80 inches of rainfall annually. The appearance of Gusiiland has been likened to that of the Scottish Highlands and, indeed, few characteristically African features strike the eye. The hills are devoid of indigenous trees, removed in the course of expanding cultivation some years ago. Nowadays dark green groves of Australian black wattle trees and scattered eucalyptus and cypress occasionally interrupt the patchwork of crudely terraced fields and pastures. Dotted across the cultivated sides of the hills, in no pattern discernible to the casual observer, are the round, thatched-roof huts and granaries of the Gusii people. The inhabitants of one such dotted hillside forming a local community were the subjects of the field study reported here from December 1955 until May 1957.

The Gusii are a dark brown Negroid people of medium height who number more than a quarter of a million. Their language places them within the Bantu-speaking * majority of subequatorial Africa, but their entry into the highlands some two centuries ago isolated them from other Kenya Bantu peoples: the Kuria, whose language is mutually intelligible with Gusii, live 35 miles to the south, while the related Logoli and Luhyia are more than 80 miles to the north, and the more distantly related Kikuyu live 130 miles away in the east. The immediate neighbors of the Gusii are tribes of unrelated language families: the Nilotic-speaking Luo to the north, west, and southwest; the Nilo-Hamitic Kipsigis to the east, and the Nilo-Hamitic Masai on the southeast. The Gusii fought with their neighbors and lost a segment of highland to the Kipsigis while leaving an uninhabited buffer strip at the boundary of low-lying Masailand. Except for intermittent cattle raids, relations with the Luo inhabitants of the lake shore were more peaceful, and no serious conflict over territory seems to have occurred.

The entire Gusii people recognize a common ancestor, Mogusii, who is thought of as the founder of the society and the person after whom it was named. Despite the recognition of this common ancestry and a common cultural heritage, however, the seven tribes of Gusiiland did not traditionally constitute a unified group. They not only combined for military operations against the Kipsigis but also engaged in warfare against each other. Each tribe, in its turn, far from being

* Bantu is a language family containing many languages which are similar but mutually incomprehensible.

a unified political group, was an alliance of the patrilineal clans in a defined area which recognized a common ancestor and totem animal distinct from those of other tribes and which acknowledged the possibility of compensation for homicide within the alliance. There were, in every tribe, one or more clans which were considered the original inhabitants of the area, directly descended from the founder-ancestor, and others who were thought of as later settlers adopted into the tribal genealogy. The "descended" clans tended to be few in number but large in population, while there were many small "adopted" clans and clan fragments in a tribe. Some of the latter were refugees from interclan conflict in other tribes. Because of their numerical strength and hereditary position, the descended clans were in some respects politically dominant, and any tribe-wide military or judicial leadership a tribe might have would be contributed by one of the descended clans.

Each clan, however, was for the most part an autonomous political unit with its own territory and powers of decision making. Clans of the same tribe feuded with one another, that is, they engaged in prolonged relationships of mutual hostility involving spear fights and the abduction of women. Interclan hostilities within a tribe could be terminated by negotiation and the payment of compensation in livestock. The fact that clans were exogamous and had to take wives from one another in orderly marriage ceremonies must have exerted some pressure against the indefinite continuance of feuds, but it did not prevent them from occurring. Thus the clans of a Gusii tribe were traditionally drawn together by intermarriage and joint participation in intertribal warfare, but nevertheless they engaged in hostilities against one another.

In 1907, Gusiiland came under British administration and became a part of South Nyanza District along with adjacent Luo areas. Each of the seven Gusii tribes became an administrative "location"; one of these is Nyaribari Location in which the community of Nyansongo is located. The population of this location in 1948 was 42,670. Much of its 100 square miles was formerly no-man's land between Gusiiland and Masai and has only been settled since 1930. The population density of Nyaribari, though varying widely within the location, averages over 450 per square mile. This is not the greatest average density in Gusiiland and does not approach the thousand and more per square mile found in other parts of the western Kenya highland, but it is a heavy population load for even a fertile soil being tilled by primitive methods.

Nyansongo is less than a quarter of a mile from Keumbu, the administrative center of Nyaribari. Located at Keumbu are the chief's office, tribal police quarters, the location assembly hall, a prison cubicle, and the official chief's residence, in which we lived. There is a Roman Catholic primary and intermediate day school where 400 students are taught by Gusii teachers. On the other side of a dirt road from the chief's office and school, there is a market, a neat rectangle of Gusii shops and restaurants bordering a grassy field where cattle are traded and soccer is played. Ordinary Gusii homesteads and fields surround Keumbu, and the public grounds themselves are used as pastures by nearby people. The road running through the area is the main route from South Nyanza to the Kericho tea plantations and ultimately to the capital city of Nairobi. It is a narrow winding road, with a dirt surface that converts readily to intractable mud during the rainy seasons.

Nyaribari Location is characterized by continuous settlement with no pronounced geographical subdivisions. To its residents, the important affiliations are to kin and work groups and to influential men. In selecting a group to study, we chose the neighboring families who were members (population 208) of a large work group. We have called this group the community of Nyansongo.

Nyansongo consists of 18 homesteads, scattered over the slopes of a long hill on both sides of the main road to Kericho. Proximity to the chief's camp and market on one side, and to the chief's private homestead on the other, figures importantly in the life of the community. The immediacy of the road is also important, for on it one can take a bus 8 miles to Kisii township, district headquarters and commercial center, or 50 miles in the opposite direction to employment on the tea plantations. Despite such easy access to organs of government and centers of Western influence, Nyansongo is relatively traditional in its way of life, adhering to many of the beliefs and practices characteristic of Gusiiland before its conquest by the British 50 years ago.

Nyansongo is roughly divided into three neighborhoods, each of which consists of a number of nearby homesteads of the same kin group who comprise a small work group for frequent agricultural cooperation. [The residents of the smallest neighborhood belong to Bonyamosicho subclan (see map 2), while those of the other two belong to different branches of Omobea subclan (designated A and B on the map).]

Each of the 18 homesteads in Nyansongo is a residential cluster of one to eight houses (see map 3). The clustering is not pronounced because the houses of co-wives and brothers are usually separated by a cultivated field, and there is also a tendency of homestead members to build their houses near a boundary disputed with another homestead. The result is what appears to be a random dispersion of houses, but in fact the network of paths almost always makes it easier to get from one house to another within a homestead than across homestead lines, which are sometimes marked by fences and hedges. The residents are usually a man, who is homestead head, his wives, their unmarried

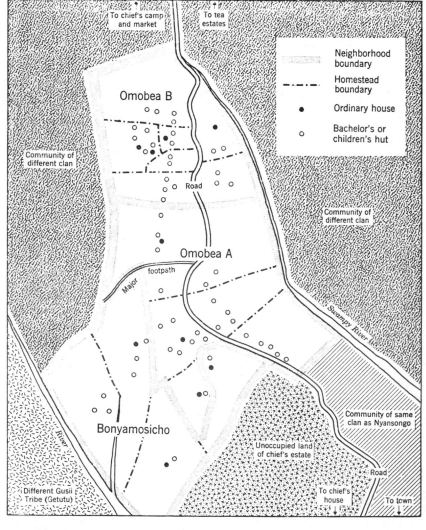

Map 2. Nyansongo community.

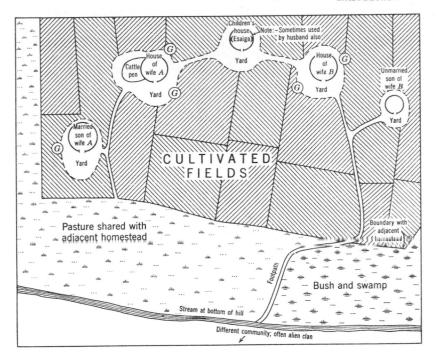

Map 3. Contemporary Gusii homestead in densely populated area.

children, their married sons with wives and progeny, and the head's mother if she is alive.

Houses are round structures with mud and wattle walls, floors of dried mud and cow dung, and water-tight conical roofs with neatly concentric thatching. They last five to ten years, the oldest one in Nyansongo being 12 years old and very shabby. There are two doors in an ordinary house but no windows, and the smoke from the fireplace drifts up to the top of the roof cone and seeps out through the interstices of the grass. The high roof of the house allows the construction of an overhead loft where grain for everyday use is stored in a large basket. There are two rooms (see Figure 1): (1) *enyomba* (which also means "house" in general), considered the wife's preserve, which contains the fireplace for cooking, the bed on which wife, husband, and small children sleep, and a partitioned entrance foyer in which the adult sons of the wife may eat without being able to see her posture while cooking or the interior part of the house containing the bed; (2) *eero,* a room reserved for the husband's entertainment of guests and where his stool, drinking tube, and other personal possessions are

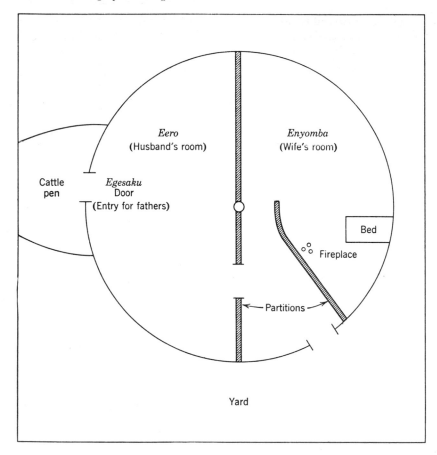

Figure 1. Traditional Gusii house.

kept. He also lies there when ill. This room has its own entrance
through the cattle pen, and classificatory fathers of the husband may
enter the house only through this door, never through the main entrance in the wife's room. The main entrance of each house faces down-
hill, toward the nearest stream or river. The yard in front of the main
entrance is the scene of many daytime activities: the grinding and win-
nowing of grain, the play of children, the consumption of food (but
not beer) with guests, and the casual visits of neighbor women who sit
nursing their infants and gossiping. From the yard one can see down
the hill, observe passersby on the road or to and from the stream, supervise the boys herding cattle in the pastures below, and even watch
people of another clan on the opposite hill across the stream.

The house described above is the standard one in which a woman, whether or not she is a widow, lives with her unmarried children. A smaller house (*esaiga*), with one room and one door, may be used as a children's house for boys from the whole homestead who are aged 6 to 12, as a bachelor's house for one initiated but unmarried male aged 12 to 20, or to house an aged widow whose larger house fell into disrepair. In the early years of their marriage a couple may inhabit the husband's previous bachelor house, but eventually he builds a standard unit for his wife, and each secondary wife must have one too. Later on he builds a children's *esaiga* in which he may occasionally sleep when he is not rotating among the houses of his wives (see map 3). Each wife has a granary near her house for storing the grain from the fields allotted to her. There is always a field beside the wife's house in which she is cultivating vegetables or grain, but at any one time about half of the fields shown on the diagram are likely to be lying fallow.

This setting of dispersed homesteads, containing separated houses and surrounded by sloping fields and pastures, is the context in which Nyansongo individuals grow up, spend most of their adult lives, and die.

⚘
⚘
⚘

Chapter 2

Basic Economy *

GENERAL BACKGROUND

Traditionally the Gusii combined agriculture and animal husbandry, and do so today although other means of earning a livelihood are now available. In the days before British administration, cattle herding was more important to the Gusii and tended to overshadow cultivation in social significance if not actually for subsistence. Economic aggrandizement was seen primarily in terms of the acquisition of large herds of cattle through breeding and raids on neighboring clans or on other

* For further material on the Gusii economy, see LeVine (1962a).

tribes. The importance of cattle, sheep, and goats in the Gusii prestige system and diet has diminished over the years in the face of a growing cash economy and because of the reduction of herds, initially occasioned by cattle epidemics and government restrictions on cattle villages, and presently by the increasing shortage of grazing lands. The young men, who once herded cattle and raided for more, now find employment on European plantations and in cities.

In the past, land was abundant; homesteads were widely dispersed across the hillsides; and cultivation was undertaken to supply the eleusine (finger millet) necessary for daily subsistence. The ready availability of land and vaguely defined property rights permitted lineage groups to move around considerably within the Gusii territory rather than remaining fixed to a particular piece of land. The pressure of a rapidly increasing population, the introduction of new crops, and the possibility of obtaining cash through agriculture have turned the primary economic attention of the Gusii away from cattle and to their extremely fertile soil. Corn, which requires less arduous cultivation, now rivals eleusine as the major food crop, while sweet potatoes, bananas, legumes, and tomatoes are commonly grown as well. Coffee is the primary cash crop, but surpluses of all crops are sold for shipment to other parts of Kenya. Thus the people of Nyansongo are now predominantly an agricultural people, but animal husbandry and outside employment serve important supplementary roles in their economy.

The Gusii standard of living is higher than that of many peoples living in "underdeveloped areas"; they are better fed, better clothed, and have more purchasing power than most peasant farmers in North Africa, the Middle East, and East Asia. Despite this relative prosperity, which is more than adequate for the satisfaction of their basic needs, the level of economic anxiety and preoccupation in Nyansongo is high. In part this is due to the economic changes of the past 50 years. The population has tripled in these years, and land, once abundant, now is fought over. The system of land tenure and land inheritance, understandably vague in the past, has in the modern era pitted brother against brother, neighbor against neighbor, and kin group against kin group in a struggle over land rights and ownership. The large amount of land litigation in Gusiiland is symptomatic of this struggle and the problems of population and economics that lie behind it. Middle-aged Gusii can remember a time when land and livestock were much more plentiful than they are now, and they witness the increasing population making them scarcer every year. Since employment and trade are regarded as supplements rather than substitutes for the life of the fields and pastures, it appears to many that the economic basis of their existence is gradually slipping away.

A further source of economic anxiety is the high value set on personal wealth. A Nyansongo man desires land, cattle, and money partly for the prestige that accrues to him. The size of his herds and number of his wives are visible signs of his affluence. The extent of a particular individual's wealth is a complex function of his father's wealth, the number of heirs with whom he had to share his father's wealth, the number of his daughters whose marriages bring in cattle, and his own personal efforts to acquire property through work and trade. In general, an individual is fiercely jealous of a neighbor who is slightly richer, deferential to one who is much richer, and fearful of the jealousy of those who are poorer. Wealthy men are respected and poor men despised: indeed, the term for "poor man" is an insult in the Gusii language.

Jealousy of a wealthy man is as great if his riches were acquired through honest work as if they were inherited, a situation which has become an obstacle to the Agriculture Department's program of encouraging extraordinarily competent Gusii farmers to develop their land to yield more than their neighbor's farm. The wealthy live in fear of poisoning, witchcraft, and sorcery at the hands of their jealous neighbors. Fear does not inspire the wealthy to share with others less fortunate, however. On the contrary, they use their wealth to dominate their inferiors through loans and threats of expensive litigation. The proverb, "The poor man's property belongs to the rich man," indicates that such domination is a familiar pattern. In spite of covert jealousy and resentment on the part of the poor, it must be emphasized that they automatically accord their wealthy neighbors a degree of respect and deference which insures domination by the rich. No poor man would dare to contradict or criticize a rich man of his own generation in a face-to-face situation unless there were a state of sustained hostility between their kin groups.

Thus in Nyansongo, as in most communities, there are one or two wealthy men who are the acknowledged leaders and whose opinions on local affairs are granted extraordinary weight. Although there is open recognition of economic inequality, there are no social classes among the Gusii. Often a rich man uses his influence (or wealth in the form of bribes) to establish legal claims to property belonging to a less influential person or to extort excessive fines from a neighbor for a minor offense. Unless such actions are overruled by a higher authority, they go unchecked, for Gusii consider themselves powerless to rebel against a person of superior wealth. Besides, those who are victimized are likely to be the influential man's debtors and dependent on his favor. This domination is prevented from persisting across generations by the likelihood of a rich man taking many wives and siring many sons. His wealth is thus fragmented in a generation. Furthermore, there is no feeling of solidarity among the wealthy, as expressed in the proverb, "Rich men fear each other." Traditionally a rich man preferred the company of his poorer relatives, whom he could dominate, to that of other rich men, who were viewed as rivals for local political power. This pattern persists, but today it is even difficult for a rich man to move his residence.

HOMESTEAD ECONOMY

The agricultural cycle in each Nyansongo homestead is based on the seasonal distribution of rain. All of Gusiiland has the two rainy seasons characteristic of Kenya highland areas. In Nyansongo the "long rains" come in April, May, and June, while the "short rains" occur in September and October. In July and August there may be occasional rain, but the December to March period is usually hot and dry. With respect to the major crops of corn and eleusine: January–February is the time for bush clearing and ground-breaking; March–April for sowing; May–June for weeding; and September–October for harvesting the grain. In July and August sweet potatoes are cultivated as "insurance" in case there is a poor grain yield. After the crops are harvested, social activities requiring food can begin, and November and December are filled with visiting and house building.

Bush-clearing and ground-breaking activity is concentrated on those fields which were allowed to lie fallow and probably used as grazing land. Once the undergrowth is cut down with machetes, the ground-breaking is accomplished either with a hoe, which is traditional and was once made by Gusii ironsmiths, or with a plow and a team of oxen. No one in Nyansongo owns a plow or oxen, but some people rent them from neighbors or borrow them from relatives outside the community. When they are borrowed from relatives, beer is served in return.

The exact time of planting is based on an individual's estimate of when the long rains will begin in earnest. Those who plant early worry about whether or not the rains will come soon enough to allow their seeds to germinate. Those who wait too long may find that the rains have come early, making the ground muddy and the planting more arduous. The sowing of corn can be performed with little additional preparation of the soil, but eleusine cultivation demands a finely pulverized soil, carefully weeded. This latter task is painstakingly performed by striking large clumps of earth with a hoe and shaking out the weeds and vines. When the whole field is soft and finely prepared, the eleusine seed is broadcast on it. In conformity with government instructions, all bushes, weeds, and vines are piled up along that edge of the field which lies lower on the hill, thus producing a crude contour terrace line.

Toward the end of the long rains, the crops must be weeded. Weeding corn, which is planted in rows, is a simple task for someone equipped with a hoe. Eleusine, which the Gusii insist on broadcasting despite the Agriculture Department's efforts to the contrary, requires a person to kneel down and pluck each weed by hand—a slow and tiresome job. By July and August, when all the weeding is finished, there is little to do but wait for the crops to ripen.

Just before the harvest, granaries begin to run low and food anxiety is common in Nyansongo. The midday meal is eliminated in most households, and all adults limit their diet drastically. Social visiting is at a minimum, since usual hospitality norms cannot be met. People know they cannot expect their neighbors to feed them or give them drink. Women visit their own kin, however, to beg for food and are usually only given bananas. These are often in full supply throughout this period, but bananas are only considered suitable for snacks, and informants took care to explain that they are not considered "food." Some women also plant small fields of sweet potatoes, beans, and peas to provide a supplementary food supply, for these can mature during the short rains. Solitary handicraft activities, such as basketmaking, may also be carried out at this time.

In October, when the harvest finally begins, initiation ceremonies provide a pleasant excuse for the resumption of neighborly social life and the consumption of large quantities of food and beer. The high point of these festivities is reached at Christmas, which is celebrated as a drinking feast even by the pagan Gusii. As the New Year begins, fences are built or mended to keep livestock away from the fields which will shortly be broken. Thus the cycle begins once more.

Today as 50 years ago before the British came to Gusiiland, work is organized according to age and sex. In the past, women and middle-aged men worked the fields, young men lived out in cattle villages to herd and raid, uninitiated children herded sheep and goats, and old men discussed cattle and settled local disputes. The abolition of the cattle-villages by the government in 1912, and the subsequent development of employment opportunities outside the district, effected some changes in this arrangement. With young men often away working for cash, children now herd cattle as well as sheep and goats, and women are burdened more than ever with agricultural activities in addition to their domestic chores. Women and children now do all the milking of cows, although women were once not even permitted to enter the cattle-villages.

Of the 28 adult males in Nyansongo, 24 have been employed at some time in their lives outside South Nyanza District. Although most have gone no farther than Nairobi (250 miles from Nyansongo), a few have been to places such as Egypt or the Congo. They have worked as artisans, policemen, and domestic servants as well as agricultural laborers. At the time of the field study, four men were Kenya policemen stationed outside the district, coming home only for vacation once every two years. Seven others worked away from home at some time during the 1955–1957 period, but these regard their employment as temporary and spend as much as a year at home before going out to seek work again. Some of the men who came home at this time never plan to seek jobs again. Five men in Nyansongo were living at home and were employed by the chief as agricultural laborers, guards, and servants on his estate. The others who had been employed outside the district had returned long since to devote themselves to their land, livestock, and lives as traditional Gusii men. Thus more than half of the adult males in the community derived income from employment during 1955–1957, and over two thirds of those employed in that period were living away from home.

Men who are at home devote themselves mainly to nonroutine tasks: the clearing of bush for a new field, plowing, building or mending fences, building houses and granaries. In addition, they take charge of the coffee garden if the homestead has one, supervise the children in their husbandry duties, and occasionally hoe corn and vegetable fields before planting.

It is women, however, who are responsible for most of the hoeing, sowing, weeding, and harvesting as well as grinding the grain, cooking, gathering firewood and wild vegetables. Children and adolescents are commandeered by their mothers to ease the female work load. However, the most difficult and time consuming of Nyansongo agricultural chores, weeding eleusine, is now performed exclusively by adult women, although it is said that in the past some men did it very skillfully.

The current division of labor by sex is the basis for the two different types of work groups in Nyansongo. Women of neighboring homesteads organize themselves into cooperative groups for the performance of routine agricultural activities. This type of group is called *egesangio,* which literally means "an equally shared thing," and a strict equality is its dominant theme. In hoeing corn, for example, the group spends a morning in the field of each of its members and then begins the round again. Each woman in the group keeps strict account of the amount of time spent in the fields of others and is jealous of any inequalities, insisting on her rightful share. When the *egesangio* weeds eleusine, the strip of field each woman is required to weed is measured with a rope, and arguments often develop over whether or not a woman has done her full share.

To perform nonroutine tasks which cannot be done alone or which have been delayed until they must be accomplished in very little time, men use a different arrangement. If a man wants to clear heavy under-brush from a fallow field or to build a house for a new wife, he will invite neighbors to come and work on the job intensively. In exchange, he will serve his visitors the beer his wife has brewed for the occasion. If the task is agricultural, the men may send their wives and daughters to do the work while they partake of the beer. The usual aim is to finish the work in one day. House building, of course, takes many days and the men do a large part of it themselves, for women are considered competent only to smear mud on the walls and are even forbidden to thatch roofs. (This restriction is apparently designed to preserve sexual modesty.) This exchange of work for beer the Gusii call *risaga,* and men recognize two groupings of homesteads on which they can call for *risaga.* There is a "small" *risaga,* restricted to the neighboring home-steads, whose women make up the *egesangio* or cooperative work group, and the "big" *risaga,* which includes more distant homesteads. The community, Nyansongo, is one "big" *risaga* which, taken as a whole, defines a territorial unit within which homesteads may exchange beer for work but outside of which the exchange does not take place.

Although much of a homestead's agricultural produce is used for subsistence, some is also bartered or traded for cash. Coffee is marketed through a tribally owned cooperative which pays individual growers for their raw coffee beans. Surplus corn and eleusine are sold at Keumbu Market to traders who pay a price fixed by the government's Maize Control Office, sold in town on the black market at a higher price, or traded illegally to the grain-hungry Luo tribesmen. Continuing a traditional practice, Luo traders bring bags of salt they mine in their country into Gusiiland on donkeys and receive grain for the salt the Gusii must have for their cattle. A number of enterprising Nyansongo women walk 10 miles to a market on the border on Tuesdays and exchange grain for Luo pots. Later in the week they take the pots to a Gusii market at Keroka, another 8 miles from their home, and sell them for cash. These women act as "middle-men" in both the physical and economic sense.

Besides dealing in surplus grain, Nyansongo women bring bananas, oranges, cabbages, and other vegetables into the Kisii township market and sell them for cash to African market traders who in turn sell them to the Europeans and East Indians of the town. Native beer is sometimes brewed and sold for cash in beer shops in Keumbu market or to men in the community. The sale of black wattle bark to the government for export as leather tanning extract was important until the end of 1956 when the permanent collapse of the world price on natural extract destroyed its market value. Thus Nyansongo families nowadays see their agricultural activities as directed toward the market and cash returns as well as toward their own maintenance.

The desire for Western consumption goods has kept apace with opportunities to acquire cash through agriculture and employment. Nyansongans want and feel they need cash for clothing, school fees, kerosene lamps, blankets, sugar, tea, medicine, bus fares, and bicycles to mention only the more common items. In the face of these desires, the developing land shortage and overpopulation are a source of considerable anxiety. The Agriculture Department estimated an average of 7 acres per homestead in Gusiiland in 1956. Nyansongo seems to be more densely populated, but many families are allowed by their chief to cultivate sizable plots on his adjacent estate, which, since they are not charged a rental fee, helps them greatly. Even if the homesteads of Nyansongo do average 7 acres when the chief's land is included, 7 acres tilled by basically primitive methods are not enough to supply the contemporary wants of a Gusii family. Thus, as mentioned earlier, many Nyansongo men seek employment on European plantations and in the cities.

Although livestock no longer occupies the central place it once held in the Gusii economy, it is still important today. Most families in Nyansongo keep a herd of three to six cows although the family herd may be increased temporarily to as many as 15 cows, when bridewealth is paid for a daughter. Such bridewealth cattle must be used quickly for another marriage, payment of debts, or sold for cash, because the grazing lands of Nyansongo are not adequate to support such herds. A few of the wealthier men in the community have larger herds, but they are kept for them by relatives living in areas of more abundant pasturage.

Cattle are useful in the homestead's daily diet, but the great value derived from their role in the marriage system makes them too expensive to be counted on for subsistence. Cow's milk is used daily; it is allowed to sour in calabashes and then eaten. Few people nowadays can afford to kill a bull simply to eat, but beef is sometimes bought in the market, though it is eaten in small quantities. Gusii conservatism has focused on the use of cattle in bridewealth, and unlike many other Kenya tribes, they refuse to accept cash as a substitute. Thus a young man whose family does not provide him with the necessary cattle must use over $400 of his job earnings to buy cattle for a legitimate marriage. Since cows are the most costly and valuable negotiable property owned by Nyansongo men, they are a great source of ambition, jealousy, gossip, quarreling, and litigation and are loaned, bartered, sold, inherited, and stolen.

The ownership and transfer of cattle are masculine prerogatives and the preservation and allocation of the herd a typically male preoccupation. Cattle are still regarded as the soundest form of investment for a man who has adequate pasturage: they multiply themselves and can readily be turned into cash in an emergency. No man is counted as truly wealthy who does not have a sizable herd to draw on for his own plural marriages and those of his sons as well as for the payment of fees to professional sorcerers, witch smellers, and medicine men. Cattle are thus marriage licenses, savings, health insurance, and prestige symbols.

Sheep and goats are less valuable than cows in terms of cash and marriage, but they have a prominent place in religious sacrifices and the entertainment of guests. Diviners usually specify the use of a sheep or goat of a particular sex and color for funeral and medicinal sacrifices, and such orders are always obeyed. A man of above-average means shows respect to his visiting in-laws or matrilineal kin by slaughtering a goat or sheep for them to eat, while a poorer neighbor kills a chicken for their consumption. A majority of Nyansongo families do not keep sheep and goats; instead they buy one or reclaim one that is owed them whenever a need arises, as when a medicine man asks for a goat as a fee for a curative potion. Every family has chickens, which are commonly given as gifts or sold in the town market, as are the eggs they produce.

In sum, the people of Nyansongo are fairly prosperous agriculturalists who supplement their subsistence and cash crop cultivation with employment and market trade and who have retained pastoralism largely for prestige and ceremonial purposes. They have a high level of economic anxiety, arising partly from overcrowding of the land and partly from economic values which emphasize invidious distinctions based on wealth.

✹
✹
✹

Chapter 3

Social Organization *

The social universe as Nyansongans see it is made up of units of increasing size and inclusiveness from the family to the nation, all of them referred to by the same term, *egesaku,* and all composed of a group of men who recognize a common patrilineal ancestor and occupy a common territory. *Egesaku* in its most general sense thus means "lineage," although it can refer to the group of father and sons in a single homestead, a lineage at one of four levels between family and clan, a clan, one of the seven Gusii "tribes," the Gusii people as a whole as contrasted with other ethnic groups (each one of which is also termed *egesaku*), or a nation such as Kenya, the United Kingdom, or the United States. Each unit within the Gusii ethnic group is spoken of as *egesaku* when considered as a separate entity, but when considered as one of several segments of a larger social unit, it is called *enyomba,* "house." Thus each social unit is thought of as subdivided into "houses," a pattern based explicitly on the polygynous extended family, as described below.

In the Nyansongo ideal, each *egesaku* has both genealogical and residential unity. Thus the Gusii people as a whole are descended from a man named Mogusii, and the territory they occupy is Bogusii. The males of Omobea subclan (the predominant one in Nyansongo) are descended from a man named Omobea, and their territory is called Bomobea. The social realities do not always correspond to this ideal.

* The structural material in this chapter owes much to Mayer (1949, 1950*b*). For additional material on the Gusii family, see LeVine, "The Gusii Family," manuscript.

For example, genealogical connections between clans and tribes are obviously fictionalized. Furthermore, the clans and many of their component lineages have suffered a certain amount of territorial dispersion, especially since the recent migrations to previously uninhabited areas of Gusiiland. There are also some local units which are based primarily on residential proximity and reciprocal work obligations and which do not correspond with lineage groups. These local groups are vaguely defined and loosely organized, however, and lineage ties still have an overwhelming influence on Nyansongo life.

Table 1 lists those social units (1–6) which are referred to by special terms (as well as *egesaku* and *enyomba*) in the Gusii language, and it also includes the two largest entities, the tribe and the Gusii people.

Table 1 Gusii Social Units
(Numbered in order of increasing scope)

SPECIALLY NAMED LINEAGE UNITS	TERRITORIAL UNITS	TRANSLATION OR MEANING
	1. Omochie	homestead
2. Abanyamatati		mourning lineage
	3. (Small) Risaga	neighborhood
	4. (Large) Risaga	local community
5. Riiga		"hearthstone" lineage
6. Eamate		clan (including numerous lineages)
	7. Tribe	alliance of clans
	8. The Gusii People	the seven tribes

Several units which are not designated by special terms have been omitted from the list. These are the mother-son unit within the homestead, which is simply called *enyomba,* and two types of lineages which can exist between the "hearthstone" lineage level (5) and that of clan (6), namely, "clan-house" and "subclan." (See Table 1.)

The composition and functions of these social units are described below, but it is noteworthy at this point to mention that adult Nyansongans are much more conscious of being members of homesteads, lineages, and clans than they are of their *risaga* membership, for both neighborhoods and the local community are unnamed ("Nyansongo" is an ethnographic pseudonym) and command no loyalty in and of themselves. The uniformity of clan membership in the local community and the rough correspondence of its neighborhoods to lineage fragments allow Nyansongans to regard these territorial units as localized lineages and provide a kinship framework for relations within the community.

HOUSEHOLD

The basic residential unit in Nyansongo is the household, consisting of a married woman and her unmarried daughters and uninitiated (prepubertal) sons. The woman's husband may also live there, but his residence is not necessarily constant, since he may be dividing his time among the houses of several wives, sleep in the children's house occasionally, or be away working for long periods. As mentioned earlier, the house is divided into two rooms, one called *eero*, in which the husband entertains his guests, and one called *enyomba*, which is the wife's room, where she cooks and performs other domestic chores. That the house as a whole and the household as a social unit are also called *enyomba* (plural *chinyomba*) indicates the primary association of the house with the wife and her activities. The children eat and sleep in the house with their mother and help her in producing and preparing food for the household. Land adjacent to the house is used for growing some of its food, particularly vegetables, but the woman is allocated larger plots of land by her husband on a yearly basis. Eventually the wife and her children become associated with those plots which are near their house and which they have cultivated, and this is the basis for later claims to legal rights over the land. When the sons marry, they build their houses near land used by their mother and use adjacent plots which have been allocated to them by their father. Granaries containing the produce of its land stand near each household and belong to it, subject to limited rights of disposal by the woman's husband. Each household also has a herd of cattle associated with it, consisting primarily of the cows given as marriage payments for the woman's daughters, and these cattle are to be used, if her husband approves, by the sons of the woman to obtain wives for themselves. As the sons grow up, marry, and establish houses near their mother's house, they continue to think of themselves as one "household," and the term *enyomba* is used to designate the sons of one mother even after their mother has died and they are all living in separate houses of their own.

POLYGYNY AND HUSBAND-WIFE RELATIONS

The mother-child household, though basic, is not an autonomous unit; it is related to the larger family by links of marriage and paternity. Polygyny is viewed as the ideal form of marriage. In Nyansongo 15 men are monogamists, 11 men have two wives each, and 1 has three wives.* Of the married women, 21 are plural wives,† 19 are monogamous wives or widows, and 3 are the unattached widows of a polygynist continuing to live as co-wives. Despite the roughly equivalent number of polygynous and monogamous adults, more than two thirds of the community's children have polygynous parents. This is due to the fact that a sizable proportion of the monogamous men are young husbands whose wives have not yet given birth or have done so only once. By the time they have many children, these men will probably have taken additional wives and thereby become polygynous parents. Thus a large majority of Nyansongo children grow up in polygynous homes. In this respect Nyansongo is not exceptional, for in adjacent communities there are men with four and five wives and even a few wealthy elders with as many as eleven wives and scores of children.

Plurality of wives and offspring is a major ambition of Nyansongo men. Four is said to be the ideal number of wives because the households of the wives are linked in successive pairs within which bridewealth loans may be contracted and which are inheritance units. Thus the first is so linked with the second, third with fourth, and so on. An uneven number of wives is considered a troublesome and incomplete situation. The first four wives are titled—first is "the ash-sweeper," second, "the helper," third, "above the cattle pen," and fourth, "the gate." Later wives have no such traditional titles.

Each wife has her own house, separated from that of her co-wife by at least one field or pasture in a conscious effort to prevent (or contain) dissension. Every wife has to bring the husband a basket of porridge at least once a day, and although he cannot consume all that is brought, he eats at least a mouthful from the basket brought by each wife. The rest of the food is then taken back to be eaten by the children. The husband sleeps with the several wives in their houses according to his pleasure, staying the longest period of weeks with the youngest and fairest. He is supposed to honor each woman's desire to have children at regular intervals, regardless of his preference.

Ideally a Nyansongo wife should obey her husband at all times and be deferential to him. She should accept his allocation of land and cattle and consult him before she takes any important action. She should respond quickly to his demands for food and drink, and pro-

---

* Two men have plural wives who did not live in Nyansongo during the period of field work; the men are counted as polygynists, but their nonresident wives are not included in the enumeration of women.

† Included are leviratic wives living with brothers or cousins of their dead husbands.

vide hospitality for his guests. He will not be pleased if she spends too much time away from her domestic duties at home, and he will be furious if she allows anyone to eat from his basket of food before he has done so, no matter how late he is.

There are several potent sanctions a polygynist can use against a wife who disobeys him or violates a cultural rule. Refusing to sleep with a wife is not only a gross sign of his displeasure but also, if it lasts long enough, a withdrawal of her only means of achieving status and prestige—her capacity to bear children. As there are severe supernatural sanctions against adultery, it is difficult for her to escape this punishment of the husband. More often, however, the husband publicly refuses to eat the food of the offending wife. He may even break the basket and throw the food on the ground. In doing so, he is said to "refuse her" (using the verb *okogira*), which literally refers to the refusal of food but carries with it the implication of sexual and emotional rejection. A 10-year-old Nyansongo boy once gleefully informed a friend of an incident in which his father, displeased by the failure of his second wife (not the boy's mother) to weed his coffee garden, had angrily spilled onto the ground the food she brought him and smashed the container in which it came. Wife-beating is also a common and socially accepted practice, and although it may accompany refusal of food or sexual rejection, the latter two are more potent in a polygynous family. Each wife wants to be her husband's favorite and to have her children favored by him over the children of other wives. Consequently, she may be easily hurt by signs of the husband's emotional rejection.

When a rebuked wife acknowledges her guilt, she goes to her parents for a goat to effect reconciliation. Bringing the goat to her husband, she cooks for him twice. The second time he eats her food and they become reconciled. An older wife may act as mediator in disputes among the wives, but there is no institutionalized pattern of seniority or authority among them.

Most Nyansongo wives are so spontaneous in their performance of the chores which are expected of them and so automatic in their respect for important masculine prerogatives that their husbands do not need to issue commands. On minor issues and family matters, a wife may loudly proclaim her opinions, but she expects to be ignored by her husband, and this is what usually happens. The taciturnity of husbands and the garrulousness of wives sometimes give the impression that women have more authority in the family than they in fact do. Husbands refrain from exercising their authority, or in some cases from even paying attention to their wives, until they feel that the wife needs correction or an important decision must be made. They then expect obedience and may use punishment if it is not forthcoming. Two Nyansongo men are notorious for having wives "who rule them." Both are monogamists, for their domineering spouses succeeded in preventing secondary marriages. The wife of old Osano, a woman in her 60's, interferes with her husband's responses to questions and answers them herself. Their adult sons have committed a number of sex and property crimes, but Osano is unable to control them. Nyakoe, a man in his 40's, who has a minor judicial position, is not so subordinate to his wife in talking to visitors, but it is obvious that she has more control over the children than he does, and he appears to listen to her advice on many matters. She is widely reputed to be a witch and has been publicly accused. Both couples are considered deviant in Nyansongo because of their reversal of the acceptable authority relationship between husband and wife.

Despite their desire for polygyny, Nyansongo men recognize that it brings them trouble. Dissensions among co-wives is one of the most common themes in Gusii folklore. One proverb is: "Another child-bearer is like an ancestor spirit at the outside wall." This is interpreted as meaning that secondary wives bring hatred which can result in murder and invoke the wrath of the spirits. There is a special word, *engareka,* which means "hatred between co-wives," and a folktale about how *engareka* caused the first cooking of porridge.

Long ago, before the Gusii cooked food, there was a man who had one wife. He wanted to take a second wife but she opposed it bitterly. He took a second wife anyway, and when she had her first baby, she naturally stayed in the house for about a week. During that time the first wife brought her food. The first wife thought that if she made the porridge very hot over a fire, it would kill the second wife. When she served it to her, she noticed it made the second wife perspire and was certain it would work. But after the week was over, the second wife was fat and healthy and said she liked the hot porridge. After that, people cooked their porridge instead of leaving it uncooked.

This folktale expresses the real emotions that characterize Nyansongo wives. Many a first wife is extremely opposed to her husband's taking another wife, and this is a frequent cause of quarreling. Women realize that monogamy gives them much greater power in the family, and some of them are determined to retain that power. The wife of a monogamous husband can punish him by refusing herself to him sexually or by refusing to work in home and garden. She most often does this by going to live with her parents for a week or more. When the precipitating quarrel has concerned the husband's taking a second wife, he may be sufficiently cowed by her desertion to give up the idea.

On the other hand, though, he may become convinced that a second wife is needed to free him from exclusive dependence on her. Once he has a second wife, the situation is reversed; *he* is the one who can punish by abandoning one for the other, and they become dependent on his favor.

For example, Manyara, a Nyansongo man in his 30's, had a rather dominant wife, Kerubo, and three children. When he began negotiating for another marriage, Kerubo ran away for some time and then came back. Manyara married the girl anyway and took her to a European plantation where he worked for a few months until she became pregnant. Being somewhat fearful of Kerubo's wrath, he wanted to present her with the *fait accompli* of the girl's pregnancy so that no pressure could dissolve the marriage. Kerubo refused to be more than barely civil to the girl, although, like a good wife, she sent food to the new house where the newlyweds were living. The new wife had a miscarriage and subsequently suffered from swollen breasts. Under such conditions she could hardly fail to assume that her misfortune was due to Kerubo's ill wishes (through witchcraft). Several months later, Kerubo complained privately that Manyara was spending all his money on fancy dresses for his bride, while she and her children went in rags and had no money to buy medicines for the youngest daughter's bronchitis. The animosity in this polygynous situation was so great from the start that only with difficulty will Manyara be able to keep it from resulting in open conflict. By his second marriage he forced Kerubo into submission but inadvertently turned her hostility against the new woman, who cannot but reciprocate eventually. Such ill feeling among co-wives is the price of polygyny.

Each wife tends to be the husband's darling when she is the latest and to maintain that position until he marries again. A Gusii proverb admonishes, "Never throw away an old grass ring (used for carrying pots on the head)," meaning that the older wives should not be neglected, but polygynists are said to "grow old toward the gate," that is, to prefer younger wives (such as the fourth, "the gate," last in the ideal pattern) as they get older. This tendency in itself causes jealousy among the wives. In addition, any inequality in the distribution of gifts or money, or in the number of children born and died, or in the amount of education received by the children, adds to the jealousy and hatred. A woman who becomes barren or whose children die almost always believes that her co-wife has achieved this through witchcraft or poisoning. She may then attempt retaliation.

Although bitter hatred may develop between co-wives, there are some Nyansongo families in which they get on well and cooperate closely. In one case, three co-widows maintain nearby households in conspicuous amity, which they attribute to their husband's deliberate attempts to foster good will before his death 17 years ago. At three homesteads where the co-wives are disparate in age—two of the older wives have children the same age as their co-wives—there are amicable relations among the women. In these cases the younger wife has accepted domination by the older, working with her in the fields, asking her advice and help in child care, gossiping casually with her in the afternoon, and so on. Where co-wives are closer in age, they may be superficially polite and cooperative but harbor grudges which result in their not talking for months at a time.

The husband who attempts to foster good will between co-wives is rare. Ordinarily he takes measures only to prevent already existing hatred from becoming expressed in violent acts. The usual provocation is the wife's refusal to do something for the husband on the grounds that the co-wife has not been doing her share. The husband, aware of the bitterness between them, takes the occasion to punish the one he regards as responsible. He may beat her or reprimand her semipublicly, so that neighbors can hear it. One morning Ogaro was reprimanding his second wife, Nyaboke, a young woman who has a girl of 12 and one of 8 and who has not been able to conceive again, while her older co-wife, Moraa, produces a child every two years. He was outside Nyaboke's house, shouting at her:

Moraa (first wife) is about to give birth and you won't work and go out drinking everywhere, coming back late at night. You may think because you don't have small children you can go wherever you want. But there are many women who have no children and they're obedient to their husbands and work hard. If you think it's me who is not giving you children, I'm not forcing you to stay here. Go somewhere else and see if you get children there.
Nyaboke: One time I was ill and Moraa didn't help me and didn't bring me anything.
Ogaro: If that is the case, then don't you go to her or help her now, but you obey me. (Turning to an old man): I'm about to leave for work at Kericho and I want you to tell her to obey me and keep feuds from occurring in my homestead. (Turning back to Nyaboke): I didn't want to quarrel, but you quarreled with her (Moraa's) daughter and you seem to want her not to have children. I didn't stop you from having children, it was God, and you can go accuse God if you want. When you were ill, I took time to take you for treatment, and most of the property, like the goat (for sacrifice), for that purpose came from Moraa's house. Well now I'm returning to work and if you follow me there I'll kick you and beat you, and you'll never see a cent from me again . . . You always claim that Moraa is given more. When I give you each five shillings, you say I've given her ten. And when I give you each a pound of sugar, you say I've given her five pounds. And it's the same with meat.

This case illustrates the troubles arising from the inequalities in child-bearing capacity among co-wives and the way in which the husband treats the jealousy when it is abruptly brought to his attention. So long as the wives have a superficially friendly relationship, however, he is unlikely to make threats or humiliate one or the other of them.

THE EXTENDED FAMILY HOMESTEAD

The extended family homestead is a clearly defined social and territorial entity which includes one or more mother-child households. It has such autonomy as a residential unit that educated Gusii refer to it in English as "village," although it is much smaller than a village in the ordinary sense. The residents of a homestead are: the man who is homestead head, his wives, his unmarried children, and his married sons and their wives and children. It is thus equivalent to the polygynous extended family as a local group. The homestead has its own land and cattle and is separated from other homesteads by boundary hedges, trees, and jointly used pastures.

Although there is a word in the Gusii language which means homestead (*omochie*), a particular homestead group may be referred to as the *egesaku* * or "patrilineal descent group" of its head. In this sense it means the head and his sons, his male descendants, who continue to live there throughout their lives and whose sons will live there too. The descent group is thought of as being divided into several *chinyomba* or "households," each one composed of the sons of a particular wife. Full brothers, who actually grew up in the same house (*enyomba*) —that of their mother—comprise as adults a symbolic household distinct from the sons of other mothers within the descent group of the homestead. This division is spatially represented (see map 3, p. 25) by the fact that married sons build their houses nearer to the houses of their mothers than to the houses of the father's other wives; it is represented in behavior by closer and friendlier relations between full brothers and their wives than between half-brothers and their wives. Many of the hostilities between the co-wives are thus passed on to their sons.

The homestead head is traditionally a patriarch with much control of family resources. He takes charge of all transactions from the nego-

* Literally, *egesaku* refers to the side entrance to a Gusii house from the cattle pen. The application of this label to the descent group apparently refers both to the identity of that group with its herds of cattle and to the fact that patrilineally related elders must enter the house through that door.

tiations for a daughter's bridewealth to the purchase of coffee seedlings. All the land and cattle of the homestead legally belong to him despite their "temporary" allocation among the several households. When he dies, the property is inherited by his sons (or closest heirs in the male line), supposedly according to his last instructions. Legitimate claims to property left by the father, however, are based by the son on which fields were cultivated by his mother and how many head of cattle, sheep, and goats were associated with her household. The cattle given as bridewealth for the daughters of a woman and any animals or grain acquired through her own efforts are thought of as belonging to her household and being reserved primarily for the marriages or inheritance of the woman's sons. The homestead head has the power to use such property for his own secondary marriages or for the marriages of sons of other households under certain circumstances (Mayer, 1950b: 27–29), but by doing so he establishes a debt between the household of the new wife and the one from which the cattle were taken. Such debts are never forgotten, and if not settled during the lifetime of the homestead head, they come up as inheritance disputes afterward. Thus the division of the homestead into mother-son units figures importantly in the allocation and inheritance of property.

In the relationship between a Nyansongo father and his adult son, formality, respect, and obedience are key qualities. The son is expected to act deferentially to his father, never contradict or embarrass him, and certainly never shout at him regardless of provocation. The father, however, may shout at the son and scold him abusively for misdeeds. Father and son may never bathe together, see each other naked, or discuss sexual topics in the presence of each other. Even their jointly hearing a sexual discussion or witnessing the copulation of animals is embarrassing. A son may want to ask his father to help him buy medicines to cure venereal disease, but he must confess his contraction of the disease through intermediaries rather than experience the shame of discussing it directly. This sex avoidance and embarrassment between persons of adjacent generations are called *ensoni* and will be discussed for other relationships later. In Nyansongo thought, the quintessence of *ensoni* in the father-son relationship is the rule that the father must never enter the house of a married son; both daughter-in-law avoidance and general privacy from the homestead head appear to be involved in this. A good son is not only deferential but also obedient, and the father's commands may involve his son's marriages, economic affairs, and the welfare of his children. The son is dependent on his father for cattle to marry with, land to cultivate, and the favor that will help him establish himself as an heir in good standing when the father dies. Although a son may go off and earn money outside the district, it is rarely enough to provide him with a full bridewealth at a young age. Furthermore, the father expects the son to bring him expensive gifts, such as blankets, lanterns, supplies of tea and sugar. Some sons are unwilling to share their earnings with their fathers, particularly because where money is concerned, they fear the father's turning it over to his other sons for immediate use in bridewealth or school fees. In general, however, sons do share their earnings, are glad to help their brothers in education, if not in marriage, and bestow gifts on their fathers. The obedience of contemporary sons may not be as great as it once was, but except in economic crises, Nyansongo filial piety would rank high on a world-wide scale.

In everyday interaction, Nyansongo adult sons and fathers do not overtly display the dominance-submission relationship which holds between them. A son will stay out of his father's way for the most part, and a father does not attempt to interfere with the daily movements and activities of his sons so long as they are not disruptive. But a father takes very seriously the rules of the relationship, refusing, for example, to enter a son's house for a chair for a visitor, even though there is no one else to get it and he wants to provide for his guest. In matters of marriage and property, the dominance of the father, and his severity if not respected, becomes manifest. The father of one Nyansongo son who sold a cow for school fees had him arrested by the Kenya police and burned down his house while he was in custody. A father may also put a curse on a disobedient son and beat the latter's mother. Most sons are keenly aware of their father's powers to punish them, and they obtain paternal permission before making any decision to allocate property.

Mother-son relations, by contrast with father-son, are more informal but also involve sex avoidance. Mother and son may argue freely without fear of offending each other so long as obscene expressions are not used. A son respects his mother but is not deferential to her, and their interaction has a relaxed, lighthearted quality that is never found between father and son. In terms of sex avoidance, the adult son may not go behind the partition (see Figure 1, p. 26) in his mother's house; he must be served food by her in the foyer of the house or outside. The explicit reason for this is sexual modesty, since the son should not see his mother squatting over the cooking fire with her dress pulled up on her thighs and should not be in the presence of her marital bed. Sexual activities and obscenity must not be an object of their joint attention, and here again deep embarrassment may be experienced if one breaks this rule or accidentally intrudes on the privacy of the other. When this happens, one party or the other leaves the scene, and the occurrence is not mentioned afterward.

The mutual loyalty of mothers and adult sons is a pronounced characteristic of Nyansongo families. A mother never admits to outsiders that her son has done wrong, no matter what the opinion of the community. One woman whose dead son had been a notorious thief would not concede this about him, even though the whole homestead was allegedly endangered by antitheft magic as a result of her refusal. A widow whose son had been deserted by two successive wives complained bitterly about the moral character of the wives even though circumstances indicated that her son was impotent, which is a legitimate ground for divorce. When rambunctious women destroyed a potato field of the same widow during female initiation ceremonies, her son ran out to chase the women and threatened them with punishment. This reciprocal protectiveness is a recognition of their common fate, for a son acquires his share of the patrimony through rights established by the mother and her daughters, while a mother gains helpers in her daughters-in-law and is dependent on her sons and their wives when she is old and feeble.

The *ensoni* feeling of sexual shame is considered by Nyansongans to be at the very core of their morality. In the homestead it is strongest between father and daughter or daughter-in-law, next strongest between father and sons, less between mother and son and weakest between mother and daughter or daughter-in-law. Among siblings of the same sex, it is only felt if there is a difference in age of a decade or more and even then may not be strong or permanent.

The homestead head uses his traditionally dominant position *vis-à-vis* wives and sons to keep conflict between the several households at a minimum. In such conflict a mother and her adult sons will act as a unit, with sons defending their mother against the father's favoritism, and the mother pleading with the father not to punish or disinherit a disobedient son even though she knows he has done wrong. Most polygynists find it necessary to maintain an attitude of impartiality with respect to their several households in order to avoid fanning the flames of family strife by undue favoritism. Those who are wealthy or have many wives have nearby houses of their own separate from those of their wives where they can spend time without arousing jealousy. A polygynist also has *emonga,* that is, land the produce from which is not allocated to the households but kept for his own use. Impartiality and a forceful, domineering manner constitute the Nyansongo formula for a successful homestead head. Even when friendly and cooperative relations among wives and half-brothers are maintained in the conduct of everyday affairs, however, an unequal occurrence of personal misfortune may mobilize latent aggression between households in the form of witchcraft or sorcery accusations. When the homestead head dies, the homestead most often dissolves as a social unit, each married son tending to form his own homestead on the land left by his father, with his mother and perhaps an unmarried brother continuing to reside there. In the acrimonious disputes over inherited property, one or more of the sons may decide to move elsewhere if land is available. Since the land is rapidly becoming filled up, more sons are now forced to remain at their father's homestead after his death, and land holdings are consequently becoming fragmented into smaller pieces.

THE LINEAGE SYSTEM

The patrilineal descent group of the Nyansongo homestead is the nucleus of an extensive system of patrilineages which plays an important part in the organization of Gusii social life. As with the descent group of the homestead, only men are full members of this system, and descent is traced through the male line to a common ancestor. Several related homesteads whose male members are descendants of one grandfather recognize themselves as a single mourning group * (abanyamatati) and observe a rule of ritual head-shaving at each other's funerals. They also eat the sacrificial meat together at the funeral and were at one time responsible for providing compensation for a homicide committed by one of their members. Two or more mourning groups together compose a riiga † ("hearthstone" lineage); its male members are usually descendants of one great-grandfather or great-great-grandfather. The riiga lineage is the largest kin group within which there is much hospitality and intimacy and was in some areas associated in the past with the joint herding of cattle by young men. Several related riiga lineages form a "clan-house"; two or more clan-houses compose a subclan; and several subclans make up a clan. The amount of subdivision within a clan varies from one area to another, particularly with size; a large clan often recognizes many more units between the riiga and clan levels than does a small clan. The clan ‡ is a large patrilineage which was often an independent political-

* For the exact relationships involved in the mourning group, see Mayer (1949: 18–19).

† Riiga literally means "hearthstone" of which a house has three, and metaphorically denotes subdivisions of a clan. See Table 1, p. 37.

‡ We follow Mayer (1949: 9–10) in using the word clan to refer to the maximal exogamous lineage, called eamate in the Gusii language.

military unit before British administration, and it is also the largest exogamous unit, requiring its members to marry outside the group, and the maximal group within which kinship terms are used. Thus the proximate Gusii lineage system is made up of kin groups increasing in inclusiveness and generational depth from homestead group to clan, all based on the principle of tracing descent through the male line to a common ancestor.

The lineage groups in Nyansongo are not intact lineages for the most part but fragments of kin groups whose other members either remained in older settlements or moved to different ones in Nyaribari during the migration to new areas that began in 1930. Every man in Nyansongo is a member of a hearthstone lineage (and hence of a subclan and clan) which has members in other communities; some persons even have fellow members of their mourning group living elsewhere. Despite their territorial dispersal and the cessation of their joint military activity, lineages of hearthstone level and below do have some corporate functions based on inheritance rights in each other's property. If a man dies without sons, his brothers inherit his land and cattle; if he has no brothers either, then property is inherited by those lineage members who stand closest in relationship to the deceased. If a whole mourning group were wiped out, its property would be inherited by a mourning group of the same hearthstone lineage, and so forth. In similar fashion are widows inherited, except that the heir must be of the same generation, and the widow has some freedom of choice. These inheritance rights, though residual, produce a sense of common interest in members of a lineage even when they are not living near one another. Many of the contemporary inhabitants of Nyansongo settled there at the invitation of fellow lineage members who took up residence there first. The military defense of joint property is no longer a consideration, but lineage members have been known to share the expenses of litigation in order to keep a disputed piece of land from being taken by someone of a different lineage. In general, a lineage of any order tends to act as a unit only when its interests are endangered by outsiders; such occasions are fewer nowadays than 50 years ago.

A striking feature of the Gusii lineage system is its use of the family idiom in the conceptualization of relations between descent groups. As mentioned above, just as the descent group of the homestead is called the *egesaku* of its head, and is made up of *chinyomba* or households, so a lineage of any order is the *egesaku* of its founding ancestor and is made up of subdivisions called *chinyomba*. This usage is perfectly consistent with the terminology referring to the homestead, since lineage members trace their ancestry back to a particular homestead head and, furthermore, often distinguish segments of the lineage by reference to his different wives and their households. The genealogy of a lineage is its history from its origin as a polygynous family to its present state. Lineages also suffer from the same internal dissensions as homesteads; the larger they are, the more segments or "households" they have, each one of which is jealous and suspicious of the other. Thus not only the same nomenclature but also some of the same motivations characterize both polygynous families and the lineages for which they are points of origin.

The family analogy also affects the rules of behavior among members of a clan. One's real father and mother are called *tata* and *baba*, respectively. All men of one's father's generation within the clan are called *tatamoke*, "little father," and clanswomen of the parental generation are called *makomoke*, which English-speaking Gusii translate as "little mother." In like manner, clansmen of the grandparental generation are called "grandmother" or "grandfather," and those of one's own generation are considered, if not called, "brother" and "sister." Nieces, nephews, and other clanspersons of that generation are called "my child," and those of the grand-nephew generation are called "grandchild." Thus for a given individual, the entire clan is made up of several generational layers, to each one of which he applies one or two terms derived from relationships in his immediate family.

There are definite rules concerning the individual's behavior toward persons in each of the generational layers. The parental generation is made up of his *abansoni*, that is, the persons in whose presence he experiences *ensoni* or sexual shame. Just as he must avoid physical immodesty and sexual discussion in the presence of his real parents, so must he practice such avoidance with respect to his "little fathers" and "little mothers" throughout the clan. The avoidance rules for classificatory parents are not quite as strict as those within the homestead group, for example, while a real father may not enter a son's house at all, a classificatory father may enter one room (*eero*) of the house and only through the cattle-pen doorway (*egesaku*). Furthermore, a man's father's brother (his "little father") may be his own age or younger, contrary to the implications of the paternity relationship. In such a case, serious avoidance does not begin until one of the parties has married, and it becomes stricter as they get older. The reserve of real father and son, however, is never reached, and a man may make passing reference to publicly known sex crimes in the presence of his father's brother while he could not do so within hearing of his real father. Hence, though behavior toward clansmen of the parental generation is patterned after customary behavior toward real parents, avoidance is not expected to be as intense in the case of classificatory parents.

Many incidents occurring in Nyansongo, where everyone belongs to the same clan, indicated that *ensoni* between adjacent generations is not merely a matter of formal etiquette but a feeling experienced by individuals. A beer party discussion of venereal disease and adultery was abruptly stopped by a group of men when a classificatory daughter of some of them arrived on the scene. When a middle-aged woman was describing supernatural punishment for adultery to the ethnographer, her real daughter and a classificatory daughter-in-law giggled for a while, then retired to another house in the homestead, and warned away other visitors of their generation. During the female initiation ceremonies, when women, especially those of middle age, are permitted to disregard verbal and physical modesty as they sing and dance in public places, the younger men—their classificatory sons—assiduously avoided these places whenever possible. When by ritual necessity or accident they were present at such occasions, the men displayed signs of acute embarrassment and fled at the first opportunity. Sexual embarrassment is more intense between persons who are not only of adjacent generational layers but also of opposite sex. An informant expressed the mortification experienced by the crowd at a magical ceremony when two chickens happened to copulate, by saying, "It was shameful; 'fathers' and 'daughters' were there."

Feelings of sexual shame can be avoided by conformity to the avoidance rules for persons of adjacent generations. With kin of the parental generation within the clan (and parents-in-law outside) one may not: shake hands (customary greeting between equals), sleep in the same house (except for adjacent generation females), bathe together or see each other naked, engage in joking insults (which are usually obscene), discuss sexual topics freely, or argue freely. The last mentioned rule is sometimes considered separately as "respect" (*ogosika*), since it is a prohibition on verbal aggression rather than sexual immodesty as such. In general, the attitude of respect is more important for conduct toward "little fathers" and sex avoidance more important with "little mothers." The maintenance of properly restrained behavior causing embarrassment to no one is facilitated by the use of an elaborate euphemistic vocabulary for sex and bodily functions in discussion between adjacent generation persons.

The rules governing relationships between clansmen not of adjacent generations require less restraint and involve less embarrassment; they lack the elements of sex avoidance and respect which characterize classificatory parent-child relations. This lack of restraint is particularly striking in relations between an individual and his real or classificatory grandparents. He may discuss sex and insult them jokingly. In fact, the characteristic pattern of interaction in this relationship involves obscene insults, humorous inquiries about sexual activity, and deprecation of the other's sexual competence. Despite the reciprocal nature of this warm, joking relationship, real grandparents may make economic demands which must be respected by the grandchild. If a classificatory grandparent is approximately the same age as the grandchild, their relations are as free and equal as if they were of the same generational status. Great-grandparents, however, are "like parents" and must be treated with the respect and sex avoidance required in adjacent-generation relations.

With clanspeople of one's own generation, classificatory brothers and sisters, one may shake hands, enter each other's houses, and argue. Sexual shame as such is not felt with these generational equals, but cross-sex avoidance is nevertheless practiced, at least in public situations. For example, a young man may bathe at the river with his male same-generation kin, sleep in the same house, and discuss sex topics with them, using obscene expressions. All of these are prohibited with *female* kin of the same generation and clan, who are barred as sex objects by the incest taboo. Despite the fact that this taboo is frequently violated by young adolescents, boys are afraid to treat such girls in a familiar way in public because of the possibility of discovery by someone of the parental generation. In general, however, it is within the same generation in a clan that relationships of the greatest intimacy and freedom are carried on.

To summarize, the Gusii lineage system is a set of organized social groups based on common descent through the paternal line and on varying degrees of common locality and mutual interest. Lineage structure and growth are explicitly conceived of in terms derived from the polygynous family homestead, which is the nuclear unit of the system. Each lineage up to and including the clan is stratified into generations whose relationships are explicitly patterned after, though not identical with, customary relationships in the family. Sex avoidance and unilateral respect characterize the relations of adjacent generations, while less restrained behavior is possible for persons of alternate generations and those of the same generation.

LOCALIZED KIN GROUPS

All of the inhabitants of Nyansongo community belong to a single clan, Abanyaribari, the largest clan in Nyaribari Location and the one to which thé chief belongs. There are three neighborhoods in the community, each one consisting of a separate lineage fragment. The smallest neighborhood, on the side of Nyansongo nearest to the chief's estate, is composed of four homesteads of the chief's subclan, Bonyamosicho, which was formerly represented in the area in larger numbers. Each of the four homesteads is closely related to only one of the others. The other two neighborhoods contain seven homesteads apiece of the Omobea subclan. In one of them the oldest males of the seven homesteads trace their ancestry to two wives of a common great-grandfather; in the other, the homestead heads are descended from three wives of a common great-great-grandfather. Many of the other descendants of these ancestors are living in similar communities elsewhere in Nyaribari Location. The lineage fragments composing the three neighborhoods of Nyansongo are on friendly terms, despite the fact that they do not have a common subclan affiliation. In fact, two homesteads have most of their neighborly relationships with homesteads outside of their own lineage groups; both are on neighborhood borders and have been involved in quarrels with their own kinsmen. Thus Nyansongo is a one-clan community composed of three lineage fragments living in somewhat vaguely defined neighborhoods.

Clan membership gives residents of Nyansongo some sense of common identity, particularly because the community borders on the communities of two alien and formerly hostile clans with whom Nyansongans intermarry. Even those families who have out-clan neighbors living nearer to them than anyone else have a minimum of contact with these unrelated people. All of their visiting, beer drinking, and cooperative work arrangements are with their Nyansongo clansmen. Where Nyansongo bounds a community of the same clan, however, active social relationships are carried on across the border, to the point that it was difficult to determine the community to which such borderline homesteads primarily belong. The social interaction of Nyansongo homesteads is thus conditioned by clan affiliation as well as by mere spatial proximity.

COMMUNITY AND NEIGHBORHOOD

The local community is defined here as the largest unit of contiguous homesteads which recognize the reciprocal obligation to participate in the trading of work for beer, known as *risaga*. The unit is thus equivalent to what the Gusii call "large *risaga*." Ordinarily, natural features such as streams or groves of trees define some of the boundaries of this group. Community members are members of the same clan, though they may be of different lineages, and as part of the *risaga* relationship, they recognize a one-day ban on heavy work for each other's funerals and hold their initiation ceremonies jointly. Each community is made up of several neighborhoods. A neighborhood is a cluster of homesteads whose members belong to the same lineage (either mourning group or *riiga*) and who work and visit with one another more frequently than they do with other members of the same community. The neighborhood is roughly equivalent to the "small *risaga*," more frequently used for trading work for beer than its larger counterpart. The women of one neighborhood tend to form a single cooperative work group (*egesangio*). Although the neighborhood is a territorial unit within the community, its boundaries may not be marked by any natural features. Homesteads at the boundaries of two neighborhoods may be more closely related to one by descent but work with the other. Homesteads bordering other communities of the same clan may shift their orientation from one community to another, causing uncertainty as to the exact boundary. Neither the community nor the neighborhood has any formal organization or institutionalized leadership.

SOCIAL SOLIDARITY

Although the people of Nyansongo cooperate in work, recreation, and ritual, and although their relations are conditioned by kinship regulations, they value homestead privacy and autonomy over neighborhood solidarity. The local community as an unnamed segment of a continuously settled area, with no formal political organization of its own, does not inspire special loyalty in its members. The settlement of dispersed homesteads has no public place or building as a spatial focus for group sociability. Accidental meetings of persons from different homesteads occur on the road, along the paths, and at the stream, but prolonged gatherings occur only at private residences and tend to be small. Despite the subdivision of the community along neighborhood and lineage lines, there is no factionalism, partly because the community has too few joint activities around which factions might crystallize. Individual homestead groups frequently develop antagonisms with one another and sometimes break off relations, but such quarrels usually arise within neighborhoods and lineage fragments rather than between them. The result is that there are no strongly cohesive groupings of homesteads in Nyansongo.

※
※
※

Chapter 4

Daily Routine

The activities of the Nyansongo family are not regulated by accurate calculation of time but by the sun and the press of seasonal circumstances. Each married woman (except the newly married, who eats at the house of her mother-in-law) has her own house, fields, and granary and is responsible for the cultivation of the fields as well for preparing food for her unmarried children (most of whom live in her house), her husband, and overnight visitors. With so many tasks to perform it is not surprising that the adult woman of the house is the first to rise in the morning, often at dawn, and after quickly dressing, builds a fire on which to cook eleusine gruel for the family's breakfast. On some mornings in the seasons of greatest agricultural activity, pressure from her cooperative work group to leave early forces the woman to provide her husband and children only with cold leftovers from the previous evening's meal.

Adult men arise later than their hard-working wives unless they have to attend a case at the African Tribunal Court, for which they may leave before dawn to make sure they arrive during the morning session. If a man does not have any specific task to do in the morning, he will eat and sit awhile, wrapped in the blanket under which he slept, before getting dressed. The children get up and eat when they want, though rarely much later than their mother, and they do not bother to dress until a few hours later. The boy or boys responsible for cattle herding must let the cows out of their pen next to the house and take them to the pasture before 8:30 A.M. Men and older children dash cold water on their faces in the morning, but washing is not considered a necessary part of the daily routine, except by adolescent girls. Each individual goes into a grove of trees or a bushy pasture for elimination, in order to insure complete privacy. Leaves serve as toilet paper.

Morning at the house is punctuated by the comings and goings of the individual residents. The woman of the house goes to work in the fields and leaves a child at home in charge. The boys are out in the pastures with the livestock, and girls carry pots of water home from the stream below. The man of the house may be occupied at home with mending fences, building a house, or tending to his coffee garden, or he may be helping a neighbor perform these chores in return for beer. If he goes to court or to see the chief or a government official for some favor, he will be away from home for the better part of the day. Despite the apparent dispersal of men, women, and children, it is often the case that no one is far from the house. The woman may be working a field adjacent to the homestead; the cattle pastures are nearby; and the stream is only a few hundred yards down the hill. Thus, except for those families who live nearer to the chief and cultivate land on his estate a mile or two from their homes, homesteads are not deserted during the daytime, for many family activities take place within shouting distance of home.

At 10:30 or 11:00 in the morning, the boys bring the cows home to be milked, and if the mother has been working nearby, she does the milking herself. She may cook a meal for the children at this time, particularly if breakfast has been inadequate and they are hungry. Such a meal may be simply boiled sweet potatoes or, if the father or guests are present, it may consist of baskets of dry maize or eleusine porridge (cooked by boiling meal in water) with beans, soured milk, or a spinach-like wild leaf called *chinsaga,* as a condiment. A large piece of dry porridge is taken by hand and cupped into shape so that it can be used to pick up some of the condiment. Meat can be used as a condiment, but the people of Nyansongo cannot afford meat; grain porridge predominates in their daily diet.

During midday, the women do not continue their cooperative cultivation but return to it either in the cool of the late afternoon or the next morning. At home, besides preparing the midday meal they attend to the grinding and threshing of eleusine, fetch water from the river, direct the work of the children in various tasks, visit one another, and pack kerosene tins full of corn kernels to be taken to the power mill two miles away for grinding into meal. If they expect to entertain guests or neighbors in the near future, the women bury grain flour and germinate eleusine in the earth for several days and fry it into small hard pieces which, when diluted with boiling water, make the beer the Gusii love so well. The boys take the cattle down to the stream to drink at noon, and girls continue the tasks their mothers have ordered them to perform. Local litigation takes place in the early afternoon and is an occasional focus of attention for adult men in the community. Otherwise there are no distinctive afternoon activities.

There is no rigid daytime schedule which the people of Nyansongo follow; each adult varies his schedule from day to day on the basis of family needs, neighborhood events, and personal inclination. As the day ends, however, individual activities converge into set routines which vary only with age and sex status. Women collect firewood in pastures and fallow fields. As they move about in the dusk, they are often frightened by the eerie shapes of bushes and trees which they imagine to be wild animals. Because of this tendency, the Gusii call the period of day in which the sun sets "women's eyes."

For married men this is the time of day for beer parties. Any Nyansongo man meeting a friend or neighbor in the late afternoon will ask where he is coming from and if there is beer there. Many men will find their way to the house of one who is serving beer to his neighbors. Each one brings his own 1-foot long bamboo drinking tube, puts it into the pot of boiling beer, and sits down inside the house to drink. Married women are allowed to drink a bit of the beer, but unmarried men are excluded from the house to avert the possibility of a quarrel with their elders when intoxicated. Despite such preventive measures, beer parties are often the scenes of bitter quarrels among neighbor-relatives, and most Gusii crimes of violence take place during or after a good deal of such drinking. Singing of traditional songs and individual dancing (mostly arm and neck movements) go on, but the pleasant atmosphere can easily be broken by a belligerent boast or deliberate insult aimed at one man by another, if both are drunk.

In the house where a beer party is not in progress, the wife prepares a meal of dry porridge and condiments for her husband and children. The children eat from one basket, and a separate basket of porridge is prepared for the husband. If he is at a party at which a large quantity of beer prolongs the gathering until late at night, the wife and children eat by themselves but leave the husband's food intact to be eaten by him on his return.

Fear of the dark drastically limits nocturnal activity in Nyansongo. Witches are most feared at night, but there is also a widespread (and incorrect) belief that hyenas are at large in the area and that they harm humans. Women are much more reluctant to go out at night than men, who by adolescence have overcome some of the nocturnal fears of childhood. Married women who walk miles away from home by themselves in the daytime are at night too frightened to go 20 yards to another house in the homestead unaccompanied. Unmarried men are the most frequent voyagers in the night, seeking sexual liaisons and arranging dancing parties with young girls whose fears must be constantly allayed. The men themselves carry kerosene lanterns to still their own apprehensions.

House-bound at night by fear, the family retires not long after the evening meal. All clothes are taken off for sleeping, and a woolen blanket covers the husband (if he is there), wife, and small children, who sleep at their mother's side in ascending age order. The traditional bed is simply a raised portion of the dung floor covered with cowhides near the hearth where cooking takes place. Most Nyansongo families, however, have purchased wooden bedsteads with hand-tied rope webbing. In the rainy season, when nights are cold and damp, the cooking fire is kept going for warmth; at other times the house is warm enough from the evening meal, since the thatched roof lets out only a limited amount of smoke and heat. Goats, sheep, and chickens sleep inside the house. Old widows sleep in their own houses but sometimes have as companions girls from the homestead who are considered too big to sleep with their mothers when the father is present in the house. The older boys sleep out in a small hut of their own.

⚹

⚹

⚹

Chapter 5

Sex and Marriage

Three traditional rules provide the setting for Nyansongan sexual and marital behavior: (1) No one may marry into his own clan, for all of its members are classified as relatives. Intermarrying clans are traditional enemies and in the past carried on blood feuds, as expressed in the Gusii proverb, "Those whom we marry are those whom we fight;" (2) At marriage the wife must go to live at the homestead of her husband and his parents. There she is granted economic rights and a legitimate social position neither of which would be obtainable had she remained at the home of her own parents. Eventually a woman becomes incorporated into her husband's kin group, but as a newly-wed she is conscious of being a stranger in the enemy camp; (3) A respectable marriage requires the payment of cattle and goats to the bride's father, in number and quality satisfactory to him, before she takes up residence at her husband's home. The bridewealth cattle give the husband exclusive sexual rights over the wife and the custody of all children to whom she gives birth. If he dies, these rights are inherited by a real or classificatory brother of the husband. The rights may only be relinquished by the husband's clan on return of the entire bridewealth.* Thus the marriage system of Nyansongo is characterized by clan exogamy, patrilocal residence, bridewealth, and the levirate.

Girls are 15 years old on the average when they marry, while males average 18 to 20 years old at their first marriage. There is more variability in age on the male side, since the possession of the bridewealth cattle is required and proves a temporary barrier for many of the less fortunate young men. For example, a youth who lacks livestock, and has no uterine sisters whose bridewealth he may use, is likely to be 25 or 30 before he can afford marriage. On the other hand, a boy from a family which is exceptionally wealthy in cattle or which has a disproportionate number of married female children may be married when he is barely pubescent and recently initiated. There is no such inequality among girls, however, because their marriages bring wealth to the family and they may become secondary wives of older men if no eligible bachelors are available.

For most individuals, sexual activity begins long before marriage, although premarital liaisons are not approved by older people and must be carried on privately. Young people are particularly afraid of having their sexual activity come to the attention of their parents or other persons of the parental generation. A circumcised boy has his own hut within the homestead and is not subjected to intense supervision by parents so long as he is discreet enough not to bring his sexual behavior forcibly to their notice. From the age of 14 or 15 onward, boys are active in seeking heterosexual affairs, concentrating their efforts at first on girls in their own community. Since such girls are of their own clan and sex relations with them constitute incest in the eyes of elders, these affairs are extremely surreptitious and fraught with anxiety. The Gusii, unlike surrounding cultural groups, do not practice partial or interfemural intercourse before marriage; with complete penetration, the fear of pregnancy and subsequent parental and community reaction are considerable.

During the female initiation ceremonies, adolescent boys of a single

---

* The amount of bridewealth returned is diminished in proportion to the number of children the woman has borne; if there are three live children, nothing is returned, and the children remain with their father's kin group.

community, in a practice called "taking by stealth," sneak into houses where groups of adolescent girls of the same community are sleeping and attempt to have intercourse with them. The girls are usually successful in rebuffing them, but a few boys achieve a hurried and fearful act of coitus with girls who pretend to be sleeping. Despite the fact that this is a traditionally condoned practice, a boy who impregnates a classificatory "mother" or "daughter" under such conditions is regarded by the community as a serious offender against sexual morality.

In Nyansongo "taking by stealth" is becoming infrequent and in any case is limited to the brief period of annual female initiation. More commonly, boys of 14 to 18 seduce younger girls of the community, taking them to their own huts at night or meeting them in a wooded place near a stream. Other boys of this age turn to cows and other livestock for sexual gratification; when discovered, they are not severely chastised, as they are considered to be just "trying out their sexual organs." The cow must be disposed of by expelling it from Gusiiland, however, and a young man who repeatedly committed bestiality or did so at a later age would be thought to be insane and possessed by spirits. Homosexuality at this age or any other is regarded as inconceivable and occurs rarely if ever. Masturbation is also extremely rare, if it occurs at all.

When a youth reaches the maturity of 17 or 18 years, he turns to girls outside his own community and clan for sexual relationships. One reason for this is his fear that continued intercourse with girls of his own community will result in pregnancy and an incest scandal. This fear has a realistic basis in the fact that, as the boy gets older, he chooses as sexual partners girls who are losing their adolescent sterility and are more likely to conceive. Nyansongans believe, however, that it is the male whose reproductive powers are increasing. Another reason for the older unmarried male to seek sexual partners outside the community is that he has more confidence in himself than he did when he was inexperienced and is therefore ready to approach strange girls in the marketplace. The youth of 18 also has more opportunity than before to meet girls outside his own clan, for he is more frequently included in the marriage parties of his classificatory brothers. In fact, such a youth, if cattle have been made available to him through the marriage of his sister, or his father's wealth, may be looking for a wife himself and is old enough to be considered a prospective bridegroom when he enters the territory of an alien clan.

The marketplaces, at nearby Keumbu or Kegati (3 miles in the other direction), located at clan boundaries and free of parental surveillance, are favored places for young men and women of different clans to meet.

Marriage feasts provide other opportunities for such meetings and for explicitly sexual encounters. Further opportunities arise out of in-law relationships and the visiting involved in them. For example, it is assumed that a young man will try to seduce the maternal cross-cousin (mother's brother's daughter) of his half-brother or paternal cousin when she comes to visit. Premarital contact can also be initiated at community boundaries, along the road and paths leading to it, and at streams used by members of different clans. The liaisons arranged at these relatively public places are consummated in the privacy of a young man's hut or an isolated grove.

Nyansongo girls are not frank about their sexual feelings; they feign extreme reluctance even when they will yield quite easily to sexual advances. Young men woo them with gifts, flattery, and serenading. The girls try to prolong this initial stage of courtship, delaying the overt sexual advances of their suitors. Some girls appear to lead on eager young men in order to procure gifts and attentions at the market-place. Even when a girl goes willingly to a youth's hut or into the woods with him, she puts up some resistance to his sexual advances. He expects this and enjoys overcoming it, taking pleasure from her protestations and cries of pain. Aside from this patterned pose, most girls have sincere misgivings about premarital sexuality. They fear the disgrace of premarital pregnancy as well as public discovery of simply engaging in coitus on a particular occasion, with the resultant reputation of being a "slut" (*omokayayu*). They also fear parental punishment for such scandals, since the parents of a girl are eager to maintain her good reputation so that a substantial bridewealth will be offered for her. To this end, parents punish their marriageable daughters for staying out too late and straying too far from home. A youth's mistaking a girl's sincere reluctance for mere pretense can lead to rape, which is very frequent among the Gusii.*

Premarital liaisons are often quite brief; a couple may have inter-course on one or two occasions and thenceforward seek different part-ners. A young man who repeatedly seeks coitus with the same girl will have his actions interpreted as encouraging her to elope with him. She may also attempt to persuade him to marry her legitimately (i.e., with bridewealth). Many young men, however, do not consider it proper to have sexual relations with girls they intend to marry; consequently, they terminate affairs quickly and are constantly in search of new sexual partners. In general, individuals of both sexes have a few sexual encounters with each of a considerable number of persons before mar-riage.

* The frequency and etiology of rape are described in detail in LeVine (1959*b*).

The sexual motive for marriage is prevalent among young Nyan-songo men. Since premarital patterns of sexuality do not permit easy access to females or protracted relationships with them, marriage is viewed as a means of obtaining a stable sexual partner. Older people often say of a rapist or violator of incest regulations, "Why doesn't he get married?"—implying that this would solve his problem. This is not to say that young men do not desire legitimate offspring, the en-hanced social status of a married person, and the labor services which a wife owes her husband. Sex is only one motive for marriage, but it is more pronounced among the Gusii than among many other African groups where premarital sexual freedom is greater.

Any discussion of contemporary marriage in Nyansongo must take account of the legitimate marriage procedure based on tradition and the increasingly frequent unions which deviate from traditional prac-tice and are considered illegitimate. In this discussion, legitimate forms will be described first and then deviant practice.

Before he can arrange a legitimate marriage for himself, a young man must be permitted by his father to use some of the family's cattle for bridewealth. Even if the marriage of his uterine sister has provided the family with bridewealth, the youth must obtain his father's consent to use that bridewealth for his own marriage. A son who does not bother to obtain paternal consent may find himself arrested for theft by tribal policemen on the basis of a complaint registered by his father. A father may withhold consent in order to use the bridewealth for his own secondary marriage or because he wants to punish a particular son; in the latter event the cattle might be granted to a different son for his marriage. A family which is cattle poor and has more sons than daughters is often rent by the rivalry of sons over available cattle. When a man has obtained paternal consent for his use of bridewealth in marriage, he can proceed to select a mate. In so doing he must conform to Gusii incest regulations, which forbid not only marriage within the clan but also marriage with cross-cousins and others of his mother's kin group. Furthermore, he may not choose as a mate any girl whom his father had openly considered taking as a secondary wife, even if negotiations for the marriage had broken off early. This means that a wife must be chosen from among relative strangers. A young man will have met girls from other clans at the places mentioned earlier, and others will have caught his eye although he has not had social contact with them.

The appearance of a girl is an important criterion of her desirability as a mate. Girls who are considered beautiful are much sought after for marriage, while ugly girls have a slightly more difficult time getting married. Characteristics considered attractive in a girl are: brown skin (as opposed to black), firm and erect breasts (as opposed to those which are too small or too pendulous), smooth, soft skin, shapely hips and buttocks (as opposed to those which are too straight or too fat), full calves and thighs (as opposed to thin ones). Some men like their women stout, emphasizing the development of hips and buttocks, but this is not general. Facial characteristics are also important although more difficult to formulate. Small eyes, a narrow mouth, and a space between the upper incisors are considered attractive in girls. Opinions of Nyansongo youths differ on preferred features, but they all take physical appearance into account in the process of mate selection.

Once a young man has decided on a girl whom he is not prohibited from marrying and whom he considers attractive, he finds an intermediary (esigani), usually a young man of her clan who is his friend or distant kinsman. Sometimes a marriageable youth selects an intermediary before he has a particular girl in mind, and the intermediary helps him choose from among available girls he knows. In either event, the intermediary is someone in a better position than the prospective groom to obtain information about the girl and her family. There are two questions the intermediary must answer: What is the girl's sexual reputation? and, Is there witchcraft in her family? In answering the first question, the intermediary reports the girl as having a bad reputation only if she has achieved some notoriety as a "slut." He may in fact know of some premarital affairs she has had; yet he will tell the prospective groom she is chaste unless her sex life has involved a scandal. This is because no Nyansongan wants to know the details of his future wife's sex life; so long as her general reputation is not bad, he is free to think of her as innocent and chaste, an image which she herself helps to foster. If the intermediary indicates that she has had premarital intercourse, which most girls have, the prospective groom is likely to reject her.

The witchcraft issue is an important one in mate selection. If there is known to be witchcraft in a girl's family, then it is deemed likely that she herself practices witchcraft and will cause trouble in any family she marries into. The intermediary is responsible for conveying information of this type to the young man and his family, and it is not uncommon for a girl to be rejected on the basis of witchcraft in her background. A Nyansongo girl whose marriage was arranged found the betrothal broken off after her mother was accused of witchcraft by neighbors. It was said that the girl remained unmarried beyond the usual age because of her mother's reputation as a witch. In many cases, however, the evidence is ambiguous, since a family believed by some to contain witches may be considered witch-free by other people in the same community. Hence the intermediary must often decide which set of rumors to pass on, and bias in favor of the girl's family is inevitable. Furthermore, the family of the marriageable young man hears rumors from sources other than the single intermediary. They must dismiss some rumors and accept others, at least tentatively. In consequence, when a bride comes to her husband's home, she may not be entirely free of the suspicion of being a witch.

A final task of the intermediary is to find out whether the girl has any disfiguring marks on her body which are not visible when she is dressed. To this end, he asks girls who are close to her and have bathed with her in a stream whether she had any childhood injuries which left scars on her body. The existence of such scars, particularly those resulting from burns, is sometimes mentioned as the cause for refusal of a prospective bride.

These, then, are the criteria which a young man with cattle uses in selecting a bride: her physical attractiveness, her sexual reputation, and the reputation of her family concerning witchcraft. The intermediary, besides giving the prospective groom information on these topics, informs the girl's father of the young man's interest. If the father has no particular objection to the youth or his family, he agrees to the match, subject to a satisfactory payment of bridewealth. Shortly afterward, the prospective groom comes with some clansmen for a dance at the home of the girl. During the dance, the girl and her female friends scrutinize the prospective groom. If the girl, seeing him for the first time, has strong objections, she may refuse to go through with the marriage, although fathers sometimes coerce their daughters into matches. One of the young men accompanying the groom sees the girl's father and invites him to come and see the bridewealth cattle on a certain date.

The inspection of the bridewealth cattle by the father of the bride-to-be is an important occasion, taking place four or five days after the above-mentioned dance. If he is an influential or wealthy man, the groom's family must slaughter a bull or he-goat for him to eat during his visit. Negotiations take place concerning the number and quality of the cattle as well as the number of goats and other articles, such as a macintosh for the father of the bride and a metal bowl for her mother. Sometimes the groom's father is cajoled into replacing inferior cows with better ones that he can borrow or increasing the total number. For example, although the maximum bridewealth set by the African District Council is 6 cows, a bull, and 6 goats (or 8 cows), several marital transactions in and around Nyansongo during 1956–57 involved 10 and 12 cows. Other times, however, negotiations break down—usually over the quality of the particular beasts offered—and the marriage is called off. If an agreement is reached, the father of the bride takes the cattle home with him. They remain at his home for a month. During that time the marriage may be called off by either side if any of the cattle die of natural causes or the intermediary brings some derogatory information to the groom's family. When this happens, the bridewealth is returned.

A month after the transfer of cattle, the bride must be taken from her father's homestead to the home of the groom. Among the adjacent Luo and other East African tribes, it is customary for kinsmen of the bride to fight with kinsmen of the groom and attempt to prevent her departure. With the Gusii, however, it is the bride herself who resists, or who hides herself underneath the roof of a nearby house, and her father, having received the bridewealth cattle by this time, may even help persuade her to go if her reluctance appears to be sincere. Five young clansmen of the groom come to take the bride and two immediately find the girl and post themselves at her side to prevent her escape, while the others receive the final permission of her parents. When it has been granted, the bride holds onto the house post and must be dragged outside by the young men. Finally she goes along with them, cying and with her hands on her head. This traditional resistance is usually token and not really intended to break off the marriage.

When the reluctant bride arrives at the groom's house, the matter of first importance is the wedding night sexual performance. This is a trial for both parties in that the impotence of the groom may cause the bride to break off the marriage and the discovery of scars or deformities on the bride's body (including vaginal obstruction) may induce the groom to send her home and request a return of the bridewealth. The bride is determined to put her new husband's sexual competence to the most severe test possible. She may take magical measures which are believed to result in his failure in intercourse. These include chewing a piece of charcoal or a phallic pod commonly found in pastures, putting either of these or a knotted piece of grass under the marriage bed, and twisting the phalluslike flower of the banana tree. The groom for his part is determined to be successful in the face of her expected resistance; he fortifies himself by being well fed, which is believed to favor potency, by eating bitter herbs, and nowadays by eating large quantities of coffee beans, valued as an aphrodisiac. His brothers and paternal male cousins give him encouragement and take a great interest in his prospects for success in the impending sexual contest. Numerous young clansmen of the groom gather at the homestead in a festive mood; chickens are killed for them to eat, and they entertain themselves by singing and dancing while waiting for the major events of the wedding night.

The bride usually refuses to get onto the bed; if she did not resist the groom's advances, she would be thought sexually promiscuous. At this point some of the young men may forcibly disrobe her and put her on the bed. The groom examines the bride's mouth for pods or other magical devices designed to render him impotent. As he proceeds toward sexual intercourse, she continues to resist, and he must force her into position. Ordinarily she performs the practice known as *ogotega,* allowing him between her thighs but keeping the vaginal muscles so tense that penetration is impossible. If the groom is young (by traditional standards, under 25), the young men intervene, reprimand the bride, and hold her in position so that penetration can be achieved on the first night. An older groom, however, is considered strong enough to take care of himself, and the young men wait outside the door of the house, looking in occasionally to check on his progress. It is said that in such cases a "fierce" girl in the old days could prevent the groom from achieving full penetration as long as a week. Brides are said to take pride in the length of time they can hold off their mates. In 1957, a girl succeeded in resisting the initial attempts of her bridegroom. His brothers threatened and manhandled her until she confessed to having knotted her pubic hair across the vaginal orifice. They cut the knot with a razor blade and stayed to watch the first performance of marital coitus by the light of a kerosene pressure lamp.

Once penetration has been achieved, the young men sing in jubilation and retire from the house to allow the groom to complete the nuptial sexual relations. They are keenly interested in how many times he will be able to perform coitus on the first night, as this is a matter of prestige and invidious comparison. He will be asked about it by all male relatives of his generation, and the bride will also be questioned on this score when she returns to visit her own family. It is said that the groom's clansmen also question the bride, in order to check on the groom's account of his attainment. Six is considered a minimally respectable number of times and twelve is the maximum of which informants had heard. They claimed that it was traditional to achieve orgasm twelve times, but that performances in recent years were lower.

An explicit object of such prodigious feats is to hurt the bride. When a bride is unable to walk on the day following the wedding night, the young men consider the groom "a real man," and he is able to boast of his exploits, particularly the fact that he made her cry.

After the wedding night, the bride remains at the home of the groom for a period ranging from two weeks to three months, following which she is allowed to return to her father's homestead (or "to her mother" as Nyansongans say) for as much as two months. When she comes home to her parents, the bride may plead for a termination of the marriage. One Nyansongo girl claimed that her mother-in-law was trying to teach her witchcraft—a common basis for divorce at this stage. The impotence of the husband is also a valid charge. The father of the bride may yield to her plea if her feelings seem so strong that she may desert her husband if forced to go back. Many fathers attempt to persuade or coerce their daughters into going back, however, particularly if the bridewealth cattle have already been used to bring another wife into the extended family. While she is at her parents' home, the bride, even if she intends to return to her husband, may accompany her unmarried friends to the marketplace, pretending to be unmarried in order to encourage would-be seducers to give her gifts. She does not have intercourse with them, however, for fear of supernatural sanctions against adultery.

Returning to her husband's home, the bride remains there and makes only occasional trips to visit her mother thereafter. If she does not become pregnant within a year, she may leave her husband for another man who offers to pay bridewealth for her. In such circumstances, the girl's father is obliged to repay the bridewealth of the first husband before or at the same time as he accepts that of the second. Many fathers do not refund the original bridewealth unless coerced, as attested to by the large number of indictments at the African Tribunal Courts for the "customary law" offense of accepting a second bridewealth without returning the first. Of the 51 legitimately married women residing in Nyansongo, 14, or 27.4%, had been married before with bridewealth paid. Most of these 14 left their first husbands because no children were born to them, but a few who were divorced already had children. Thus the first stage of marriage is a trial period during which the bride, who was so carefully selected by her husband and his family but had little say in the matter herself, can take steps to dissolve the union if she finds it unsatisfactory.

Up to this point the discussion has centered on the ideal case of the young man with an adequate bridewealth who is arranging his marriage in the traditional manner. In contemporary Nyansongo this ideal is no longer the most frequent practice. Scarcity of pasturage and the prohibition on raiding have put cattle into short supply. As the same time, cattle are absolutely required for a legitimate marriage, and the bridewealth rate has risen sharply. It takes the entire pay of a tea plantation worker for at least 40 months to purchase the cattle necessary for a minimal bridewealth. In consequence, many young men are priced out of the marriage market, at least until their sisters grow up and get married. Since fathers do not want their daughters to be married without bringing in bridewealth, they are tempted to arrange matches with rich old men who want second, third, fourth, or fifth wives and who are willing to pay considerably more than the going bridewealth rate for them. The young girls themselves want neither old husbands nor positions as secondary wives, if they can help it, so they tend to run off with young men who cannot afford the bridewealth and live as their concubines. This does not necessarily mean that they are renouncing sexual virtue, however, for the young men with whom they elope often promise to pay the bridewealth to legitimize the union as soon as they can raise the necessary cattle. In many cases this promise is fulfilled, and concubinage becomes legitimate marriage.

When a young girl has been persuaded by a youth to elope with him, she goes off to his house secretly and begins living there as his wife. She is accepted by the young man's family as if she were his wife. The elopement infuriates the father of the girl, who has been cheated of the bridewealth. He makes inquiries, finally comes looking for her at the homestead of her lover. Usually she has been forewarned and has hidden herself; the irate father cannot find her and eventually leaves. Sometimes he takes some valued articles from the homestead, feeling that he has been deprived of his source of bridewealth and might as well get some compensation. Some days later, the lover visits the girl's father, admits she is living with him, and offers a reduced bridewealth for her. The father may well accept in order not to lose everything. Even after such an agreement is made, however, one or the other party may renege. The father, on his side, may lure the girl home with the pretense that her mother is ill and then let her be taken by some young men who carry her off to a man who has paid the bridewealth. Or, he may get the chief's tribal police to retrieve her and arrest the lover on the "customary law" charge of removing a girl without the consent of her parents, which is punishable by the African Tribunal Courts. The young man, on his side, might never follow through on his promise to give bridewealth, in which case the girl may leave him after a few months or years to live with another man who promises her eventual legitimacy or to marry one selected by her father on the basis of his ability to make the bridewealth transfer immediately.

Romantic love appears to be a factor in elopement. Not only do girls dislike the idea of marrying older men but they are also positively attracted to particular young men because of their appearance, manners, and personalities.* There are cases of girls who have repeatedly run away from legitimate unions arranged by their fathers to live as concubines with particular youths by whom they are attracted. A girl may also leave her lover for a man with bridewealth only to return to the lover when he has raised the bridewealth needed to ransom her.

Of the 51 legitimately married women living in Nyansongo, 4 were known to have lived in concubinage elsewhere before their marriages. At least 5 women were living in the community as concubines at one time or another during 1956–57. Several Nyansongo girls eloped with men of other clans, and one of them was acquiring a reputation as a "slut" who runs from man to man, a reputation that would make it difficult for her to contract a legitimate marriage later on.

When a girl is first married, she sleeps with her husband in his bachelor's hut but cooks and eats in the house of her mother-in-law. During the first year of marriage, before she has harvested her own fields and has her own grain store, she and her husband will eat food grown in his mother's fields. Afterward, the bride is allotted fields to cultivate in her father-in-law's homestead, and she is then no longer dependent on her mother-in-law's food supply. If she gets along well with her mother-in-law, the new wife may cook and eat in the older woman's house until shortly after the birth of her first child. If their relationship is not a close and amicable one, the young woman may begin cooking in her own house sooner.

A legitimate bride is told by her parents, "We have been given their cattle. Stay there, obey them, do as you're told, and don't do anything to displease your in-laws." In consequence she acts shy and submissive to her parents-in-law at first. This shyness is said to disappear with her mother-in-law when she first becomes pregnant and with her father-in-law when she has given birth to her first child. No one gives orders to the newly arrived bride, for she is eager to do everything without being told. When there is no water or wood, she will fetch it, and she goes to work in the fields when she sees the others going. Her domestic work is scrutinized by her husband and parents-in-law, but they do not openly

---

* Girls prefer men who are young, have regular facial features and (preferably) a space between the top incisors, act in a suavely provocative manner, give them gifts, and make promises of material well-being and of attention to their desires.

criticize her. The young women in the homestead, wives of her husband's brothers, may jokingly criticize her lack of skill. They may call her by nicknames indicating that she grinds coarse flour or cooks bad food. Such an appellation embarrasses her greatly, but not so much as if her parents-in-law or husband had used it, in which case it would be so humiliating that she would report it to her parents and have the marriage called off unless an apology were made. As a married woman grows older and bears children, her confidence within the homestead increases. She develops an egalitarian and jokingly intimate relation-ship with her mother-in-law, although deferring to her on important occasions. With her father-in-law, avoidance and respect continue strong, but overt deference may not be as pronounced as when she first arrived.

A married woman never loses contact with her parents and blood relatives. They visit each other; they bring her gifts when her children are born; she borrows food from them when her granaries are running low; she attends their funerals. The brothers of a Nyansongo wife who had loudly complained that her husband was neglecting her in favor of a new concubine came to visit her husband and urged him to take good care of their sister. When a young widow was too pregnant to hoe her fields, her brothers brought a plow and oxen and did the job for her free. A woman has a special relationship with a wife purchased for her brother with the bridewealth provided by her own marriage. She may take food from this sister-in-law's granary without asking. Thus a married woman makes a new life and set of relationships for herself at her husband's home but does not give up her ties with her family of orientation.

In contrast with his wife, who comes to be on relatively intimate terms with her parents-in-law, a Nyansongo man always maintains a most formal and deferential set of relationships with his parents-in-law. They are always strangers and must be treated as honored guests when they visit. They may not enter the house of their son-in-law. They do, however, carry on a joking relationship with his parents. In like manner, a man has an egalitarian, joking relationship with his wife's brothers and sisters; with the latter, elaborate sexual joking is carried on.

In days gone by, and nowadays in areas of Gusiiland more con-servative than the one in which Nyansongo is located, the final wed-ding ceremony could take place any time from days to decades after the start of cohabitation. It included an additional payment of cattle, aggressive interaction between the affinal groups in the form of wres-tling matches, dancing contests, and reciprocal insulting of the bride

and groom, as well as the placing of anklets of iron on the bride to indicate her married status. Many of the old and middle-aged women in
Nyansongo wear such ankle rings. They are viewed as a symbol of
marital fidelity, although the same degree of fidelity is required of a
wife who does not wear them. The Nyansongo wife is not allowed to
have intercourse with any man but her husband, although he is free to
engage in extramarital sexuality. The possibility of sexual attraction
between a woman and her husband's brother residing in the same
homestead is recognized in some lewd songs but is actually considered
a heinous offense.

The fidelity of the wife is ensured by a supernatural sanction described in Chapter 9. This punishment does not go into effect until the
adulterous wife resumes intercourse with her husband. Thus it has the
effect of inhibiting a wife's adulterous impulses unless she is willing to
desert her husband and run off with a lover. When she does the latter,
the husband can sue her father for return of the bridewealth and/or
sue the lover for adultery, a "customary law" offense defined as living
with a woman who is legally married to someone else. The bridewealth
may be returned and a divorce granted, with the original husband re-
taining custody of the children. If the husband does not want a divorce
and has other wives, he may do nothing, feeling that the woman will
eventually return because her children will not be welcome at any
homestead but that of their legal father, and she will want to be with
her children (especially sons). When a repentant wife returns, a puri-
fication ceremony must be performed before the husband can resume
sexual intercourse with her.

A Nyansongo woman may remarry after divorce, but if her husband dies, she cannot be married again. She may choose a genitor for
her future children from among her husband's brothers and paternal
cousins, but his responsibilities are purely sexual and procreative; they
do not extend to her economic and social welfare. Children fathered by
the levirate are known as sons and daughters of the deceased, who paid
bridewealth for their mother, rather than of their physiological father.
If a widow is very young, she may move her residence and live as a
wife with a brother of her husband. If she is middle-aged and has a
number of children, however, the man who is given sexual rights over
her often does not live near her and she simply lives by herself with
her children and co-widows, if any. Some widows are sexually promiscuous, but this is not widespread among them, for the same supernatural sanctions apply to their leviratic relationship as to an ordinary
marriage.

Since the exclusive sexual rights of the husband over the wife are emphasized by Nyansongans, the manner in which these rights are exercised is of interest here. The conception of coitus as an act in which a man overcomes the resistance of a woman and causes her pain is not limited to the wedding night; it continues to be important in marital relations. Wives in monogamous homesteads never initiate sexual intercourse with their husbands, and they customarily make a token objection before yielding to the husbands' advances. The wife does not take an active role in the foreplay or coitus. Touching the husband's penis with her hand, for example, is punishable by ancestor spirits and must be expiated by a sacrifice. Most importantly, it is universally reported that wives cry during coitus, moaning quietly, "You're hurting me, you bad man" and other such admonitions. The men find this practice sexually arousing. The following statement by a 36-year-old husband suggests the attitude of the Gusii male toward his wife's sexuality.

During coitus the husband asks her, "What do you feel? Don't you think it's good?" The wife says, "Don't ask me that." She will never say yes. When the woman cries and protests during intercourse you are very excited. . . . We are always mystified as to whether women enjoy it. But the wives in polygynous homesteads complain when their husbands neglect them, so they must like it.

There is good reason to believe that the reluctant sexual pose of wives is not feigned in all cases. Young husbands claim to desire coitus at least twice a night, once early and once toward dawn. In a number of monogamous marriages, however, this rate is not achieved, due in part to the stubborn resistance of wives. There are married women with reputations for refusing to have intercourse with their husbands for up to a week at a time. Such husbands are eventually moved to beat their wives and even send them back to their parents. In one case of this kind, the wife's distaste for coitus was the only major source of conflict between husband and wife. Among those monogamous wives who do not have antisexual reputations, however, refusal to have intercourse with their husbands usually occurs when they have quarreled over something else. Since family modesty prescribes the performance of intercourse in the dark after the children have fallen asleep, wives enforce their refusal by pinching a child awake if the husband is insistent. Such evidence suggests that for some wives at least the resistant and pained behavior in marital intercourse does not represent a conventional pose or an attempt to arouse their husbands but a sincere desire to avoid coitus.

✤
✤
✤

Chapter 6

Religion

The people of Nyansongo continue to believe in and practice the religion of their forefathers despite the efforts of Christian missionaries. Of the 70 adults living in the community, 28 have at one time or another been members of Christian churches. This group includes a few who were baptized during severe illnesses experienced while outside the district but who never practiced their new religion. By the broadest definition then, only 40% of Nyansongans can be considered Christians. Of the 28, nine (mostly women) attended church services during the period when fieldwork was carried out.

The Bonyamosicho neighborhood tends to be Seventh Day Adventist, since the chief and his elder brother had been Seventh Day Adventist evangelists 30 to 40 years before and had converted many in their subclan. The Omobea people tend to become Roman Catholics, and there is a growing trend in this direction among young girls who enjoy and look forward to the rituals and white dress of the Catholic wedding service. Two wives of Omobea men are from the Logoli tribe of North Nyanza District and belong to the Friends African Mission which is dominant there.

The Seventh Day Adventists and the Friends missionaries enjoin Africans to refrain from drinking native beer or liquor, making sacrifices, marrying more than one wife, and engaging in witchcraft and sorcery. With the exception of drinking, the Catholic mission sets the same standards for Christian behavior. The rules notwithstanding, everyone in Nyansongo drinks beer and participates in sacrifices; polygynous marriage is common even among younger men; witchcraft and hired sorcery are at an all-time high. Those who were once practicing Christians have for the most part given it up either because of involvement in polygynous marriage or of a pragmatic return to Gusii ritual to deal with illness or death. As a sophisticated Nyansongan remarked, "I don't believe they're good Christians when they're in trouble or sick. When a man is well off he can be a pure Christian." Although Christianity is not widely practiced in the community, monotheism has begun to permeate the Nyansongo belief system. Some Nyansongans assert that it has precedent in their traditional beliefs, but regardless of the validity of this claim, the word *Nyasae*, used by African Christians of western Kenya to denote "God," is often heard. Nyasae occupies a position in Nyansongo thought equivalent to fortune or luck in our own, and events are attributed to Nyasae when an individual feels he has and can have no influence on their outcome.

The traditional religion of Nyansongo consists mainly of an ancestor cult which coexists in Gusii belief with a witchcraft-sorcery complex described in the chapter Death, Disease, and the Supernatural. The Gusii do not have an organized cosmology in the sense of a comprehensive set of conceptions of the universe and the beings and forces in it. They have a traditional history going back to Mogusii, founder of the national lineage, and continuing through the southward migration of the Gusii people, their segmentation into tribes and clans, their feuds, wars, and heroes. The personages of traditional history are the ancestors, and it is their spirits (*ebirecha*, sing. *ekerecha*) who are the major supernatural beings recognized by the Gusii. There is, however, little connection between the history and ritual observances concerning ancestor spirits, just as no connection is made between the ancestor spirits and the witchcraft and magic of living people. There is no priestly hierarchy nor are there any shrines in Gusiiland.

The people of Nyansongo view their religion as a set of demands made on them by the ancestor spirits—demands which must be detected and fulfilled in order to avert disaster. Characteristically, though, they do not resort to religious practices until the onset of misfortune or the appearance of a sign indicating that it is imminent. In consequence, religion is not an object of daily attention for Nyansongans, but rather a set of beliefs and practices which spring into action during an emergency when supernatural punishment is feared.

The ancestor spirits (*ebirecha*) are immortal beings lacking shape or substance, "like wind," living in a volcanic formation atop Manga, the most prominent escarpment in Gusiiland. In its most general sense, this category of beings includes all dead Gusii, but practically it refers to the male ancestors of the living members of one's lineage. In this sense, the ancestor spirits are simply the dead members of the lineage who in their postmortem form continue to take an interest in the affairs of its living members. They are not personified, however, and are identified only as "our grandfathers" rather than by any specific name or kinship designation. Like living "grandfathers," ancestor spirits make demands (especially concerning food) on their juniors, are easily displeased, and contribute little to the physical well-being of the homestead. The attitude of the living toward them is one of fear and deference, involving unquestioning obedience to their demands. The ancestor spirits are always considered right no matter how unreasonable their behavior might seem. They are to be appeased in order that they might not bother living members of the lineage.

A major source of displeasure to the ancestors is failure to perform funerary and other customary sacrifices to them or failure to sacrifice the right kind of animal. This is viewed as a deprivation of the food they desire. They are also displeased by intraclan homicide, adultery, and incest but may be propitiated by sacrifice after the commission of such crimes. When offended and not properly propitiated, the spirits can kill members of the offending homestead through disease or disaster (such as being struck by lightning or drowning), drive them insane, kill their cattle, ruin their crops, and afflict them with sterility. Before using such drastic punishments, the spirits send an omen to the offender as a sign of their displeasure; if he recognizes it as an omen, he has time to take remedial action and prevent major disaster. An aardvaark, python, or hyena seen in the daytime is considered a bad omen; the sight of a crane standing with its young, peculiar sounds emanating from a civet cat, jackal, or owl, the striking of one's granary by lightning, a hawk defecating on one's head—all these indicate that an ancestor has been offended. Some omens are linked to a specific type of punishment which follows if the omen is ignored. For example, if a man sees snakes mating and does not take the proper action, he will be made impotent.

When a man suspects that he has incurred the displeasure of the ancestor spirits or when he or his family are visited by misfortune, his only recourse is to visit a divine (*omoragori*). An intermediary between men and spirits, the diviner diagnoses the cause of the omen or misfortune and prescribes the type of propitiation needed. Diviners are middle-aged or elderly women who have learned their skill through a sort of apprenticeship to older diviners. When their apprenticeship is over, they are initiated into the profession by at least five senior diviners of the area in a ceremony called *enyangi,* a word referring to childhood initiation ceremonies and marriage ceremonies as well. In the ceremony, both senior diviners and novices rhythmically shake gourd rattles until they become possessed by the ancestor spirits and scream loudly. This part of the ceremony is private except for three mature men, but the next day a big feast is given, to which anyone can be admitted who leaves a small amount of money at the door step, and there is much eating, drinking, and dancing. The initiate can henceforth wear an iron clip on her necklace which signifies her status as an established diviner. Some women later go through another ceremony to become senior diviners who wear large cowrie-shell collars and can conduct the initiation of apprentices into the profession.

There are many female diviners throughout Gusiiland. In Nyansongo there was one well-established diviner, another who was initiated in May, 1957, and a third who began her apprenticeship at that time. They meet secretly with senior and established diviners from adjacent communities, but each woman practices by herself at her own house. The role of diviner is the most important role outside the family that a woman can occupy, but though it is a respected position, it does not endow her with extraordinary power or prestige. Since diviners' services are often required and usually paid for, the position carries with it monetary rewards.

Typically the diviner is confronted by a client whose wife has not given birth for an unusually long time. Her first task is to determine the cause of this affliction, and she does so by means of an oracle. One type of oracle involves the spinning of a small cup on the handle of a knife blade, which is stuck into the floor. Questions concerning possible offenses and omens are asked while the cup is spinning, and its coming to rest during a particular question indicates an affirmative answer by the spirits. In a variant of this, a gourd is balanced on a sharp implement in the floor; its falling off means "no" to whatever question is asked. Some diviners throw cowrie shells on the floor and read spirit messages from their configuration. Regardless of the method used, the diviner uses her knowledge of her client, first to demonstrate the efficacy of her technique and then to suggest a plausible explanation for his misfortune. She may be aware that he was out of the district when his grandfather died and thus unable to perform the customary role in the burial; she may have heard that the sacred fire went out during his initiation into manhood. Since both of these events are among the many ritual sources of irritation to ancestor spirits, the diviner can plausibly attribute his present misfortune to one of them. She also uses the oracles to search for omens with the prompting of the client himself, who may be eager to recall that he saw an aardvaark or found a lizard in his fireplace. Indeed some anxious people rush to the diviner as soon as they detect an omen. If the diviner, from her knowledge of the client's situation, believes that witchcraft is indicated, and if there are the proper omens to confirm it, she may suggest that her client is the victim of human witches rather than the offender of his ancestors.

Having struck on a credible explanation, the diviner prescribes a remedy. Unless witchcraft is considered the cause, in which case another type of practitioner must be consulted, the proffered solution is appeasement of the spirits through animal sacrifice. The animal to be sacrificed is specified in extreme detail: a black hen, a white ram, and so on. If the client desires propitiation of the spirits for a serious offense, such as incest, the animal is more likely to be expensive, that is, a sheep or goat rather than a chicken, and will also be rare, for example, an all-white he-goat.

A sacrifice to the ancestor spirits is conducted at home by the eldest male member of the homestead concerned, although younger men and men from other homesteads do some of the work involved in it. If a sheep or goat is to be sacrificed, it is suffocated with leaves outside the house and placed on its side inside the husband's room. The elder carefully cuts off the skin of the exposed side and inspects the visceral lining for an auspicious spot. If the spot is not found, another animal must be sacrificed, but this is rare. Many ritual details are attended to, which will not be recounted here. Stomach contents of the animal are smeared on the foreheads and chests of the individuals most directly involved in the occasion for the sacrifice, and the meat is divided among all relatives present. Much of the meat is eaten immediately without cooking, as Nyansongans also eat nonsacrificial meat. Although the meat is said to be drained of flavor by the spirits, who are "eating" it simultaneously, women and children greedily devour the intestines and forequarter, while the men who took part in the sacrifice haul away the choicest meat for later consumption.

The ancestor cult, whose role in social control is discussed below, does not encompass the entire traditional magico-religious system of the Gusii. Supernatural beliefs are involved in curing and preventing disease, ensuring agricultural success through the control of weather, and preventing crime within kinship units. Each of these functions has its supernatural specialists: professional sorcerers and witch smellers in the area of medicine, rain makers and hail stoppers for weather protection, magical detectives for theft control. Other part-time experts, who know rituals for removing different types of curses and protecting against specific misfortunes, abound in Gusiiland and are widely used by Nyansongans.

To summarize, the religion of Nyansongo in its essentials consists of belief in unpersonalized ancestor spirits who occasionally punish the living for ritual neglect or certain moral crimes, female diviners who interpret ancestor-sent omens and prescribe remedies for disease and sterility, and animal sacrifices to propitiate the spirits and thereby effect a cure. These essentials have not been markedly affected by Christianity, probably because they do not require constant observance but spring into action in times of stress when the desire to try anything that might help is very strong. Religious aspects of social control are described in the chapter dealing with that topic, and the most common magical beliefs and practices are considered in the chapter on Death, Disease, and the Supernatural.

$$\ast$$
$$\ast$$
$$\ast$$

Chapter 7

Recreation

There is little formalized or ritualized social life in Nyansongo. There are no drums, no group singing in the fields, and few organized group dances. Furthermore, even festive activities are not adorned by masks, wood carvings, or decorative art, all of which are virtually absent from Gusii culture. The people of Nyansongo generally take their pleasures in informal settings requiring little in the way of preparation, coordination, or ornamentation. Some of the situations which are arranged for pleasure are surreptitious; others are thought to be dangerous as well as enjoyable. Only the most superficial and fleeting forms of recreation are free from the danger of immoral or injurious consequences.

The sex and age divisions among Nyansongans are conspicuous in their recreational activities. Married men attend beer parties, occasional soccer games, and big public gatherings; married women visit each other, go to markets near and far, and conduct a few of the more expressive ceremonies. Young men and women meet each other in the marketplace, have parties of their own, and engage in sexual relations. Unmarried men are also involved in soccer as participants and interested spectators. Even when events like sacrifices and initiation rites bring whole groups of neighbors or kin together in what is partly a recreational context, the men and the women, the young and the old, have their distinct roles to play. Sex differences in expressive behavior are particularly striking, for the festive occasions in which women play a large part are characterized by much more gaiety, noise, and uninhibited words and movements than those presided over by men.

Every married man in Nyansongo has his own bamboo drinking tube, about 4 feet long and with a filter at the end, and some men carry them about, always ready to partake of some beer when it is offered. The beer is made of the fermented flour of maize and finger millet, roasted into hard, round balls, which are sometimes eaten between meals. The women, who make beer, put these granular balls into a large pot, which is placed in the middle of *eero,* the husband's room in the house, and pour boiling water into it. The top of the hot brew is poured off and drunk separately from a calabash or cup. Then the man of the house and his male guests, sitting on stools, put their tubes in and begin to drink. Although the filter in the tube keeps out the coarsest part, the hot beer is nevertheless very thick, sometimes approaching the consistency of oatmeal.

At most times of the year there are beer parties going on in Nyansongo every late afternoon, and a man may go to drink without being invited if he is on good terms with the host, particularly if they are close kinsmen or neighbors. Three to ten men usually sit around, sucking on their tubes and discussing events of the day. If the men are all of the same generation, they talk of sexual matters both real and fantasied, laughing moderately and enjoying the gossip. Such discussions are often terminated by the arrival of an old man or of a woman who is a classificatory daughter of someone present.

Although in the past women were excluded from drinking parties, nowadays they are permitted limited participation but are clearly there on sufferance. A woman enters the room, stands by a man whom she knows well, takes his tube when he is resting between drafts, and drinks some of the beer. She does not sit down, and she usually leaves in a few minutes to rejoin the women in the other room of the house, where they are boiling water and preparing food. If the liquid in the beer pot runs out, the men may shout at the women to bring more hot water. Occasionally an intoxicated man barks abusively at the women and tries to chase them out of the room in which the drinking is taking place. In spite of the fact that they must stay in the background during beer parties, Nyansongo women manage to drink enough on such occasions to get drunk regularly. A few of them are notorious for the frequency with which they get drunk and subsequently neglect their duties as cooks and mothers, and one woman was severely reprimanded by her husband for this behavior.

Unmarried young men are barred from the room in which their elders are drinking, although the youths are often given some of the beer to drink outside or in a nearby house. The old men say this prohibition is to prevent the outbreak of disrespectful behavior by the younger men when they become intoxicated. It also serves to heighten the exclusiveness and importance of the mature men as a drinking group.

When beer is plentiful and guests are many, a drinking bout is enlivened by singing and dancing. This is particularly likely to happen if a man has brought his lyre, a traditional Gusii instrument, to accompany the singing, but unaccompanied singing is also frequent. One man starts a song, then everyone joins in. The songs are traditional Gusii melodies; some extol the virtues of famous leaders of the past, while others have reference to contemporary figures, sometimes in a satirical vein. The women join in the singing, and in the dancing that begins soon after. During a song, one person gets up and moves his arms rhythmically to the music, taking an occasional step forward as he does so. The persons recognized as the most skillful dancers vibrate the muscles of their necks, shoulders, and arms, while making very few gross movements. A number of persons may dance simultaneously, but each one does so individually; there is no coordination among them. At a large, crowded party, there is little space for dancing, and someone who wants to dance may have to wait until another leaves the floor. At the height of such activities, however, everyone is participating by either dancing or singing, and the atmosphere is one of restrained hilarity.

Beer parties in Nyansongo have three dangers: violence, poisoning or witchcraft, and adultery. Alcohol is thought to make men aggressive, and quarrels among them are regarded as inevitable, beginning with pugnacious boasting and ending in physical combat. The presence of respected outsiders and authority figures, such as in-laws, ethnographers, and chiefs, has the effect of inducing a degree of restraint which is absent when only close neighbors and kinsmen are there. Even then, men become more garrulous and bold, for example, daring to ask the ethnographer questions about how Americans live, which they had not previously brought up, and familiarly giving him advice, which they did not do when sober. No aggression was observed. In the absence of the ethnographer, however, incidents occurred in which brothers attacked one another while drinking beer, as bruised

faces testified the following day. Drunken brawls are not taken lightly
and often lead to litigation. Many men in Nyansongo openly express
the opinion that beer parties should be kept small in order to prevent
the occurrence of large-scale brawls.

A danger of beer parties less openly talked about is that one will be
poisoned or bewitched. Some men believe that using their own drinking tubes avoids this, but the opinion is general that too much participation in beer parties exposes one to the secret poisons of one's
enemies.

Women are thought to be made sexually uninhibited by alcohol, so
that there is a danger that they may expose themselves indecently while
dancing or be susceptible to seduction after the party. Typically an
intoxicated woman who has left the party to urinate or to go home is
accosted by a man who tries to take advantage of her condition by
forcefully suggesting sexual relations. It is said that wives who are
otherwise faithful to their husbands may be subjugated in such circumstances, but the only known case in Nyansongo during 1955–1957
involved a young mother of three children, widely regarded as sexually
loose, who was seduced (raped, she claimed) by an unmarried man
after she left a beer party. The young wives who get drunk most frequently are also those with generally bad sexual reputations. It is
more acceptable for older women to become intoxicated, and they enjoy more toleration from the men at beer parties. By and large it is the
sexual and aggressive potentialities of the men and women under 40
years of age that are considered most dangerous at beer parties.

Beer drinking in Nyansongo is not limited to the late afternoon and
evening. If a man has a kinsman visiting him from afar or some neighbors helping him in the fields, he may serve beer in his house in the
morning or early afternoon. In the months following the harvest, and
particularly around Christmas, drinking may go on all day long. This
daytime beer consumption is even more of a male activity than the
parties described above, since the domestic activities of women prevent
their taking part.

The unmarried people have their own parties at night in the bachelor huts of young men. Such parties are organized by a few youths
who pick up girls in the marketplace and persuade them to attend.
European beer is drunk rather than the traditional kind, and lively
phonograph music provides the setting for dancing and eventual seduction. Some young men play guitars and accordians at such parties,
adapting Gusii songs to vaguely Latin-American rhythms and melodies.
In the 1930's unmarried men and women performed traditional dances

publicly at markets, but an outbreak of rape in 1937 resulted in a permanent prohibition on such activities; nowadays they are much more private and somewhat clandestine.

Although Nyansongo women participate in the men's beer parties, this cannot be called their major form of recreation. The women more frequently mix pleasure with their work, which is very demanding and time consuming. While men meet over beer, women come together daily in their cooperative working teams, which give them the opportunity to chat, gossip, and joke with one another while cultivating the fields. In the afternoon, when they relax a bit or do some chores around the house like spreading grain on mats to dry, one or two women may drop in on another and spend some time talking. If she goes to the power mill, a woman engages in conversation while waiting in line to have her maize ground. However, going to the market in town or beyond one or two days a week is the greatest recreational event for a Nyansongo married woman. She gets dressed up in her best clothes and goes with a group of her female neighbors. There is always an economic justification for the trip—exchanging grain or vegetables for money, pots, or chickens—and a 15- to 20-mile walk is often involved, but seeing the town, looking over European goods in the shops, and the good-natured banter en route provide enjoyment over and above its ostensible purpose.

Apart from their weekly routine, married women conduct the most elaborate and raucous ceremonies in Nyansongo life. The initiation of girls, described later, is an annual revel for the females in the community, and they violate proprieties on that occasion as men never do. Initiation of female diviners, which occurs less regularly, provides another occasion for great rejoicing and, like initiation of girls, involves singing, dancing, and feasts. Unlike the latter, however, the festivities of diviners' initiation are held mainly indoors, and men must drop some money at the entrance in order to be welcome. The gayest and most elaborate indoor party attended by the ethnographers in Nyansongo was a diviners' initiation.

In ceremonies conducted by men, women often take a lighthearted attitude which is recreational for them and inconsistent with the seriousness of the males in charge. At the sacrifice of a goat to the spirit of a recently deceased Nyansongo homestead head, the women scrambled with each other for the pieces of meat allowed them. They devoured the raw intestines and forequarters voraciously, then complained about not getting more. The widow of the deceased took the lead in this good-humored fun, while the men solemnly performed the ritual and divided the meat according to traditional prescription. The female tendency to be boisterous in a formal ritual setting is also exhibited during the leading-in ceremony of the male initiation rites (see Chapter 16) and in the traditional marriage ceremony as described here and in Mayer (1950a). Women are expected to be highly expressive and even obstructive on such occasions.

Big public events outside the community attract men more than women and play a small but increasing part in the recreational life of Nyansongo men. Soccer is the most important of these; some of the younger men play it on the field at Keumbu market, where the two semiprofessional champion teams sponsored by the chief practice. Men young and old watch the game there and go to the stadium in Kisii Town to see the championship games, especially the intertribal matches. On one occasion when we drove a number of men to a soccer game in town they sang traditional Gusii war songs along the way. A year later, groups of Gusii and Luo spectators fought at an intertribal match. The indications are that soccer evokes great interest of the kind that men formerly had concerning military contests.

Political and judicial proceedings, regardless of their functional significance, attract male spectators on a large scale. The most regular of these is the Monday *baraza* (assembly) held by the chief, which is attended by men, especially older ones, from all over Nyaribari, who use the occasion to see their friends and kinsmen and to gossip as well as listen to the announcements and speeches which the chief makes in the formal session. Litigation at the African Tribunal Courts, a frequent activity of Nyansongo males, can be viewed as a diversion for many of the plaintiffs and witnesses, although it is obviously also much more than recreation. When the provincial commissioner visits Keumbu or the governor of Kenya Kisii Town, large crowds of men gather to watch and listen, and some of them bring huge calabash horns to sound as they dance in his presence or after he has left. On the occasion of the visit of Princess Margaret to Kisumu, the provincial headquarters 80 miles away, several young married men in Nyansongo donned their defunct policemen's uniforms and set off to see her. These events allow men in Nyansongo to relate themselves to the wider society in which they live, but it must be noted that a number of them participate only slightly in this form of recreation.

$$ \begin{array}{c} \maltese \\ \maltese \\ \maltese \end{array} $$

Chapter 8

Political Organization and Social Control

The Gusii are one of the many African peoples who did not have a centralized political organization before coming under European colonial administration. Political integration was at the clan, sometimes even local community, level, and there were no permanent governmental offices. Each clan and community had its own authority system in which elders and wealthy individuals had more power than anyone else. Warfare occurred among the seven Gusii tribes, and blood feuding was carried on between clans and sometimes between subclans and smaller lineage segments as well.

Beginning in 1907 the British pacified the area, established courts for the peaceful settlement of disputes, and appointed chiefs and other officials to rule the people. The Gusii political system of 1955–1957 was a combination of indigenous patterns of political behavior with the governmental structures introduced by the British. On the local level, particularly, the colonial system may be said to have been grafted onto pre-existing authority patterns rather than eradicating them. For this reason it is necessary to describe the traditional authority system of Gusiiland before proceeding to the contemporary political setting of Nyansongo.

TRADITIONAL LEADERSHIP PATTERNS

Leadership in traditional Gusii society was not institutionalized in a set of permanent positions with fixed powers.* An early district report states, "The chiefs have extremely little power and are far too

* A partial exception is Getutu tribe, which developed a limited form of hereditary chieftainship in the nineteenth century. Statements here refer primarily to Nyaribari tribe.

numerous." In fact, however, these were not tribal chiefs or clan chiefs in the usual sense but only nonhereditary local leaders who assumed power and performed some political functions. The indigenous authority system of Gusiiland is best understood by beginning with the extended family homestead, where the lines of authority were most clearly drawn, and then proceeding to larger units in the political system.

The traditional Gusii homestead was an internally self-governing unit. All disputes and rule violations arising within it were handled by the homestead head (backed up by the ancestor spirits) unless he called in an outside authority. The powers of the homestead head vis-à-vis his wives and sons were great and have been described previously. Unless he was a man of little forcefulness or discretion, his orders regarding the economy, defense, and marital affairs of the homestead were commands which had to be obeyed. Defiance of his will could bring punishment to wives and sons. He had supernatural and economic sanctions to use against recalcitrant sons, and he could beat his wives, humiliate them publicly, and reject them sexually. These sanctions the homestead head used to deter threats to his authority as supreme decision maker and to quell conflicts among his wives and sons. He did not need to use them frequently because his wives and children usually feared him and did not disobey him or come into open conflict with one another. Minor infractions on their part might provoke a threat by the homestead head; more serious or repeated infractions would lead him to apply sanctions. When the most serious crimes within the homestead occurred, however, the homestead head did not punish. Fratricide and incest within the homestead were considered punishable only by the ancestor spirits; propitiatory sacrifice and a peace-making ceremony would be performed. With respect to fratricide, the restraint of the homestead head is said to have stemmed from his desire to restore peace to the family rather than to perpetuate conflict by punishing one side or the other. A homestead head who was not a dominant personality or who wanted to impress his sons with his impartiality might call in his elder brother or some other closely related elder to help him adjudicate a case within the homestead. Extended families in which the father had died also called on similarly related elders for the settlement of internal disputes.

Cases of conflict or rule violation involving members of more than one homestead were brought to the attention of the "lineage elders" (abagaaka begesaku). This term did not refer to a council with a definite membership but to a group of homestead heads and other elders ("men with gray hair") whose membership would depend on the nature of the case being heard. If the case at issue was an inheritance dispute between two brothers, then several closely related patrilineal kinsmen of their father would sit as the lineage elders because they were representative of the small-scale lineage involved. If the case was an assault or witchcraft accusation involving two homesteads whose blood relationship was not very close, then all the older men in the community would be the lineage elders involved and would judge the case jointly. The composition of the group of lineage elders involved in adjudication could be expanded beyond community boundaries to the largest unit within which lineage ties and classificatory kinship were recognized, namely, the clan, but this of course did not mean that all the older men of the clan actually heard the case. This pattern of adjudication by elders is still operative in Nyansongo.

In the past, when the lineage elders sat as a court, they had no specialized agencies to enforce their decisions. Instead they relied on (1) self-help by the successful litigant, (2) general community respect for their age and the legitimacy of their role, (3) fear by the unsuccessful litigant of their power to curse, (4) oaths invoking the supernatural sanctions of the ancestor spirits, and (5) the military threat posed by certain wealthy and powerful men (known as *abatureti*, hut elders, because they provided a hut for meetings of elders) who played a large part in community decision making.

The lineage elders had the power to curse an unidentified thief or arsonist or someone who refused to comply with their order to pay a debt. Once they had decided to curse him, the plaintiff provided a pot of beer for them, and they would drink some but not all of it. Then they would hold their fingers over the holes in the tops of their drinking tubes, utter the words, "Let him become emaciated and die," and walk away without drinking any more from the pot. Holding the finger over the hole is said to be an imitation of suffocation. If an offender so cursed did not confess and attempt to put himself right with the elders, death or a great misfortune would befall him, since the ancestor spirits were believed to carry out the curse. If the offender decided to confess and reform, he brewed beer and killed a bull or he-goat for the elders. They would come and eat at his house, and after his public apology, they would spit beer on him to remove the curse. It appears that the actual uttering of a curse by the lineage elders was less frequent than their threatening to do so, which inspired sufficient fear in the offender to make him comply.

In many cases the elders did not have to render a decision themselves but were able to allow the litigants to take an oath which would be enforced by the ancestor spirits. The accused in a Gusii trial rarely admitted his guilt; consequently there was often a factual question to be settled. If someone accused of an offense or involved in a debt dispute were certain of being in the right, he could offer to swear an oath which would kill him if his testimony were false. When the litigation concerned whether a cattle debt had been contracted and was really owed, both parties might remove their clothes near a small, flowering tree called *omotembe* (*erythrina abissinica*). The plaintiff would seize the tree and challenge the defendant, swearing his own claim to be correct. When the turn of the accused came, he might demur, fearing death for a false oath. His refusal would be tantamount to confession, and he would be required by the elders to pay the debt. If he also seized the tree and swore he was telling the truth, then there was nothing more to be done except wait and see which one died or had death in his homestead. The first one to be visited by disaster might well settle the debt to prevent the total destruction of his family by the ancestor spirits. There were many different kinds of oaths, depending on the type of offense and the category of person involved. For example, an accused married woman could lay her unweaned child on the ground and step over it while denying the charge. If she were lying, the child would die. Ordeals, that is, supernatural tests by which the accused can reveal his innocence or guilt, were also used by the elders in certain cases and also freed them from the necessity to make judgments themselves.

A Gusii homestead was thought of to some extent as a military unit with the younger men being warriors under the command of the homestead head. On some occasions, for example, when homicide occurred, young men from the victim's homestead might attempt to retaliate against the family of the killer. This was not considered right, and the elders would try to prevent it, but everyone was aware of this possibility. The degree of deference accorded a homestead head by his neighbors thus depended on the military might he commanded as well as on his wealth and number of wives. A man who was wealthy in cattle could obtain many wives, who could bear many sons to augment the military capacity of his homestead. Thus a man with four to ten wives might have a formidable army of warriors bound in loyalty to him by the father-son relationship. If his community or lineage segment were attacked from outside, his sons might be largely responsible for the defense of the area. His poorer neighbors with their smaller families were aware of the fact that incurring his displeasure might jeopardize the protection from violence thus afforded them. Such wealthy men tended to dominate the judicial proceedings of the elders; hence defiance of the elders' decision was also defiance of them. Although they would rarely use their sons as officers of the court, the threat that they might do so was ubiquitous and aided the enforcement of the judgments reached by the lineage elders.

Regardless of his authority outside his local community, the most wealthy and forceful homestead head was dominant within it. He helped his poorer neighbors by making loans to them, judging their cases, and aiding materially in the defense of the area. At the same time, he used their dependence on him to dominate them and, to some extent, to exploit them. Two Gusii proverbs illustrate this: "The property of the poor monogamist is owned by the powerful man," and, "The property of the pauper is used by the rich." In all likehihood he infringed on the property rights of others in the cause of his own aggrandizement, yet so long as his wealth and military power were unequaled, no one dared challenge his authority. Furthermore, it was often his son who was acknowledged leader of the cattle-village in which the young men jointly herded cattle.

Disputes and offenses involving individuals of different local areas within the clan were more likely to result in armed conflict than those occurring within local communities. An alternative, however, was the peaceful resolution of the conflict by conducting a trial with hut elders from the areas concerned (and from other areas, too, to lend impartiality to the proceedings) sitting in judgment. Poor elders with reputations for judicial wisdom might also be included in the impromptu tribunal, which was also thought of as the lineage elders. The success of such procedures in maintaining peace within the clan was apparently not very great, at least compared with those few areas of Gusiiland where something like hereditary chieftainship existed.

Traditional Gusii leadership was viewed as successful when it could contain and subdue the conflict resulting from lineage segmentation. As clans and their component local lineages grew in size over time, segments of equal size tended to break away from one another, to stress their autonomy and unity at the expense of the larger unit, and to view each other as enemies. This occurred in the minimal lineage of the extended family, where co-wives and their sons came into conflict with their coequals, as well as on the higher levels of lineage structure right up to the clan. The leader at every level was faced with the problem of maintaining order among conflicting segments, using his power to induce people to submit their disputes to him and the lineage elders rather than settling them by force. This order was more frequently achieved at the levels of the homestead and local community where the needs of economic cooperation and defense and the influence of supernatural sanctions reinforced the efforts of leaders to keep the peace.

Above the local groups, social control (in the sense of nonviolent settlement of disputes) was only achieved when a leader arose who was not
only acknowledged as wealthier and more powerful than anyone else in
the area but who also was willing to use severe physical punishments
of offenders to maintain respect for his judicial authority.

CONTEMPORARY POLITICAL ORGANIZATION

In 1907, after the Gusii attempted to assassinate the district commissioner, who was establishing a government station in their territory,
a British-led police force defeated them in battle and opened a new
era in the political history of Gusiiland. Thenceforth the Gusii were
administered by the district commissioner of South Nyanza from headquarters on the eastern edge of Nyaribari. He was the first man to
command an effective monopoly of military power in the area, and he
used this power to stop warfare and feuding among the Gusii, to
abolish their cattle-villages, and to introduce a new form of government.

Gusiiland was rapidly transformed from its fragmented, stateless
condition to a set of chiefdoms with specialized political roles operating
within a system of colonial administration. Fifty years after the trans-
formation began, however, many features of the indigenous authority
system could still be observed in operation. The seven tribes of Gusiiland were converted into seven administrative "locations," each with
its own chief. The chiefs are appointed by the Provincial Commissioner,
but only from among the descended clans of the tribes they are to
govern. Each chief has under him a number of "subheadmen" who
used to function only in their own clan territories but were recently
given multiclan territories in an action designed to reduce clan pa-
rochialism.

Three African Tribal Courts have been established in Gusiiland,
each with its president, vice-president, and two to four panels of elders,
all drawn from the Gusii population. Although a specialized judiciary
is an innovation, much of its procedure is indigenous. Traditional
oaths are used in civil cases over land and custody of children. An
omotembe tree is grown outside each courthouse for the most commonly used oath. Finally, "customary law" regulations are enforced
Although the offenses covered in them are not traditional, these regulations seek to uphold with slight modification Gusii customs regarding marriage and property. On the other hand, however, the Tribunal
Court is radical because it does not recognize the jurisdiction of the

homestead head and because it is supposed to treat all individuals as equals before the law. Thus a son can sue his father and a wife her husband, actions which would have been unthinkable in earlier days. The role of the wealthy judicial leader or hut elder (*omotureti*) has been formally recognized in the contemporary judicial system. Each one is supposed to be elected by the people of a given territory, and he hears cases in conjunction with the elected hut elders of adjacent areas. The lineage elders usually sit jointly with the hut elders and often influence their decision. Nowadays this local judicial arrangement is used as a court of first instance in land and property damage (usually cows eating crops) cases and can hear minor criminal cases as well. The hut elders have the power to award damages up to 200 shillings ($28.00) and can order prison sentences of up to three months, which must be confirmed by a Tribunal Court. They report their findings to the chief weekly at a public meeting, and he decides where the case should go from there. The hut elders in Nyansongo and elsewhere have a reputation for being eminently bribable and are little trusted by the people.

Over the chiefs and African Tribunal Courts is the district-wide apparatus of colonial government. This consists of the district commissioner and his administrative hierarchy, the resident magistrate and Kenya police, and the African District Council. The last is a legislative body, presided over by the district commissioner, on which all the tribes of South Nyanza (Luo, Kuria, and Suba, as well as Gusii) are represented by their chiefs and elected members.

Aside from the Council, other branches of district government are staffed at their top levels by British officials. Under the district commissioner there is a district officer in charge of Gusiiland, a district officer in charge of courts, and agricultural, medical, education, revenue, maize control, and public works officers. The district officer in charge of Gusiiland deals mainly with the chiefs, and the courts officer with the African Tribunal Courts, whose decisions he may reverse. The resident magistrate is the supreme judicial authority in the district, operating a court which hears all cases involving Europeans and Asians as well as the more serious African criminal cases. These latter include murder and manslaughter, arson, rape, theft, official corruption, the cultivation of marijuana, and the illegal distilling of "native spirituous liquors." The resident magistrate can give prison sentences up to 15 years and retains the power to order flogging, which he uses in cases of petty theft and other minor offenses. Cases of homicide and rape in which a sentence of greater than 15 years may be given are referred by him to the Supreme Court of Kenya. African cases are brought to the resident magistrate by the Kenya police, who have British officers, a number of outposts in the district, and considerable military equipment. This contrasts sharply with the African Tribunal Courts, which depend on complainants to bring their own cases to court.

In spite of the extensive British officialdom in South Nyanza, much of the responsibility for administration and law enforcement falls on the shoulders of the chiefs, who have considerable autonomy in the governing of their respective locations. There is no paramount chief or ruling council of Gusiiland; hence location chiefs are responsible only to the district officer and district commissioner but not to any higher chiefs. The district commissioner and district officer are infrequent visitors to any particular location, however, and this gives chiefs the opportunity to develop relationships with the people they rule which are independent of the dictates of colonial administration.

One of the outstanding characteristics of Gusii behavior within their contemporary political system is their litigiousness, for which they have been notorious in Kenya for decades. With a population of 260,-000, the Gusii supply their tribunal courts alone with almost a thousand cases a month and $50,000 to $60,000 a year in court fees. Many cases are appealed to the South Nyanza African Appeals Court and even higher; and the Court of Review, highest native appeal court in Kenya, visits South Nyanza more frequently than any other district. Almost every Gusii adult male has been involved in a court case; many have had ten or more. Land litigation and suits for the custody of children are most common, but assaults and sex offenses are also brought into court in great numbers. Lawsuits may be said to be a major preoccupation of the contemporary Gusii, and one of the reasons that the litigations are so protracted is the reluctance of persons to admit being in the wrong. The Gusii proverb, "No one cuts his own boil," applies to trial behavior, where the defendant will protest his innocence and fabricate stories in support of it to the end. A resident magistrate who had judged many Kipsigis cases in Kericho District was amazed and chagrined at the greater length of Gusii criminal trials due to the refusal of defendants to plead guilty regardless of completely incriminating evidence.

SOCIAL CONTROL IN NYANSONGO

In the 1930's, when the African Tribunal Courts were established, Gusii chiefs were deprived of their formal judicial powers. People continue to bring cases to the chiefs, however, according them a central role in the judicial process. This is especially true in Nyansongo, partly because it is under a powerful chief who has been in office for 30 years and partly because the community is located in the 2 miles between the chief's private residence and his official headquarters. The subheadman in charge of Nyansongo and the *etureti* (hut) elder of the community are both members of the chief's subclan, appointed to their posts by the chief without popular support, and are passive individuals commanding little respect from their neighbors. One is held in contempt by Nyansongans because he is dominated by his wife who is reputed to be a witch. Community residents by-pass the subheadman and hut elder living among them and take their cases directly to the chief.

When someone in Nyansongo has a problem with possible legal implications, his first impulse is to see the chief about it. Whether it is a land dispute, assault or stock theft, witchcraft accusation, or the elopement of a daughter, he will move as quickly as possible to see the chief. In the early morning there is a long line of litigants waiting at the chief's house, later in the day at his office, and they sometimes awaken him at night as well. For some, the chief is a legal expert who can advise on whether a case should be taken to the Tribunal, Kenya police, or hut elders. For others, who are themselves sophisticated in judicial procedure, a letter from the chief to the court or police is considered a necessity.

In many cases, however, the chief acts not as an intermediary but as a court, settling disputes, punishing, and issuing warnings. His actions in these cases go far beyond the legal powers granted him by the British authorities. Most frequently he is called on to adjudicate family squabbles and enforce the traditional obligations of nuclear family relationships. In Nyansongo a son quarreled with his mother over the fact that money he sent home was used for his brother's bridewealth. Tempers flared, and he struck her on the arm with a hoe. The homestead head, a weak old man, reported the incident to the chief, who had his tribunal policemen lock up the son for a few days in a brick hut at the chief's camp which is reserved for such purposes. During those days the son worked around the chief's camp under guard while the chief consulted the parents and tried to settle the case. In another case, two wives of a middle-aged man complained to the chief about their husband's neglecting them sexually in favor of a concubine from Ruanda-Urundi who, they were certain, was using love magic to hold his attraction. The chief ordered the concubine out of the district and gave her the bus fare for the trip. Such cases are everyday occurrences, often involving sons taking their father's cattle without permission, brothers fighting one another, cousins suspecting one another of sorcery. The chief deals with them firmly, often giving support to flagging paternal authority by dressing down sons, "discovering" their poll tax delinquency, or locking them up for a while. He also gives permission for persons to consult witch doctors of various types. Sometimes he reverses the decisions of the hut elders or insists on sending a case judged by them to the Tribunal Court. Despite the fact that his administrative location contains almost 50,000 people, no matter is too trivial for the chief to concern himself with, and he manages to dispose of the large number of matters which persons from Nyansongo and many other communities bring him daily.

The power of the chief is of benefit to himself as well as to others. He is by far the wealthiest man in the location, having 14 wives, a Chevrolet sedan, large herds of cattle, a sizable·coffee plantation, and five power mills for grinding corn. He is always well-dressed in expensive European clothing. The Gusii consider it appropriate for a chief to be wealthier than other persons, and if not outstandingly wealthy when appointed to office, he takes steps to acquire wealth as soon as possible afterward. The chief in charge of Nyansongo has been rich for many years, and some of his kinsmen have reaped economic benefits from his chieftainship as well. He does not share his political power with anyone, however, whether kin or not. His subheadmen tend to be obedient to the chief but not effective with the people, and it is said that he chooses men with such qualities in order to keep power concentrated in his own hands.

Except for some elders, the chief tolerates no contradiction or criticism at the weekly assembly meeting of the location. Most people are extremely deferential to him, but those who have defied him in some way find themselves ordered to court for tax delinquency or even told to leave the district if they wish to avoid dire punishment. The chief is surrounded by assistants—clerks, tribal police, bodyguards, chauffeurs, domestic servants, and field hands—who are available to do his bidding. Being a member of the chief's entourage is considered prestigeful and a means of eventually obtaining a political office, such as subheadman or elder of the Tribunal Court. One Nyansongo man gave up a job outside the district to become the chief's chauffeur; another did the same to become his cook. Ordinary residents of the location are sometimes pressed into service to perform an immediate task for the chief or one of his assistants. The tribal policemen, uniformed and armed but ill-trained guards which every chief is allowed to have, are most blatant about using their position to take advantage of fearful shopkeepers anxious not to offend them, and to extort bribes from suspected criminals.

The autocracy of the chief is resented by some but opposed by no one. Most people regard his power as vast, being backed up by the even greater power of the district commissioner. They respect his authority and appeal to it when they need to rather than protest against it. In spite of this, the chief is covertly suspicious of his subjects. He will not eat in the house of any person in his location, reportedly because of fear of poisoning, and he hires witch doctors to protect him from his enemies. This is consistent with the belief that the wealthy and fortunate are subject to the envious witchcraft of the less fortunate, but it is carried to quite an extreme in this instance. The private life of the chief is discussed by people in Nyansongo and elsewhere, but he is not expected to be a paragon of Gusii moral virtues. As with Gusii leaders of pre-British days, he is reputed to violate important kinship rules in the course of his own family life, but this does not seem to shake anyone's respect for his authority. Since his power is unsurpassed, there is no one who would dare attempt to correct his behavior.

The chief with his tribal police and the Kenya police with their patrol cars cooperate in law enforcement. In spite of their activities, however, criminals can evade arrest by escaping to the tea plantations 50 miles away where, as employees, they are protected from arrest by the European management or by bribing the policemen. To a large extent, then, the apprehension of offenders is dependent on the great responsiveness of the population in reporting offenses to the chief and the lack of willingness of criminals to resist arrest. Communities like Nyansongo do not have organized peer groups which aid in the detection and apprehension of criminals, and even the informal sanctions of their elders are nowadays authorized by the chief. Magical sanctions used by individuals and supernatural interpretations of death and disease remain important elements in the social control system, and their role in the control of specific types of offenses will be discussed below.

AGGRESSIVE OFFENSES

Despite their traditional pattern of feuding, Nyansongans believe that violence and aggression are evil and should be avoided. Women argue loudly with one another, though usually without strong emotion, but the men are particularly subdued and polite people. They rarely raise their voices to one another, and public brawls are extremely infrequent. There is no feeling that two men with a dispute should settle it with their fists or by any other direct expression, and when two men attempt it, there are always those who hold them back and try to calm them down. In transactions such as the selling of a cow, when bargaining has reached a deadlock and feelings are beginning to run high, the tension is relieved by smiling and laughing rather than by shouting. On many occasions we were amazed to see how polite and friendly a person could act toward someone with whom he was currently engaged in a serious dispute. It can be said that Nyansongo interaction, under conditions of sobriety, is generally characterized by an atmosphere of quiet and superficial good humor.

Such nonaggressive behavior often belies deep-seated ill feelings between Gusii individuals. This is recognized in the proverb, "People may be seen together but their hearts do not know each other." A case that arose in Nyansongo (described in Chapter 9) illustrates this concretely. When Mogaka died, his older widow made it known to numerous neighbors that she blamed two male neighbors, closely related to the deceased, with having killed him by sorcery. The two men knew of her charges, and they issued counter-accusations to other neighbors, imputing foul deeds to the widow's family. This was a serious and notorious situation in the community. But, a week after the death, when the sacrifice for the dead man was performed, not only were both men present and assisting in the ritual, but at the informal meal afterward, the widow was joking with them, good-naturedly encouraging one of them to take her younger co-wife as a leviratic wife, and so on. Their interaction betrayed none of the hostility they felt toward one another. Shortly afterward, the older widow was the sole complainant in the trial of one of the men for sorcery, and she uttered her charges publicly. This is a striking illustration of the Nyansongo ability to suppress aggression in direct interaction with the object of the aggression and their tendency to express it in back-biting and litigation.

Nyansongans are not highly sociable people, and they view their neighbors with considerable suspicion. "Homesteads are secret hiding places" is one oft-quoted proverb, and another warns, "A thicket has eyes," counseling caution about speech in the manner of our own wartime slogan, "The walls have ears." Sociability is equated with danger in two proverbs. "He who enters doors will be found with a swollen intestine," refers to a postmortem sign of death by witchcraft as the consequence of going into other people's houses. "Eat like the hide-dresser," is considered an admonition to stay out of trouble by eating at home like the dresser of hides, whose work prevents his visiting his fellows. Few Nyansongans follow the extreme advice of such proverbs, but they share anxieties expressed in them. Privacy is desired and available, and it gives individuals the opportunity to conspire and talk against each other. Everyone is aware of this, and thus when people come together for work and entertainment, which is rather frequently, each one comes with at least a slight feeling of distrust.

The unsociability which appears to give rise to aggression is itself a reaction to aggression, and the preferred method of handling it. "Bitter squash is of a different pot," means that people with a grudge will separate and not see each other. The hyperaggressive person is dealt with in the proverb, "A biting snake is pushed away with a stick," meaning, "Keep your distance." There is a definite tendency for Nyansongans to avoid volatile persons and alleged witches and to break off social intercourse with a family with whom they have a dispute. As soon as trouble between homesteads arises, paths leading from one to another are blocked, and visiting stops, at least for a while. When one of the men in the case mentioned above was judged guilty of the sorcery responsible for the death of the widow's husband, the elders ordered that there be no further social intercourse between the adjacent families, as a means of preventing any more aggressive action. If persons holding a grudge are forced into interaction by an accidental meeting along a path or at the homestead of a third party, they will ordinarily be polite and friendly. This is not considered wrong, as "insincerity" is in our own society, but a necessary expedient in order to avoid aggression. If one person is an alleged witch or notoriously quarrelsome person, the other would definitely be friendly in order not to provoke aggression, but he would also get away as quickly as is consonant with politeness. Mention has been made of the conscious spatial separation of the homes of co-wives in order to reduce their aggression. Young unmarried men are also spatially excluded from beer parties to prevent their becoming aggressive to their elders under the influence of alcohol. Nowadays they are given some beer, but must drink it outside the house or in another house. In the past, of course, young men lived in cattle-villages apart from their elders, which may have served the function of preventing intergenerational conflict on a daily basis. Currently, not only the presence of young men at home but also the overpopulation of the land makes separation more difficult than before and open aggression therefore harder to prevent.

A strong paternal authority is connected with the prevention of aggressive offenses within the homestead. Those homesteads in Nyansongo in which open conflict broke out most often between brothers were those in which the homestead head was senile or simply lacking in forcefulness when dealing with his adult sons. Where the father was a dominant person, he did not tolerate open quarreling, and the sons tended to remain peaceful under his authority. After the death of such a homestead head, the sons are quite likely to engage in aggressive encounters or to break off relations with one another, at least temporarily.

Although Nyansongans profess a negative attitude toward killing, in pre-British times homicide was often a necessity for defense and other military operations against out-groups. The extent of what might be considered an "in-group" varied from time to time and place to place in Gusiiland, depending on the balance between authoritarian leadership and divisive lineage tensions. Consequently the line between homicide as a military operation and homicide as an offense to group morality was difficult to draw. It can be said with certainty that homicide involving anyone outside the social unit here called the tribe was always part of legitimate warfare and homicide within the homestead was always a "criminal" offense involving expiation via sacrifice and other rituals. Intermediate cases within the tribe but outside the homestead might be settled by the payment of compensation equivalent to the bridewealth for one wife and sometimes by sacrifice as well, the probability of settlement being dependent on the relations between the lineage segments of murderer and victim.

Homicide under contemporary conditions in Gusiiland is treated as a police offense and is punishable by death (hanging) if the Supreme Court of Kenya decides it is murder and not manslaughter. That the retaliatory motive is still present is indicated by the fact that it is mainly in *intra*familial homicide cases that efforts are made to conceal, or bribe the police to conceal, the offense from the authorities. The family of the deceased wants to see the killer punished. Nyansongans, however, regard the process of Western justice with respect to murder as absurdly ineffective. Two middle-aged women once complained to us:

> When a man has committed murder, he should be hanged in front of a crowd of people rather than taken to Nairobi for hanging. When they are taken to Nairobi, people don't know whether they are really killed. If they were hanged in front of a crowd, people would know that bad things await those who murder others. Murderers should be taken to town, and everyone in the tribe should see them killed there. Now, when a man kills intentionally he's taken to prison for a year, and then people hear he has won his case and is free. Or he may bribe and get free, which is wrong.

Further investigation revealed that even among the semieducated Gusii there is strong doubt that convicted murderers who are taken to Nairobi are really killed there. Rumors are circulated to the effect that convicted murderers are kept in a large padded room in Nairobi and fed a great deal of food to make them fat while samples of their blood are taken. This is considered a far superior fate to being killed. Furthermore, cities like Nairobi are regarded by Gusii as corrupt places where one could bribe one's way out of execution, and they feel this theory is confirmed every time a killer is reprieved or acquitted for lack of evidence. Thus there is general disbelief that execution for murder is ever carried out.

The current Gusii homicide rate is fairly high. Table 2 is a comparison of the average annual rate of Gusii murder and manslaughter indictments during 1955 and 1956 with the rates for adjacent tribal groups, the Kipsigis and South Nyanza Luo, and with the rate of murder and *nonnegligent* manslaughter indictments in the urban United States during the same period.*

Table 2 Average Annual Homicide Rates per 100,000 Population Three Kenya Tribal Groups and the Urban United States, 1955 and 1956

Gusii	5.5
Kipsigis	4.8
South Nyanza Luo	4.5
United States, urban	4.85 *

* Statistical Abstract of the United States, U.S. Department of Commerce, 78th Annual Edition, 1957, p. 139.

Murders in Gusiiland ordinarily occur during or after beer parties at which relatives and neighbors are present. If in-laws or other respected visitors are present, there is little quarreling. But when the drinking group includes only intimates, sharp words are the very least that is inevitable. Alcohol seems to transform the quiet Gusii man into a loud, pugnacious braggart and to bring out his pent-up aggression. Intoxication in a familiar group is the most usual setting for murder in Gusiiland.

The motivations behind murder and other aggressive outbursts against neighbors and relatives usually involve economic factors. Land disputes and cattle debts can be at the root of bitterness that has been aggravated by years of litigation. A recent case from outside Nyansongo illustrates a fairly typical set of conditions that can lead to murder. An old man whose wife was dead lived for ten years with a widow at her

* Negligent manslaughter, mainly homicide due to auto accidents in United States, is extremely rare in rural Kenya. Population estimates used for the Kenya tribes are 1948 census figures plus 10%.

house. They quarreled bitterly and decided to divide their wealth in half. He took his share of movable articles to the homestead of his adult sons. One day he decided to return to live with the widow, and *her* adult son was home from work at the time. The son was annoyed, especially because he feared that the old man would stake a claim to half of the land which his mother worked, which according to custom belonged to the son. At a beer party, the son said, "They have divided the wealth and now he returns. I want to kill him—do you all agree?" The others present, who were drunk, laughingly agreed with him, thinking he was not serious. After drinking, the son found the old man going to sleep, hacked him to death with a machete, and carried the body to a river, where he deposited it in the water, first tying one leg to a tree. Eventually the body was discovered and the son arrested. This case contains the elements of economic anxiety, intoxication, and close relationship between murderer and victim that are typical of Gusii murder cases.

In traditional Gusii judicial practice, assault and mayhem were recognized offenses, and compensation could be obtained by the victim through litigation. If a person were badly injured and the services of a professional medicine man were needed, the assailant was required to pay the fee for his services as well as the compensation itself. The goat, sheep, bull, or grain that the elders awarded was intended to be food to help the victim recover from his wounds. If he died later on, full homicide compensation could be claimed. Thus there was traditional precedent for the concept of assault as a legitimate ground for civil action introduced by British administration.

The contemporary treatment of assault in the African Tribunal Courts combines Gusii concepts of compensation and the Western idea that it is a crime punishable by legal sanctions. The courts can order fines, damages, and prison sentences after one hearing. The fines and damages are commensurate to the injury and range up to $70; the maximum prison sentence is one year. Some assault and all mayhem cases are taken to the Resident Magistrate's Court, which has the power to order corporal punishment and longer prison sentences but does not award damages. The vast majority of assault cases, however, come to the African Tribunal Courts, where they constitute the most frequent category of criminal offense.

Assault is frequently committed by Gusii, and it is even more frequently a grounds for litigation. Some assault cases occur when men are drunk, and these are fairly likely to involve real injury. No matter how drunk or how slight the injury, it will be reported to the chief and an assault litigation will begin. The most frequent kind of assault case occurs in the following manner. Two neighbors with adjoining land disagree concerning their boundary; they may or may not be involved in a civil suit over the land itself. January arrives and it is time to break ground. Masoti begins plowing a pasture which he and Obwoge have been using for communal grazing and which contains the disputed boundary. Obwoge is aghast at this; he comes down with a machete and argues with Masoti about his right to cultivate the pasture. Masoti is adamant and pushes Obwoge away; the latter threatens him with the machete. Friends and relatives intervene and try to calm them down. The one who reaches the chief first claims he was assaulted and badly injured. At the hospital with a police form, he details an injury to his back or arm for which the doctor is unable to find evidence. At court the elders read the doctor's report, hear the complainant, eventually decide to dismiss the case for lack of evidence. Cases of this type pour into the courts in January and February, the plowing season. A variant of it is the case in which two neighbors have had a boundary dispute which has caused bad feelings. The cattle of one get into a field of the other. The owner of the trespassed property gets furious and shouts at the careless boy herder. He may slap the boy or threaten the neighbor if he himself is present.

The tendency of Gusii individuals to instigate assault litigation on trifling grounds is extremely strong, and Nyansongo seems typical in this respect. In a three-year period, 1954–1956, one of the three African Tribunal Courts in Gusiiland heard 1306 assault cases, of which only 478 or 36.6% resulted in convictions. At the Resident Magistrate's Court, where the more serious assault cases are taken, the Gusii surpass adjacent tribal groups in per cent of nonconvictions. This is shown in Table 3.

Table 3 Per Cent of Nonconvictions in Assault Cases by Tribal Group, Resident Magistrate's Courts of South Nyanza and Kericho Districts, 1955 and 1956 *

Gusii	39.5%
South Nyanza Luo	35.7%
Kipsigis	18.6%

* Court Records.

A certain number of Gusii (and Luo) nonconvictions for assault may be due to testimony so perjured that the court is unable to determine what took place. But the fact remains that the majority of Gusii assault charges are dismissed because there is no evidence that an assault occurred. The doctors who examine assault plaintiffs at the Kisii Hospital are rarely able to find marks of a determined attack.

Another category of aggressive offense, recognized by the Gusii though not by the British-imposed judicial system, is witchcraft and unjustifiable sorcery. There are many stories of young men who met witches at night and killed them with clubs. This is regarded as entirely justifiable, in fact commendable, homicide. In the daytime, however, a witch is not distinguished by dress from any other woman and is treated much like anyone else, even though people suspect she is a witch. To offend a suspected witch by accusing her or treating her impolitely would be to invite her wrath. In many ways she may be excluded socially, but this is done with extreme subtlety and discretion so that matters do not come to a head. Many divorces and separations occur because the wife is considered a witch by the husband, but this would not be stated overtly until she was gone. In general, the feeling is: If you are not prepared to kill a witch, do not offend her by revealing what she is. If a number of deaths in a community are attributed to witchcraft, then some action is felt to be necessary. In the past the most usual course of action after a public accusation was an ordeal called "going to the river," in which the accused had to pull an iron ring out of a pot of boiling water with both hands. If the hands were scalded, the verdict was guilty. Another kind of ordeal was used if a sick person were certain he was being bewitched but did not know who did it. Suspects drank a bitter liquid (ekeroro) and then ran around. Falling down and fainting was a sign of guilt. Persons incriminated by ordeals would be subject to lynching (riyoyo), that is, being clubbed to death by a mob of neighbors. The sons of the convicted witch might successfully defend her from the mob, but then they would have to pay compensation for anyone she killed. The mob execution of a witch was only done when she was notorious for killing people, but it was considered necessary at such a point because witches are thought to be incapable of reform.

Under the British administration, witch killing is murder, and since chiefs and elders no longer support it, alternative remedies for witchcraft have become popular. One is the hiring of a professional sorcerer (omonyamosira), a man, to bury medicine (omosira) which will combat the witchcraft poisons and act at a distance to kill witches. This is done not by the group, because elders disapprove of it, but by individual men who suspect their neighbors of witchcraft. Because of the high level of suspicion in the community, no one trusts his neighbor to use the sorcery only against witches but fears that it will be used to do away with anyone he hates or envies. In other words, each person fears that the other will use sorcery not for its ostensible purpose, to kill witches, but in the unjustifiable way that witches themselves use their magical powers. The use of sorcery, which has been largely imported from other tribes, has been increasing as has its concomitant suspicions. The professional sorcerers themselves are most feared as "witchcraft" murderers, and when death occurs in a community, the sorcerer may be blamed. One night in 1954, under such circumstances, a group of men smashed the skull of a wealthy sorcerer who had a reputation for unwarranted killing. His sons informed the police of the murder, but the culprits were never found because everyone refused to talk. Thus sorcery has become an increasingly popular witchcraft antidote, but it acts to bring new sources of aggressive conflict into Gusii communities.

Another contemporary way of dealing with witchcraft is to call in a professional "witch smeller" (omoriori). The witch smeller has the gift of being able to detect and root out the medicines hidden by the witch in the victim's house. He removes them in a dramatic way and warns the assembled throng, especially the women, to stop their witchcraft activities or he will have to identify the culprits. In general, however, he avoids fixing blame and focuses attention on removal of the injurious substances. This procedure has the general approval of Gusii constituted authority because it does nothing to increase suspicion or encourage witch killing.

Sometimes accusations of witchcraft or sorcery become public and have to be dealt with by authority in order to prevent witch killing. The Tribunal Courts refuse to hear witchcraft cases, but they will hear defamation cases brought by women who have been accused and want to clear their names. More frequently, however, the chief will order the elders to hear the case, as he did on several occasions in Nyansongo in 1957. If they decide the person is guilty, they issue warnings that such things must cease and sometimes order the alleged victims to stay away from the witch or sorcerer. No penalties are recognized for such offenses. The elders publicly oppose all witchcraft and sorcery and try to keep cases of it *sub rosa* as long as possible, for if they admit that it exists, they are encouraging retaliation. When a case becomes public, they try to reduce the conflict that led to the accusation rather than punish one side or the other.

SEXUAL OFFENSES

The sexual behavior of the Gusii is discussed in other sections of this work (Chapters 5 and 9) and elsewhere (LeVine, 1959b); hence this section will be limited to a review of those aspects which are relevant to social control and are not covered elsewhere.

Legitimate sexual intercourse among the Gusii is limited to the marital relationship; under any other circumstances it is theoretically punishable or a source of shame if discovered by someone of the parental generation. On the level of the family and neighborhood group, the social control of sex continues to be effected by traditional means: punishment by the ancestor spirits; *amasangia,* death because of adultery; intergenerational shaming. Father-daughter incest, for example, of which one contemporary case was reported to us, is treated as an affliction caused by the ancestor spirits who must be placated by a sacrifice. The offending father is not punished except for being forbidden to eat or drink milk from the cows in the daughter's bridewealth. Intraclan premarital incest outside the extended family is common but must be clandestine to avoid punishment.

The sanctions that can be used when classificatory father-daughter incest becomes public information are illustrated in a case where it resulted in pregnancy. A young man of 20 had a leviratic wife but was otherwise unmarried. One night during the time of female initiation he joined in *ogochabera,* "taking by stealth." He was drunk and had intercourse with a girl who was his classificatory daughter. She became pregnant while still unmarried, which is in itself a disgrace, and had a difficult delivery. During her labor, old women, in accordance with the belief that unconfessed sex offenses make childbirth difficult, had questioned her about her sex affairs. She confessed to having intercourse with 12 young men, whom she named, but the birth still did not take place. It is said that when she finally admitted intercourse with her classificatory father, delivery was immediate. This was taken as a sign of his guilt in the matter, and he was made to feel it. The girl's father and his own family reprimanded him harshly. He denied it at first and tried to run off, but he was ordered to stay home for three months so that the baby's resemblance to him could be noted. It is said that it was so strong that he had to confess. The girl's family contemplated accusing him in front of the elders but decided not to. In any event, he was stigmatized throughout the community and told when he came to beer parties, "You are useless; you may even steal our wives!" Because of this, he stayed at his own homestead and did not go out to beer parties until after the girl got married. Before the child of a supposedly incestuous union marries, the culprit will have to apologize at a feast in front of the child, its mother and legal father, and people from his own community. Such an apology (called *ogosonsorana*) is only necessary when the incest cuts across adjacent generation lines and has come to be known publicly; incest within the generation, even if publicly known, would not occasion such severe sanctions.

In the past, a Gusii man who discovered his wife *in flagrante delicto* had the right to spear and kill her lover. If he merely suspected a man of having sexual relations with his wife, he would question her about it. If she admitted it at all, she would claim to have been raped, and the husband would accuse her alleged rapist before the lineage elders. The elders could order an oath to be taken in which the woman stood naked astride a trench and the defendant, also naked, would pass through the trench between her legs, carrying a spear and shield. If his denial of guilt were false, he would be killed by the ancestor spirits. His refusal to take the oath indicated his culpability as a rapist, and the elders could slash and kill his cattle; no one of the husband's minor lineage could eat the meat of such cows.

Nowadays a husband may no longer kill his wife's lover under any circumstances. A Nyansongo man was told that his wife had sexual relations with an unmarried man in the community after a beer party. She claimed that she had fallen asleep in the house after leaving the beer party and that the young man had raped her while she was asleep. An indecent assault charge, to be heard by the local elders, was ordered by the chief. During their hearing they learned that the wife had the reputation of being promiscuous; the charge against the young man was immediately dropped. Had her reputation been cleared, the elders would have awarded damages to the husband. The latter would then have to perform a sacrifice with his wife before resuming marital relations.

While traditional means of controlling sexual behavior remain effective at the local level, where kinship sanctions are operative, increased contact between persons of different localities has resulted in a rise of premarital sexual activity, including rape. In the past, interclan rape or abduction would touch off a blood feud; today the typical rapist who is convicted of "indecent assault" serves six months in prison and pays a fine of $70. Many are able to escape the district before arrest, so that the charges are eventually dropped. The high frequency of rape has been a major problem in Gusiiland for over 20 years. Table 4 gives a comparison of the Gusii rate of rape (including indecent assault) indictments with the rate in the United States.

It can be seen that the Gusii have a phenomenal amount of rape. This fact is also revealed in Table 5, which compares the number of Gusii rape indictments in the Resident Magistrate's Court with those of adjacent tribal groups.

Table 4 Average Annual Rate of Rape Indictments per 100,000 Population, Gusii and United States, 1955 and 1956

Gusii *	47.2
United States, urban †	13.85
United States, rural †	13.1

* This is an extremely conservative estimate; the procedures by which it was arrived at are described in LeVine (1959*b*).

† Statistical Abstract of the United States, U.S. Department of Commerce, 78th Annual Edition, 1957, p. 139.

Table 5 Number of Rape Indictments in Resident Magistrate's Courts, 1955 and 1956 and Populations, 1948, Gusii and Adjacent Tribal Groups

	TOTAL NUMBER OF RAPE INDICTMENTS 1955–1956 *	1948 POPULATION
Gusii	13	237,542
South Nyanza Luo	6	270,379
Kipsigis	4	152,391

* A small proportion of the rape indictments are entered in the Resident Magistrate's Court, but this is the only court for which comparable figures are available.

This clearly indicates that the Gusii surpass adjacent tribal groups in rape rate.

THEFT

The Gusii traditionally had a clearly defined sense of private property with reference to domestic animals and grain. In each homestead the several "houses" had traditionally recognized claims to stock, but the homestead head was the formal owner of all herds and could allocate them as he saw fit during his lifetime. Theft within the homestead was dealt with only by him, while interhomestead theft brought judicial agencies and magical sanctions into play.

The Gusii are not shocked or revolted by the idea of stealing each other's cattle, as their Kipsigis neighbors are. Theft of cattle among the Gusii was only more serious than the theft of goats, sheep, or chickens in economic rather than emotional terms, and Gusii cattle were as fair game as those of another tribal group.

The rules of theft were relative to social distance. Raiding of alien tribal groups, Luo and Kipsigis, for cattle was highly approved of and frequent in the past. Cattle raids on other Gusii tribes were also permissible and frequent, although retaliations often resulted. Even the raiding of other clans within the tribe for cattle was proper under most circumstances, though not in areas where there was supraclan political authority. Within the clan, taking cattle, other animals, or grain belonging to another homestead was an offense and is more properly designated theft than appropriation outside the clan.

Controlling the theft of movable property in any society presents two distinct problems: identification of the thief, and treatment of the thief once he has been identified. In Gusii society there was no police force and no scientific method of detection; thus the identification of an unknown thief was difficult.

The solution was the application of magico-religious sanctions which were believed to affect only the thief himself and his family, although his identity was not known to the persons applying the sanctions. The thief would become so frightened that he would identify himself and could be dealt with as a convicted offender. Three procedures of this type were in general use before British administration. First, if a person found an animal or some grain missing and strongly suspected that it was taken by someone in the immediate vicinity of his homestead, he could summon his neighbors to a meeting. He would use the *obomera* oracle, rubbing leaves up and down on a greased stick and calling out the names of all neighbors present. The person whose name was called as the leaves stuck was the guilty one. In a variant form known as *amaera,* everyone present was asked to drink a potion (containing some earth that had touched the stolen article) which is supposed to kill the guilty one. The thief usually incriminates himself by refusing to drink. Second, in the case of a serious theft of several cattle that had not been committed by neighbors, the victim would invite the lineage and hut elders to his house to drink beer and curse the unknown thief. They would perform the drinking-tube curse, which would act to kill the thief. Ordinarily the thief would confess because of fear of the effect of the curse. Then he had to brew beer and kill a bull for the elders, and they would come and spit beer on him to remove the curse. The next day he would sacrifice a goat to the spirits and wear a goat-skin bracelet. Third, if the theft victim preferred private sorcery to the elders' curse, he could hire a practitioner known as an *omokengi* to perform a kind of sorcery called *ogokenga,* which was used only against thieves. In one form of *ogokenga,* a hole was made in the watery stem of a plant called *omokubo,* and toads, ants, grasshoppers, snails, and crabs were inserted, along with rope from the stolen cow and earth from its footprint. The stem would be swollen with the articles introduced into it, and in like manner the thief's viscera would become swollen and he would die. Before a large crowd, the *omokengi* would hold up the stem and say to the anonymous thief, "You will die!" Elders in the crowd would shout, "Eeee! (Yes!)." An alternate procedure was to extract the bones and internal organs of a mole through a hole in its skin, fill it with the same articles just mentioned, and inflate the moleskin with air through a reed. It was taken to the top of a hill, where the *omokengi* shouted, "When the toad dies, you die!" Sometimes, instead of performing these laborious operations, he would shout a warning of the thief's death in the early morning for everyone in the area to hear. If this did not have the desired effect, he would undertake the rituals described. If the stolen animals were returned, the *omokengi* was given a hoe. This specialist in antitheft sorcery has been replaced in Gusii-land by the professional sorcerer (*omonyamosira*) and witch smeller (*omoriori*), both of whom are highly eclectic practitioners who perform any kind of magic (much borrowed from other tribes) for which people are willing to pay. One sorcerer is very fierce-looking and cultivates his reputation as a powerful, terrifying individual. Though he did not want to give away any secrets, he did make the following statement.

I am frequently called for in cases of theft. I mix a poisonous powder with the roots of certain trees, and then mix in earth from the place where the stolen article had been. I dig a hole there and put in the mixture and the freshly cut head of a black chicken. Then I put a curse on the thief and when he gets ill he confesses. But first I warn all the people around in a loud voice. Everyone is frightened; women ask their sons if they committed the theft. Most of the times after this the thieves return the stolen articles.

These, then, represent the range of magical procedures used to frighten thieves into confessing or returning the stolen property intact.

The second major problem in theft control is what to do about the thief once he is identified. In the past, if the owner caught someone in the process of stealing his animals, usually at night, he had the right to kill him without payment of compensation. Usually, however, this was not done for intraclan theft; litigation was more frequent. If the elders convicted a man of theft, he had to return what was stolen, or an equivalent, and provide a goat for the elders to eat. Both offender and victim ate it with the elders, and the thief was humble and quiet at the feast. If the convicted thief refused to repay the animals, the owner could either take them back himself with the moral support of the elders, persuade the elders to curse the thief, or, in some areas, appeal to the judicial chief (*omokumi*) for the use of his powerful wand to enforce repayment. An incorrigible thief would be warned by his family, who would eventually make it publicly known that he could be killed by anyone in the clan who discovered him stealing; alternately, he might be sorcerized by one of his victims. In general, however, the sanctions for occasional theft were rather mild, mainly involving repayment, provided the thief admitted both his guilt and the authority of the elders' order to repay what was stolen.

In many cases where the owner of a stolen animal claimed to know the identity of the thief, the accused maintained his innocence. Litigation before the elders was then necessary, and since in many cases perjured evidence made the facts difficult to ascertain, oaths and ordeals were often resorted to. If a stolen cow were found alive in a particular homestead, and the person in possession of it claimed it as his own, elders might order the following oath. The accused would hold the horns of the cow while the plaintiff cut off a piece of its right ear with a spear. As the animal shook the ear, throwing blood on them, the parties would state their claims in the form of a challenge. The animal could stay at the homestead where it was found, while the plaintiff retained the piece of ear. If at a later time trouble or deaths in the family caused one of the parties to concede that he was wrong, a cleansing feast would be held and the piece of ear produced at that time. When a person was accused of deliberately killing an animal belonging to someone else, he might be challenged to eat a piece of flesh cut from the wound on the body of the animal and stitched onto a sharpened stalk of napier grass. His refusal was a virtual confession of guilt; his eating it put him in danger of the usual spirit sanctions if he were guilty. In cases where the accused admitted taking the animal but claimed it to be rightfully his, the *omotembe* oath (described previously) would be used.

It is difficult to estimate the comparative incidence of Gusii theft. Statistics are not comparable to those available for American populations. In gross amount of theft complaints and theft convictions at resident magistrate's courts, the Gusii ran slightly behind both Luo and Kipsigis for 1955–56. The validity of the comparison is weakened by the fact that a breakdown for in-group and out-group theft is not available, and by the presence of European farms presenting unique temptations in Kipsigis reserve but not in the other two areas. The Gusii appear to have a reputation for an exceptional amount of theft among European farmers, and it may be that their theft rate is higher when they are living outside home territory. No type of theft is unknown in contemporary Gusiiland: organized rings of cattle thieves were discovered by the police during 1955–1957; robberies of shops and restaurants took place; sons frequently stole from their fathers. People in Nyansongo keep locks on their doors and do not leave valuables unguarded outside; children are sometimes left at home to protect the household against theft. Yet it would not be accurate to say that theft is an everyday occurrence nor that there is a pervasive fear of theft.

Nowadays the Kenya police are often called on for theft cases, and they provide a system of natural detection and enforcement which did not exist in the past. Belief in supernatural sanctions for theft have by no means died out, however. We administered a story-completion test to 27 Gusii high school pupils, who are among the most educated persons to be found in Gusiiland. One story they were requested to finish told of two teenage boys who steal a chicken undetected. Almost half of the pupils finished the story with the boys being identified through the use of the greased-stick oracle or poison ordeal and having to confess the theft. Thus magical means of identifying thieves play a part in the fantasies of even the more educated Gusii when confronted with the possibility of their own involvement in theft. The use of professional sorcerers for theft cases is common and is generally believed to be effective in causing the deaths of unconfessed thieves. The death of a Nyansongo man in 1956 was attributed to such a cause. Furthermore, traditional oaths are fully accepted and commonly used in the Tribunal Courts (at the request of the defendant) in civil cases of debts which often border on theft accusations. In general, then, there is a high level of belief in supernatural sanctions against unconfessed thieves.

CONCLUSIONS

The Nyansongans cannot be described as an extremely law-abiding group of people; many types of crimes occur in their community as well as in the wider society of which they are a segment. They are preoccupied with accusing each other of offenses, in court and outside, and no one is expected to admit his guilt. There is great reliance on the chief and courts, as well as on magical procedures, for the enforcement of cultural rules regarding sex, aggression, and property.

Chapter 9

Death, Disease, and the Supernatural

Nyansongans concern themselves with the interpretation of deaths and illness, and they see in the pattern of such events meaningful purposes and designs. No death occurs without firmly expressed opinions as to its "cause," and serious and chronic diseases often call forth interpretations as well. In the Nyansongo belief system, the same categories of supernatural explanation apply to all serious misfortunes and anomalies; thus a disastrous crop failure might be attributed to the same cause as human and bovine fatality, sterility, and congenital deformity.

This chapter covers Nyansongans' reactions to death and disease and their customary ways of coping with such events. The following topics are taken up: (1) medicinal practices which do not involve the supernatural; (2) emotional and ceremonial responses to death; (3) beliefs concerning witches (mentioned previously in Chapter 8), which are basic to an understanding of disease theories in Nyansongo; (4) theories of disease, involving not only witchcraft but ancestor spirits (discussed in Chapter 6) and sorcery (discussed in Chapter 8); (5) the ways in which contradictory diagnoses are resolved in concrete situations.

MEDICINE

A good deal of "naturalistic" medicine is practiced in Nyansongo. Medicine men (abanyamoriogo) have potions and pastes for sprains, diarrhea, pulmonary complaints, and heart ailments; indigenous surgeons (ababari) set fractures and cure backaches and concussions by the removal of sections of bone from the spinal column and skull. One Nyansongo woman whose head had been injured had two skull operations by a Gusii surgeon who removed sections of her cranium. Furthermore, even conservative Nyansongans are eager for Western medication, particularly injections and operations, and they pay exorbitant fees to poorly qualified Indian doctors in Kisii Town for remedies ranging from penicillin to diathermy. But these practitioners have little effect on the bulk of disease in Gusiiland. Although its elevation and coolness protect the inhabitants from sleeping sickness and other tropical ailments of the low-lying lake shore, Gusiiland is ravaged by pneumonia, typhoid fever (in the rainy seasons), bovine tuberculosis, intestinal parasites, and dysentery. Chronic malaria (with resultant enlargement of the spleen) is not uncommon, rabies is spread by numerous wild dogs, and fear of tetanus is the traditional explanation for the custom of removing the two lower incisors. Infant mortality is high, and so is the death of women during childbirth. Nyansongans are pragmatic about treatment and will try anything that promises help and that has the faith of someone they respect. When one remedy fails, they try another, running through injections, mepacrine tablets, sacrifice, and sorcery with no feeling of inconsistency. Diseases are so often in advanced stages before treatment is sought that even the best medical care would be of little use. Death from disease is thus a common occurrence,* and the outcome of any illness is fraught with uncertainty.

REACTIONS TO DEATH

Despite the high death rate in Nyansongo, death is not taken casually; on the contrary, it occasions elaborate ritual and the expression of intense emotions. The degree of ceremonial elaboration and emotional expressiveness varies with the social status of the deceased. The funeral of an infant, buried in the floor of the house, is humble, with little wailing and few people attending. When a wealthy, middle-aged man dies, however, kinsmen come from far and wide, and expressions of grief are profuse. Funerals of others fall in between these two extremes, with more elaborate funerals for married persons than unmarried, for men than women, and so forth. The corpse of an adult is buried just outside the house in which he lived, on the right side of the house for a man, on the left for a woman. Burial takes place in silence almost immediately after death, although the autopsy mentioned below may be performed first. The women of the family usually begin their wailing, which can be heard from far away, while the person is dying, but they must restrain themselves during the burial.

* This characterization is based on field observations; no death statistics were available.

After the corpse is buried, the women resume wailing, now even more loudly, sometimes sobbing and sometimes chanting in a stylized sing-song. They sing improvised eulogies of the deceased and attribute his death to the ill will of others. A Nyansongo mother wailed of her married son: "I'll never give birth again, and he's the one who caused me so much trouble in labor." Then she knelt on the grave and shouted, "You were my favorite son, you used to bring me sugar and salt and good blankets. Now you've gone below here. Why don't you listen to me and come back?" She ran into the son's house and emerged holding ashes in her hands, exclaiming, "These ashes—that's where I warmed myself last night hoping you'd come back, but you didn't." She ran back to the grave sobbing: "My Mogaka (his name), my Mogaka." The wife of the married but childless man chanted, "I'll never find a man who will love me as my husband did. I would have had a child by him, but maybe people were bewitching him." At another funeral, a married daughter of the dead man cried, "There was no one like my father, father, father! He was bewitched because he had so many cattle." When a woman is chanting a eulogy or wailing, she often goes into a slow, shuffling dance, moving her arms in rhythm with her legs. The wives of the deceased remove much of their clothing and either tie around their waists or actually don pieces of their husband's clothes, such as shirts, jackets, and hats. They continue to wail for 12 to 18 hours, sometimes longer, until they are too weak to go on, and yield to the urgings of the other women who want to give them food. Wives and daughters of the dead man have tears streaming down their faces while wailing and appear genuinely distraught, but women outside the immediate family wail loudly without other signs of deep grief. At night older brothers and sisters of the dead man stay with the widows to reassure them about the future and "keep them from killing themselves."

During the day of the burial, the males of the homestead and surrounding homesteads are silent and subdued. Their expression of grief is limited to facing the grave at one point and uttering a single note— "oooo"—which they hold for about a minute. The rest of the time they stand about silently, watching the women or chatting among themselves in low voices.

The day after the burial, the public funeral occurs. When the deceased is a married man, his wives and certain other close kin have their heads shaved at the grave. Some of the deceased's personal property is put on the grave. It may be his bed, if he had one, or the chair he most often sat on, with his clothes draped over it. His drinking tube and walking stick may also be included. By this time news of his death will have spread to his kinsmen near and far. Women from the community and from related families outside it will have gathered at the house of the deceased during or before the head shaving. Afterward, as other women join them during the day, this group wails with the widows of the dead man. The wailing on this day is more stylized and less grievous than the day before, although similar eulogies and accusations are sung. Men attend the funeral with spears, machetes, horns, whistles, and bells, as well as a few head of cattle apiece. They drive the cattle over the grave of the dead man while making a din by shouting, blowing the horns and whistles, and ringing the bells. Then they run about the grave thrusting the spears and machetes into the air.* Other men attend the funeral without cattle and pay their respects by facing the grave and singing one note, as mentioned above. Immediate relatives sacrifice two goats to propitiate the spirit of the deceased. Afterward the wives undergo a period of mourning of one to four weeks during which time they receive visitors and must not travel or bathe. A sacrificial feast at which the widows pick their leviratic mates ends the mourning period.

WITCHES

When a Nyansongan dies or is stricken by a serious illness, alternative explanations may be offered. One type involves the unprovoked aggression of witches or the wrongly directed magic of sorcerers; the other points to the patient's own acts as having caused either the ancestor spirits to punish him or a live person to retaliate through sorcery. Both explanations have an equal claim to validity in Nyansongo thought, but in specific cases one may be favored over the other. In this chapter we outline the alternative types of explanation and describe the process by which one interpretation rather than the other comes to be accepted in particular cases.

Before discussing Nyansongan theories of disease, it is necessary to describe their beliefs concerning witches. People in Nyansongo fear witches greatly and talk about witchcraft very frequently. In their belief, a witch (*omorogi*) is a person with an incorrigible tendency to murder his neighbors by secret means and with little provocation. In

---

* Although Gusii informants were not able to give reasons other than tradition for this behavior of the men, Wagner (1949: 453–458) describes similar phenomena for the related Logoli, attributing the cattle drive to a desire to pay respects to the dead man by wealth display, and the sham fight to recall the deceased's prowess in warfare.

theory a witch may be either male or female, but persons real and myth-ical to whom witchcraft is attributed are invariably women. Such women are believed to run naked at night, speechlessly carrying fire-brands and knocking on the doors of houses with their buttocks. Large groups of them are said to meet secretly at night to plan murders and to exhume and devour corpses. The eating of human flesh is supposed to enable them to run fast, although some are old women, and their muteness is attributed to their having eaten human hearts, which have stuck in their throats. Anyone who meets a witch may kill her if he can catch her, but a club must be used so as not to shed her blood. If you utter a sound while confronting a witch, you will die.

A person whose mother is a witch learns the evil art from her in childhood, but many women are believed to learn it later in life. A mother-in-law who is a witch may enlist her daughter-in-law, and women who have had great misfortune, such as the loss of many chil-dren, are regarded as specially susceptible to recruitment, since they want to retaliate against a world that has treated them badly. It is said that a woman who wants to become a full-fledged witch must first kill a close relative, usually her own child. After that she partakes of the conspiracies and cannibalism of the local witch group. Murder by witchcraft is effected by the planting of a "poisonous" substance in the roof, floor, or walls of the victim's house; it is thought to act at a dis-tance to cause disease and eventually the demise of the victim. The articles planted may be hair or feces of the victim, dead birds, bones of exhumed corpses, or actually poisonous powders, to mention but a few possibilities.

The question of whether there are women who conceive of them-selves as witches and run about naked at night is a real one. Highly educated Gusii youths claim to have seen them and relate detailed plausible accounts. Three living women in Nyansongo were mentioned as witches. One of them confessed to being a witch while drunk and later retracted the confession. Another indirectly admitted participa-tion in a witch group during an interview. Even if there are "real witches" in Nyansongo, suspicions and accusations run far ahead of substantiation. This is particularly obvious in cases where two families quarreling over land accuse each other of witchcraft, although none of their members may be considered witches by the community at large. Community opinion is fluctuating and inconsistent on the identity of witches, however, so it does not play a definitive role in settling such disputes.

An important aspect of Nyansongo witchcraft is that it is believed to be practiced by closely related neighbors against one another and by members of the same family against one another. The most frequently ascribed motive for it is jealousy of good fortune—greater wealth, better crops, more children—by a less fortunate person. A woman who becomes sterile is thought likely to practice witchcraft against those of her co-wives or wives of her husband's brothers who give birth regularly. Inheritance quarrels among brothers and half-brothers may also involve witchcraft accusations among their wives and mothers. Wealthy men fear the witchcraft of their poorer kinsmen.

THEORIES OF DISEASE AND DEATH

Witchcraft (*oborogi*) is always suspected when a Nyansongan has died. The proverb, "No one dies without carrying someone on his back" is interpreted to mean that all deaths are traceable to witchcraft. If the deceased were a homestead head or if the family has been suspecting witchcraft prior to the death, an autopsy may be performed. The examination is conducted to ascertain whether any of the internal organs are swollen. If so, the suspicion of witchcraft is confirmed. Regardless of what is found, however, the close female relatives of the deceased invariably make accusations of witchcraft in the course of their wailings at the funeral. At one funeral in 1956 the widow recalled that a neighbor woman quarreled with the deceased over trespassing cattle, and chanted her conjecture that the woman had bewitched him. At the funeral of a girl who had died in childbirth after we took her to the hospital, we were accused by her mother of having conspired with hospital attendants to kill her (no means were mentioned). Such behavior is an immediate expression of the grief and frustration of women at funerals, but it is often forgotten later on.

In some cases, however, accusations of this nature lead to violence at funerals. When a married woman dies without children, her kinsmen are extremely chagrined because they have to refund her entire bridewealth, no matter how long she has been married. If she had been living in a polygynous homestead and had been infertile or unable to bear viable offspring, her kinfolk are doubly angered because they suspect witchcraft by her co-wives as the cause of death. When her sisters attend the funeral, they may destroy all her valuable possessions and grain stores to prevent the co-wives from benefitting by her death. In one such case the husband of the dead woman was attacked physically as well.

When an autopsy has been performed and signs of witchcraft are discovered, the men may decide to act on the confirmed suspicion, particularly if the deceased were a relatively rich and important person. A professional sorcerer * (*omonyamosira*) from outside the community is called for two reasons: (1) to retaliate against the witch, and (2) to protect members of the deceased's household from further effects of the witchcraft. The retaliation is accomplished by burying *omosira,* anti-witch medicine, in the grave itself or at some other place very near the house of the deceased. The *omosira* varies from one sorcerer to another; it may be a freshly killed black chicken wrapped in an article of the deceased's clothing or it may be a bottle containing a seed and some water. It is believed that when the seed germinates and splits, the witch will die. The sorcerer also performs a protective ritual known as *okoosia,* the making of incisions into which a powder is rubbed on the bodies of members of the immediate family. Just as an identical ritual protects a husband and adulterous wife from further supernatural sanctions, in this situation it wards off the future effects of the witchcraft that killed the deceased. Once the sorcerer has buried *omosira,* deaths and illnesses occurring in the next few months at nearby homesteads may well be attributed to its effect. The family which hired the sorcerer may be pleased at the success of the retaliation, but the family newly stricken by misfortune may not admit their responsibility for the previous death. The latter family may claim that the medicine is killing innocent people and report it to the chief. When the person is dying, they may ask the sorcerizing family to save his life by calling the sorcerer to take out the buried medicines and administer protective powders. If the sorcerizing family refuses, great bitterness against them will result, and they may come to be regarded as being like witches themselves. Thus a death may be attributed by family members to the illegitimate use of sorcery as well as to witchcraft by their neighbors; indeed, the distinction between witchcraft and sorcery may become quite vague in such cases.

Certain kinds of nonfatal illnesses may also be attributed to witchcraft. While dysentery, bronchitis, and malaria are believed to be susceptible of naturalistic treatment, if the family has previously suspected witchcraft or has had a series of misfortunes, a severe onset of such a disease may be thought of as witch-caused—particularly if the illness does not yield to naturalistic remedies. Sterility and mental disease, however, are always regarded as supernaturally caused, and the diviner rather than the medicine man is first to be called on in such cases.

---

* A professional sorcerer differs from a witch in being a male who can be hired to commit a magical murder; his profession is known and openly stated by him. Some sorcerers, however, have been suspected of using their powers to kill personal enemies and have been killed by their irate neighbors.

The diviner may diagnose either ancestor spirit affliction or witchcraft as the cause, but diviners always live nearby and know the situations and fears of their clients well. The client is questioned about omens and mentions dead rats on the path, cut pieces of snakes and dogs found near the house, if witchcraft is his primary fear, whereas quite different omens point to ancestor spirits. If the first diviner does not give a satisfactory diagnosis, another will be consulted; thus the eventual interpretation of the disease is more dependent on the fears and anxieties of the patient and his family than on the arbitrary judgment of the diviner and her oracles. All three cases of mental disease which we had the opportunity to observe were attributed to witchcraft. In one, sorcery was used to combat it; a witch smeller removed the poisons in the second; and in the third case, that of a boy suffering from either mental retardation or psychosis, no remedy that we know of was resorted to. A witch smeller was also called in to cure a case of sterility. One young couple in Nyansongo had several infants who died and then a hydrocephalic child with a grotesquely enlarged skull. A diviner pronounced the deformity of their only living child the result of witchcraft by its grandmother, and the father of the child was reported to be learning professional sorcery to combat his mother's evil influence. Nonfatal but relatively incurable conditions, such as mental disease, sterility and deformity, then, are often attributed to witchcraft and less serious diseases may also be if patient and family are disposed to suspect witchcraft.

When a person suspects that he or his family are the objects of sorcery, he views it as unprovoked and illicit malevolence, distinguishable from witchcraft only in that professional services were required for the evil magic. When a dead or dying person is known to have committed certain offenses, however, he is regarded as having brought sorcery on himself. This has already been mentioned for witches; a woman widely reputed to be a witch may die because of legitimate retaliation through sorcery. Sorcerers are also hired to kill unidentified thieves through magic, and the death of a man known to have committed theft may be attributed to sorcery by one of his victims. Finally, a man who refuses to pay a sorcerer for his services may become the latter's victim, and it is generally felt that his death was his own fault. Several deaths in Nyansongo were interpreted as the results of legitimate or justifiable sorcery: one of an old woman for witchcraft, one of a young man notorious for theft, and one of an elder who had failed to pay a sorcerer. Interpretations of this kind resemble the ancestor spirit explanation of disease (discussed below) in that the affliction is regarded as punishment for an offense.

When a diviner diagnoses death or disease as punishment by ancestor spirits, she always names a misdeed of the patient as the ultimate cause. Sexual offenses, homicide (other than magical), and perjured oaths are the most serious of such offenses.* Another misdeed invariably punished by ancestor spirits is the neglect of proper mortuary rituals or the omission of a sacrifice for a dead ancestor. This is a residual category of offense, named by a diviner when she can think of no real misdeed committed by the person, because no one is entirely certain that he has done everything necessary for dead relatives. In addition, such ritual negligence is believed to be indicated by the occurrence of an intrafamilial offense, such as father-daughter incest or parricide, which is so serious that it is classified as a "madness" sent to punish the family by a displeased spirit. Numerous deaths and diseases in Nyansongo were attributed to supernatural punishment. A 10-year-old girl told us that her mother's co-wife had died in childbirth because a woman with whom her father was having an affair stepped over the birth blood. (This is *amasangia*, the spirit-caused punishment for adultery.) Even more frequent is the interpretation of impotence and sterility as spirit-caused conditions by diviners. Sacrifices to make up for ritual omissions are prescribed and performed over and over again until the condition improves or the patient gives up (or turns to witchcraft explanations). In general, when death occurs and the deceased is known to have committed a serious offense, the death and the offense will be linked in terms of ancestor spirits or justifiable sorcery; when an incurable but not fatal disease occurs, diviners are likely, if no serious misdeed is known, to fabricate a ritual offense to which they ascribe the condition.

Amasangia, the supernatural sanction against the infidelity of a wife, involves a somewhat special and elaborate set of beliefs. It can be incurred at any time after the transfer of bridewealth to the bride's parents. *Amasangia* literally means "sharing" and refers to the consequences of illicit sharing of a married woman's sexual attentions. *Amasangia* is caused by the adulterous behavior of a woman, but it directly affects her husband and children rather than herself. Nyansongans believe that if a woman has sexual intercourse with a man other than her husband and continues to cohabit with her husband, then when the latter becomes ill, her presence in the same room may cause his death. It is said that the sick husband begins to sweat pro-

---

* The homicide of a non-Gusii can lead to his spirit afflicting the family of the killer in exactly the same way as ancestor spirits do, but propitiation may require the performance of a special ritual in addition to sacrifice. It should also be noted that venereal disease is regarded as a punishment for sexual licentiousness without specific involvement of ancestor spirits.

fusely when approached by his adulterous wife; if he has cut himself, her attempt to bandage the wound will promote bleeding rather than arrest it. Some of the older polygynists will not allow their wives to visit them when they (the husbands) are ill, since they jealously suspect their wives of adultery. The "shared" wife may also unintentionally kill her child by her proximity to him when he is ill, and miscarriages are regularly attributed to adultery. Belief in *amasangia* appears universal among Nyansongo women, including Christians. They see it as punishment directed against themselves, for no woman wants to be a widow or to lose children. When a woman has committed clandestine adultery, she can avoid the evil consequences either by confessing to her husband and having a purifying sacrifice performed or by running away with her lover.

A second type of sanction enforcing marital fidelity is also part of the *amasangia* complex but is directed at men rather than women. When two men of the same clan have had intercourse with the same married woman, regardless of whether or not she is married to either of them, it is believed that a visit by one to the sickbed of the other will result in the death of the sick one. This is unimportant if the two men are distantly related and do not in any case visit one another, but it enters significantly into the relations of brothers, half-brothers, and first cousins. If one of them has an affair with a married woman, he must concern himself with whether any of the male clansmen whom he often visits has also had intercourse with her. Sometimes suspicion of adultery with a wife is aroused when a man becomes ill and finds that a particular half-brother or paternal cousin of his has not visited him. We knew of two young married men who were constantly seeking extramarital affairs and who would tell each other of the married women they had intercourse with so as to avoid sickbed visits if any of them were the same. Such collaboration to prevent supernatural punishment is rare; ordinarily *amasangia* acts as a check on male access to the wives of others.

DECIDING DIAGNOSES: PATIENT RESPONSIBILITY VERSUS BLAME OF OTHERS

There are, then, alternative theories of disease causation extant in Nyansongo, and they are equally valid by Nyansongo standards. How is it decided which theory applies in a given case? No hard and fast rules of interpretation are laid down, and there are few simplistic formulations of the type which allowed medieval Europeans to conclude automatically that a leper had sinned. For example, when a woman has a miscarriage, she may attribute it to the witchcraft of her jealous co-wife, but her husband may see in it grounds for suspecting her of adultery, particularly if he has been away and has some anxiety on that score. Thus the theory selected to interpret a particular misfortune depends on the position and status of the person making the interpretation, and it often happens that a single event has entirely different meanings for different persons. Most frequently the patient himself (or, in the case of death, members of the immediate family) defensively blames the affliction on the witchcraft or unjustifiable sorcery of others, while neighbors, particularly men, are more likely to attribute it to misdeeds of the patient. When a thief dies, the women of the homestead immediately begin wailing and claiming that the deceased was bewitched. But neighbors, knowing that the dead man had committed theft and fearing that the sorcery medicine which they suspect killed him will kill anyone who goes to the funeral, refuse to take their usual part in the burial and other mortuary practices. Members of the deceased's homestead may not at first accept the fact of his guilt, but lineage elders will come and tell them that unless they make restitution and persuade the victim of theft to dig up the sorcery medicine, it will kill the whole homestead.

A case occurred in Nyansongo which illustrates this process. A young married man, Ongaki, son of Mogaka, was a notorious thief. He became seriously ill with a mysterious disease and seemed to be dying. Some elders came to him and urged him to confess so that his life could be saved by the appropriate measures of restitution, digging up the sorcery medicines and administering protective medicine. He maintained his innocence and blamed his illness on the unjustified sorcery of a neighbor whose family had a reputation for witchcraft. In January 1956 Ongaki died. His mother, the elder of two co-wives, wanted to bury sorcery medicines to kill the neighbor who killed him. Mogaka, father of Ongaki, opposed this on the grounds that the young man had probably been killed by the sorcery of a victim of his theft. Ongaki's mother insisted her son was not a thief and said she would take Mogaka's refusal as a sign that it was her co-wife, a much younger woman, who had killed him by witchcraft. Mogaka, realizing that his senior wife was threatening disruptive accusation within the homestead, agreed to hire a professional sorcerer so as to keep peace in the family. The sorcery medicines were secretly buried, but Mogaka, feeling that they would do no good, postponed payment of the cow that was the sorcerer's fee. In December of 1956 Mogaka had a severe attack of malaria and was suffering from pain due to a swollen malarial spleen. He refused to eat and became extremely emaciated. When a lineage elder asked him if he had any medicine buried, he denied it vigorously at first but intimated that he wanted to pay the sorcerer shortly before his demise in January of 1957. Almost simultaneously, Ongaki's widow bore a child (by her leviratic husband), which died a few days after birth. The funerals were poorly attended because of the widespread belief that the professional sorcerer had killed Mogaka in retaliation for the unpaid debt. Mogaka's widow steadfastly accused neighbors of killing him by unjustified sorcery and even ignored the fact that the two accused neighbors buried Mogaka to prove their innocence. (To bury someone whose death you have caused magically is believed to be fatal.) Eventually Mogaka's oldest half-brother returned from working outside the district and forced the widow to hire a witch smeller who removed poisonous substances from houses in the homesteads of the widow and the men she accused. The brother made a public speech about the evils of accusing others for troubles you yourself have caused. Later the widow confessed to several lineage elders that Mogaka did owe the sorcerer a cow, and it was duly paid. After confession and restitution, involving the widow's capitulation to the interpretation that Mogaka and she herself were responsible for the two recent deaths in their homestead, protective medicines were administered and accusations ceased.

Another case had similar elements. A young married man named Ogise came home to Nyansongo after having fought with British forces against the Mau Mau. He had had pains in his legs even before his military experiences and had reportedly been to doctors for them, but on his return he claimed a battle wound in his leg. He suffered for several months with an earache for which we gave him sulfa pills, but he refused to go to the hospital. When he seemed to be dying, he revealed that when he had killed Kikuyus for the government (not considered an evil act), the bodies had been left unburied, and perhaps their spirits were killing him. A diviner was consulted, and a hen sacrificed, but he died anyway. His older brother and another lineage elder inspected the corpse but did not find the battle wound he had reported. The elder brother said he simply died of disease, but a lineage elder said consensus was that he died of venereal disease contracted in his affairs with "low women" outside Gusiiland, had been ashamed to admit it to doctors, and had made up a story about a battle wound as a defense. Since no accusation of witchcraft was made (except the funerary ones of the bereaved mother) and since no magical sanctions were believed to be operating against the whole family, there was no need for the elders' interpretation of his death to be forced on the family if they wished to believe differently.

SUMMARY AND CONCLUSIONS

Nyansongans maintain contradictory explanations of disease, one of which views disease as a punishment for sexual, aggressive, property, and ritual offenses, while the other, more frequently used, blames it on the unwarranted malevolence of others. When a person becomes seriously ill, he tends defensively to adopt the interpretation which attributes the evil to others, much as a Nyansongo defendant in a trial always insists on his innocence. Lineage elders tend to adopt the punitive interpretation, especially if the patient is known to have committed offenses, and they try to persuade him to confess and perform the rites of absolution so as to save his life. When the patient dies without having confessed, close relatives, particularly women, often accuse others of murdering him magically. The elders then work to convince the survivors that their lives are in danger if they do not admit the dead man's guilt and do what is necessary to protect themselves from the sanctions that are continuing to operate. In doing this, the elders attempt to achieve two aims: (1) to save the homestead from annihilation by the supernatural punishment which the elders sincerely believe was incurred by the deceased and (2) to turn the blame of others into self-blame and thereby keep peace within the lineage. Thus, despite the fact that Nyansongo patients do not ordinarily blame themselves for their diseases, it is the role of authority figures to make them confess their guilt when it endangers the welfare of their family.

⚜
⚜
⚜

Chapter 10

Formal Education

The Gusii did not take eagerly to the Western schooling which was first offered them in 1910. By World War II, the neighboring Luo were far ahead in education. In the 1940's the Gusii began to perceive the material advantages of schooling, and the desire for education grew rapidly until it now surpasses the government or mission ability to provide instruction. A contemporary myth tells of a great Gusii prophet who lived before the Europeans came, but who predicted that white men would come, take away Gusii children and give them white mushrooms. This prophecy, incomprehensible when it was uttered, is now understood to mean that schools would be established and that the children who attended them would be able to earn many shillings ("white mushrooms"). This story is typical of the Gusii view that education is a pathway to lucrative employment, and those parents who want their children educated emphasize the monetary rewards awaiting the educated man. Thus the payment of school fees is seen as an investment which will bring cash return.

In spite of this belief, however, and although Nyansongo is located a quarter of a mile from a school with eight grades and 400 pupils, only one child in the community was attending school in 1956. This 8-year-old boy was later joined by two adolescent boys who were first graders. Of the 28 married men in Nyansongo, 12 had attended school, a majority for two years or less, and this group included a few who attended for only one term and did not become fully literate. Four men claimed to have become literate without schooling. The married women are all unschooled and illiterate. The unmarried population includes only five males (other than the three boys who were pupils in 1957) and two females with a year or two of schooling. Thus Nyansongo is predominantly an illiterate community and does not show signs of change in this respect.

The most educated person in the community is a married man in his late twenties who went through seventh grade, speaks some English, and works sporadically as a brick mason on the Kericho tea plantations. He is not accorded unusual respect, in fact, his reputation is extremely low because of his numerous violations of sexual taboos among close neighbors and kinsmen. His education commands less attention than his deviant behavior, which is viewed as immoral and slightly mad.

When asked why they send so few children to school, Nyansongan parents plead lack of money for school fees, but this explanation is at odds with fact, for there are relatively well-to-do families whose children do not attend school, and poor families whose children do.* For the poor and powerless families education is seen as the path to wealth and prestige.

* The lack of education among Nyansongans is also related to their lesser involvement in Christian missions than many people in surrounding communities.

Many of the local economic opportunities in Nyaribari location are controlled by its chief, who in his thirty-year incumbency has acquired tremendous economic and political power. Much new land was opened for settlement by Nyaribarians, markets and power mills were built, and coffee cultivation was introduced during this period. Many persons of all the local clans shared in the benefits of this economic development, but the chief has favored members of his family and lineage, and to a lesser extent people of his subclan and clan, in the allocation of shops, jobs, and loans. His great prestige with the colonial government and his important positions in the African District Council and the Kisii Farmers Cooperative Union give him influence in the choice of persons for many well-paying jobs. He has used this influence on behalf of the selection of his own kinsmen and in barring persons of subordinate or "adopted" clans of Nyaribari from access to economic advantage.

The members of the lesser clans, some of whom have suffered from discrimination by the chief, have shown great determination to advance economically despite the obstacles he puts in their path. Some have explicitly encouraged their children to work harder than the other pupils at school, and to compensate for their membership in a less favored clan by advancing in education to the point where they have unique qualifications for important positions. These are usually obtained outside the district or in open civil service competition. This encouragement has had striking results. One young man from a poor family in a low-ranking clan, who grew up in a community adjacent to Nyansongo, received a B.A. from Makerere College, an M.A. from the University of Bombay in India, and became a labor relations executive with a large corporation in Nairobi. He is the most educated Gusii. Two men of a different low-ranking clan are regarded by the chief as special enemies. The son of one graduated from high school and was the only Nyaribari student in Makerere College during 1955–1957; a daughter of the other is one of the few Gusii women who has gone beyond primary school and speaks some English. Both of these educationally advanced individuals also grew up within a half mile of Nyansongo. By contrast, only one of the chief's numerous sons completed secondary school, and none of his daughters has had much education. Altogether, the educational advancement of his children has not been commensurate with the financial capability of their father to provide them with schooling. This is also true of the sons of the chief's brothers.

Thus the over-all picture of educational recruitment in Nyaribari is as follows. Young people from low-ranking clans, whose opportunities for economic advancement are blocked by political discrimination, have tended to go farther in school than the children of politically powerful families. Boys of the latter families obtain good jobs in local government despite their lack of high educational qualifications. In this context the educational backwardness of Nyansongo can be properly understood. Its people belong to the same clan as the chief, and one of its neighborhoods is made up of persons of his subclan. A number of Nyansongo men are employed by the chief as cook, chauffeur, guards, foreman of his field hands. Several families are allowed to use the chief's land without payment of rent. Certain men in the community who are not generally considered able have been appointed to minor political positions by the chief. In other words, residents of Nyansongo have access to the chief's favor and derive some economic benefits from their relationship with him. Given this relationship, which provides a sense of security unknown in the low-ranking clans, Nyansongans are not disposed to invest their scarce monetary resources in school fees or to push their children toward educational achievement.

The largest school near Nyansongo is a Roman Catholic mission school, but several smaller schools run by the Seventh Day Adventists, Friends African Mission, and African District Council are within a few miles. All of these, including the Catholic institution, are day schools staffed entirely by African teachers. The number of Nyaribari parents who want their children to go to school is so much greater than the number of places in the schools that many must be refused. Parents plead with the schoolmasters and attempt to bribe them in an effort to get a child into first grade or to win the readmission of one who was dropped for poor performance. This situation gives the teachers considerable power and even higher social status than they would otherwise have.

Most of the families in and around Nyansongo cannot afford to send more than one child to school. When asked which of their children they would choose to send, parents answer, "The most obedient child." No mention is made of specifically intellectual qualities, such as ability to learn. Parents seem to view schooling as a series of commands by the teacher which, if they are obeyed by the child, result in success. Failure is attributed to disobedience rather than to stupidity. The parental attitude is partly a recognition of the real dangers of truancy, for a disobedient child will go to the market or play with some friends rather than attend school, thus wasting the money invested in school fees. Truancy is a big problem, and though parents and teachers cooperate in controlling it, it is less costly to select a child whose obedience has been proven in the family setting than to risk sending to school one who seems likely to pursue his own pleasure and lie about having gone to school. Nevertheless, the adult view of education in terms of obeying commands is more general than a realization of the risk of truancy, and it sometimes results in the selection of a well-behaved child for schooling over his more clever and mischievous brother.

The first few grades are now taught in the Gusii language (Swahili used to be the norm) by teachers, most of whom have not gone farther than eighth grade themselves. English is introduced in fifth grade, and by eighth grade an average student can write a passable essay in English and carry on a limited conversation. The English of the eighth grade student in day school, however, is inferior to that of students in the mission boarding schools near Kisii Town. Academic subjects in the higher grades are taught by Gusii teachers who have completed high school and gone to teacher training college or liberal arts college. In addition to the standard British academic curriculum, the Catholic mission school near Nyansongo offers carpentry, agriculture, music, and physical education. Training in music is obtained by spending long periods in a drum and bugle corps which marches on the school playground. At morning recess and lunchtime, many of the boys play soccer, using small rubber balls when nothing better is available. They are great soccer enthusiasts and seem to play at every opportunity.

Pupils of both sexes must wear uniforms in good repair. For boys, who predominate at the school, this means a khaki shirt and khaki shorts; for girls it is a blue dress with white collar and cuffs. Children are sent home by teachers if they are not wearing the uniform on a particular day, but greater lenience is shown those whose uniforms are torn or frayed. Clothing is one of the school expenses of which parents complain, and many of them do not understand why uniforms are needed or that school authorities are firm in their demand for them. Children who do not go to school often have torn and tattered clothing and generally wear less than pupils. The school has pupils who walk as far as 10 miles every day from home to school; lunch is not provided by the school, and their mothers do not give them lunches to take along either. The wealthier boys are given a few pennies to buy bananas at the market during the noon recess; a fortunate few have relatives who are shop owners at the market and give them a meal. The majority, however, get nothing to eat from early in the morning until they get home in the middle of the afternoon or later, and this must have some effect on their performance in afternoon classes.

School discipline is strict. Teachers demand complete attention and order in the classroom. When the teacher walks into class, the pupils rise in unison and remain standing until told to be seated. Officially, only the headmaster is allowed to administer corporal punishment, and he must record each administration in a ledger which is examined by a visiting school supervisor from the mission. In fact, however, each of the teachers in the lower grades uses corporal punishment daily without even getting permission from the headmaster. Those children who have talked in class or otherwise caused a disturbance are made to line up in front of the class and one by one stand by the teacher to receive a few strokes with a wooden switch. Even outside the classroom the pupils are deferential to their teachers and responsive to their commands. Students in the seventh and eighth grades are put to work on the school's agricultural instruction plot as a punishment for misbehavior.

If the teacher derives some power by being the dispenser of a currently scarce and valued commodity and a classroom disciplinary agent, this power is augmented by the fact that the pupils do not return home for lunch and that many of them are 14 to 24 years old. In other words, he has daytime control over a number of physically mature individuals, and customary checks on personal power do not operate in his case because he is living at the school, away from his community and kin group. The seduction of girls in the 15 to 18 age range by their first or second grade teachers is a recognized abuse, and teachers are dismissed for such offenses when they are discovered. Many other extracurricular uses of the docile students are locally regarded as legitimate. For example, some of the teachers use the older boys to cultivate plots of land loaned to the teachers by persons in nearby communities. The boys are not paid for this, and the teacher reaps the harvest. Male students are also used as domestic servants in the houses of the resident teachers, even cooking for those who do not have their wives with them. In general, the older boys at the school are viewed by the teachers as a labor force which may be assigned to tasks personally required by the teacher. Neither the students nor their parents seem to take strenuous exception to this practice. In this sense, then, schooling is, as parents believe, an exercise in obedience rather than intellectual development.

Part II

Child Training

Chapter 11

Pregnancy and Childbirth

Nyansongo husbands and wives share a strong desire for offspring. Procreation is considered essential to marriage, and parents want as many children as possible, which is related to the dramatic population growth of the Gusii over the past half century. Both male and female children are considered valuable, males because they have a permanent stake in the welfare of the homestead, females because their marriages bring cattle to enrich the family. Insofar as mothers have a preference, it is for a boy, "to bury me when I die," "to take care of me when I'm old," "to bring a wife who will help me in work," "to build houses and mend fences." A girl is said to "go away (in marriage) as soon as she gets big enough to be helpful," and "she may even elope without giving us cattle." It is through her sons that a woman achieves an honored status in the family. Men traditionally want boys to perpetuate the lineage and defend its patrimony, but they realistically point out that having children of both sexes is far better than having too great a predominance of one sex. With all daughters, the minimal lineage dies out and its property is inherited collaterally; there is no one at home to help the parents when they are too old to grow their own food, and they become dependent on kin who are less interested in them than their sons would be. With a predominance of sons, the family has difficulty in raising bridewealth cattle for them to use in marriage, and they may remain unmarried until the age of 30 or longer. Short-range domestic considerations may also influence a mother's preference: if there are cattle and no boys to herd them, she will want a boy; if there is no one to help with fetching water and gathering firewood, she will want a girl. In general, however, Nyansongo parents desire to have both sons and daughters.

Women want to give birth once every two years until menopause, and their husbands actively concur. No formal post-partum sex taboo exists, but polygynists tend to stay with wives who are not currently nursing children. Many wives are eager for sex relations only when they want to conceive, and they do not want to become pregnant again until the child is about 2 years old and has developed some physical independence. Sometimes the space between children is less than two years, due partly to the Gusii belief that conception can take place only during menstruation. In monogamous families, children are more likely to be close in age, but women who have children too often are said to be oversexed.

Any unusual delay encountered by a woman who has been actively trying to conceive is viewed with alarm by husband and wife even if they already have several children. Childlessness is one of the standard supernatural punishments which can be inflicted by the curse of a father on his disobedient son, by the lineage elders on a serious offender against morality, and by the ancestor spirits on a man who has failed to make appropriate sacrifices, ignored omens, or sworn a false oath. Difficulties in conception, in addition to their frustration of the procreative impulse, arouse fears of such punishment and lead to efforts to propitiate the ancestor spirits. The husband goes to a diviner for diagnosis and often makes expensive sacrifices in order to cure the condition. If one sacrifice does not work, he will consult a different diviner. After several such attempts fail, the husband may begin to suspect witchcraft.

Childbearing is a matter of invidious distinction among co-wives in a polygynous family, and they are sensitive to any inequalities in the distribution of living children. Suspicions of witchcraft arise among them when a wife becomes sterile or has a miscarriage or stillbirth. A survey of Nyansongo women past menopause indicated that approximately half of the children born alive live to maturity. In this situation there are some women who have given birth repeatedly but have few or no children, and they often blame this on the witchcraft of their co-wives. When a woman first suffers a procreative disaster, she is likely to suspect the evil machinations of others. Should she become incurably sterile at a young age or lose so many children that her plight is abnormal, others may accuse her of witchcraft when they suffer similar disasters because it is assumed that jealousy has made her wish evil to them. Thus children are so desired by Nyansongo women that in polygynous families childbearing is competitive and gives rise to hostilities among co-wives.

The sterility or impotence of a husband is likely to result in the dissolution of the marriage. A young woman is not expected to remain with a husband who cannot father her children, since both her desire to have children and her marital fidelity are regarded as imperative. A young man in Nyansongo who was reputed to be impotent was deserted in turn by two legal wives, with consequent return of bridewealth. When a man becomes sterile or impotent later in life, the need for his wives to have more children may be honored by a clandestine breach of their obligation to remain faithful to their husband. Although it is regarded as shameful, the impotent man may allow his wives to have sexual relations with other men of their own choosing. Nowadays such a husband often takes employment outside the district so as not to be at home while his wives are being impregnated by other men. The adult children of such women may not accept this practice; they have been known to insult and even stone the men who are thus serving their father's wives. Children born of these unions are legally children of their mothers' legal husbands and have no relationship with their physiological fathers. All men suffering from impotence and sterility consult diviners (diagnosis usually involves snake omens) and perform sacrifices, usually without effect. Among the older bachelors are to be found those who proved sexually incompetent or sterile in an early attempt at marriage. Thus a procreative failure on the part of a man is disruptive to the marital relationship.

The need for procreation throughout their fertile years is felt so deeply by Nyansongo adults that irregularities in the ideal reproductive cycle arouse strong anxieties and cause disruptions in family relations. Despite the high mortality rate in infancy and childhood, the loss of a child at any stage of life is taken as a serious event. In order to establish a stable marriage, avert fears of supernatural punishment, and minimize dissension among co-wives, viable children must be produced regularly. The significance of childbirth for the Gusii of Nyansongo must be viewed in this context.

Infanticide is not approved of by the Gusii in any circumstances (unlike many other East African tribes) and does not occur. Such an act figures in cultural fantasy as characteristic of witches who are said to order a new witch to kill her own child in order to prove her power. Abortion is also considered bad and occurs only in cases of unmarried girls and brides who are about to escape the husbands chosen by their parents. Women deny the existence of indigenous abortifacents and claim that most abortions are attempted by deliberate jumping and falling. Since the girls who attempt abortion want to conceal their pregnancy and can confide in no one of the older generation, it may be true that abortive techniques have not been highly developed. It also appears to be true that most premarital pregnancies are not arrested but result in childbirth. Infanticide and abortion, then, as methods of disposing of what Nyansongans want most to preserve,—children—are disapproved of and rarely occur.

Illegitimacy, that is, the birth of a child to an unmarried girl, is regarded as an extremely disgraceful situation. The girl who discovers that she is pregnant may frantically plead with her lover to marry her or even come to live in his house without being invited. Sometimes this results in marriage or concubinage, but more frequently young men, cherishing an ideal of marriage to a girl with whom they have not had sexual relations, run away to plantations or the city to avoid such involvement. If the girl is young, her parents may press charges of defilement in court and thereby scare the young man into marrying her. Often, however, the pregnant girl will not disclose the name of her lover, and the best her parents can do is to try to marry her off to a young man before her pregnancy becomes visible. If their attempts fail, the girl has her child at home. She wears dresses which conceal her condition as long as possible and afterwards remains at home, not even visiting her girl friends, spending much of her time indoors to avoid being seen. Her shameful condition is known and discussed throughout the community. If she does not induce an abortion or miscarriage, she must undergo the ordeal of an illegitimate childbirth.

Nyansongans believe that a girl who conceives before marriage cannot deliver until she has revealed the name of her child's father. It must be the name of the real father or delivery will not take place. Thus when the girl who has previously refused to name her lover is in labor, old women of her family and neighborhood demand her confession in severe terms: "Talk quickly or die!" They may even pinch her and slap her in order to get a confession. If the man named is someone of the same clan as the girl, the women will look for resemblance between the infant and the putative father during the first few months after birth. If a strong resemblance is found, then the man is disgraced (see Chapter 8, p. 103, for the handling of a case of this kind). If the accused is of a different clan and the girl is young, a defilement case may be brought against him at this late date, using the resemblance as evidence in an attempt to obtain damages or force a marriage.

Most frequently the unmarried mother is simply taken as a secondary wife by an elderly man wealthy enough to pay a high bridewealth rate for proven fecundity but too old to be able to demand a girl of high moral virtue. The child becomes a legal part of the family of his mother's husband, but he has a lower status in the eyes of many in that family. Despite the social disgrace, then, the unwed mother may benefit her father by bringing an unusually large amount of bridewealth.

The Nyansongan desire for children is one of the strongest motivations in their culture, but it does have limits. The high value which they set on human fertility and reproduction is exemplified by their attitudes toward sterility, impotence, infanticide, infant mortality, and abortion. At the same time, their drive to have as many children as they can is modified by a concern for infant welfare, which prescribes a two-year interval between births, and by disapproval of nonmarital sexuality, as shown in the attitude toward unwed motherhood. Women who violate these limits on procreation are viewed as lacking in proper sexual inhibition.

Conception is believed to be a union of male semen and female blood; hence it can take place only while the female is menstruating.* There is no fear of menstrual blood. The male contribution to the child's heredity, that is, appearance and temperament, is considered greater than that of the female; in fact, resemblances to females are overlooked while those to the father are noted and mentioned. Menstruation is understood to be a monthly occurrence and is called *omotienyi,* which means "moon" and "month." When a woman who has resumed menstruation since the birth of her last child and has been cohabiting with her husband (or another male) finds that she has not menstruated for two or three months, she assumes she is pregnant. She is happy and tells her husband, who is also pleased.

A pregnant woman is not treated specially and is not subject to any restrictions. Women continue arduous physical labor until they no

---

* Even many of the more educated Gusii retain the belief that conception takes place only during menstruation.

longer feel capable of it. Although illness during pregnancy is a valid excuse to refrain from work, all women observed in Nyansongo performed normal domestic and agricultural tasks until about a week before giving birth. Some women claim they are "stronger" during pregnancy and can work harder. If a pregnant woman felt weak and wanted to sleep more and work less than usual, her husband and related women would help out. Cravings for particular foods, such as bananas or eleusine grain, are recognized and indulged. Some women are said to be more quarrelsome when pregnant, and others demand that their husbands stay at home throughout the gestation period. Morning sickness is known, and one particular form of it involves the wife vomiting whenever she sees her husband or even when she sees his clothes in the morning. There is no medicine used for such conditions.

A miscarriage is considered a pitiful event, though not as grave as the death of a living child. The foetus is buried in the floor of the house rather than outside because it was not yet ready to "leave the house," that is, the womb. If the woman who suffers the miscarriage has been suspected of adultery, she will be encouraged to confess her misdeed so as to prevent further harm from befalling the family. If she has had bad luck with previous births, the possibility of witchcraft or spirit affliction may be seriously entertained.

Human parturition (*okogonkia*) is distinguished in the Gusii language from that of animals (*okobiara*). When a woman feels the labor pains and contractions, she notifies her husband's mother. Birth is to take place in the mother-in-law's house (which is in the same homestead) because it is not proper for a mother to enter her son's house, and she is required to assist in the delivery. If a woman is visiting her own parents when she goes into labor, she may give birth there, but her mother-in-law will be called to assist. The first time a woman gives birth is a big event because her fear of the process is very great and also because there is no way of predicting what difficulties may develop. While only two or three women are present at a later birth, the first one may attract a large crowd of older women. At first the mother-in-law is in charge of the situation, with the wives of husband's brothers and of husband's paternal uncles also present. A skin is laid on the floor near the mother-in-law's bed (not on it), and the woman in labor lies on it, flat on her back with her knees bent. It is common for a woman who has not given birth before to be terrified, crying and holding her legs together. When this happens and labor has gone on for a while, women in the community are called and the woman's mother is sent for. On one occasion of this kind, at least 15 women were present, including the oldest woman of Nyansongo, who came from the most distant part of the community. A middle-aged neighbor was sitting behind the 18-year-old girl in labor and was supporting her in a sitting position identical to that used in the clitoridectomy operation. Under such circumstances the women tell her to be brave or, she will kill the child. In particular, they say that holding her legs together will suffocate the baby. Sometimes they pinch her, beat her, or slap her to force her to aid the contractions. They often hold her legs apart forcibly. To add to the commotion, some woman may impatiently urge her to confess adultery in order to ease the delivery. An experienced woman may take charge of the situation; if her measures result fairly immediately in birth, she will be rewarded with flour.

Men are not called on in childbirth unless an emergency develops, and even then their role is a limited one. The husband is supposed to stay out of the house in which his wife is in labor, not because of a taboo but because the wife does not want him to see her at such a time and would be extremely angry if he approached. When delivery is long and difficult, however, the women attending will tell the husband to dig up the roots of a bush called *chinsaga*. It is believed that such difficulty is caused by the baby being stuck some distance from the opening, and that the juice of these roots, which are chewed and sucked, will dissolve adhesions in the womb and allow the child to come out. Another remedy for prolonged labor involves a man who is a classificatory brother-in-law; it must not be the husband or an adjacent-generation person. The man is to hold the woman's nose and force his breath into her mouth to make the baby emerge from the womb. This is frequently resorted to, as it was on the occasion mentioned above, although men do not relish doing it. Thus a variety of medical and moral measures, some of them involving men, are used to hasten delivery, particularly when it is the woman's first childbirth.

The old women attending are so anxious to remove the child from the womb that when it begins to emerge, they sometimes deliver it too rapidly, causing the placenta to be retained. Such cases are common and, before the advent of Western surgical aid, resulted in the death of the mother. If hemorrhaging occurs, the mother is fed porridge and water, as much as possible, "to make blood." If she becomes weak from loss of blood and loses her appetite, she may be fed the internal organs of a goat and the soup in which they were cooked; this is also believed to replenish her blood supply.

Under normal conditions, when the child is delivered one of the attending women cuts the umbilical cord with a knife and puts ashes and colostrum from the mother's breast on the navel. The women clean the substance from the child's mouth and wash the whole body with water. Juice cooked from the leaves of a pumpkin squash plant is fed to the child to wash out his first feces. On the evening of the day of birth, a bit of liquid porridge is put into his mouth to stimulate the food he will be taking before long. Actually, however, the child is nursed at the breast from its first day. Colostrum is considered healthy; "it makes the child fat." When the afterbirth emerges, the new mother herself wraps it in leaves and throws it into the bush while on her way to the stream where she will bathe. On returning to her mother-in-law's house, she will rest there with her newborn child for four to five days. During that time she will do no work except to gather some firewood and leaves to wipe away the child's excrement. If the mother-in-law is dead or feeble, the woman will stay at her own house during this period and will be helped by her co-wife or other nearby women. There is no seclusion or prohibition on visiting, and the husband may be sleeping in her house at the time.

Once the child's umbilical cord drops off, food is prepared for guests, and the women who attended at the birth come to name the child. Up until this time the neonate is called *Mosamba Mwaye*, "the burner of his own home," indicating that he has left his previous habitat (the womb) and cannot return to it. Now one or two names are chosen with the approval of the child's paternal grandmother and mother. There are many criteria for determining the name: the weather conditions or other events occurring at the time of birth, evil omens seen before the birth, previous condition of the mother with respect to childbirth. Most frequently, however, the name of a recently dead person of the same sex in the father's family is used for the first name and the name of a dead person on the mother's side for the second and less important name, which may later be dropped. The women eat, and then the child's paternal grandmother or a classificatory grandmother shaves its head and bounces it up and down in her arms, saying, "We shall call you _____." If the mother has had numerous infant fatalities before, a small top knot will be left on the child's head and maintained until his initiation. No men are present at the naming and shaving ceremony. After it, the new mother returns with her baby to her own house and begins to work as soon as she is able, doing even the hardest chores usually within a month.

Nyansongans conceive of the neonate as a fragile thing, especially susceptible to malevolent influences which can kill it through disease. Thus there is no idea of beginning to train it at this stage, for every effort should be expended to satisfy its needs and ensure its survival.

※
※
※

Chapter 12

Infancy

The infancy of Nyansongo children can be characterized as the period between birth and weaning, when the greatest amount of attention is paid to their needs and the least effort is directed toward their training.

In this stage the health and survival of the child are a source of anxiety to the parents, although this is not apparent until the child actually becomes ill. With the exception of an occasional amulet worn on the wrist to prevent stomach trouble and teething pain, few measures are taken which are specially designed to protect the child from disease; action is reserved until the onset of the disease. When an infant develops diarrhea that lasts for several days, the mother becomes extremely worried and usually hires a medicine man (*omonyamoriogo*) to administer potions orally and make small incisions on the child's body. The practitioner may be paid a goat or two, a substantial measure of the mother's concern. In general, such minor diseases inspire greater worry and more immediate action in infantile cases than in those of older persons.

Infants are particularly susceptible to the "evil eye" (*okobiriria*), not because they are young but because their skin is still light brown and therefore delicate. Adults whose skin is light brown are also thought to be affected by it, as are light-colored animals and trees with red flowers. When the child's skin develops a darker hue and rougher texture, however, the evil eye is no longer a danger. Although men have been known to have it, it is mostly women who have the evil eye. When such a woman looks at a child whose skin is still brown, any small things near the child—grain, feathers, flowers, wool of a blanket, ticks on a domestic animal—will cling to his skin. If not removed in time, the objects will work their way through the soft brown skin, lodge in the visceral organs, and kill the child. The practice of the evil eye is said to have been introduced by Kipsigis women who were sold into the tribe as wives when there was famine in Kipsigis territory. It is unconscious and not controllable by the person who has it, so that when such a woman gives birth she is forced to focus her eyes on eleusine grain held in front of her to absorb the evil effect and prevent it from reaching her infant. Therapy for the effects of the evil eye on infants resembles that used among the Kipsigis. When parents notice the adherent substances on the child's body, they rub his whole body with clarified butter, which is thought to remove the harmful materials. This process, called *okongura*, must be done without talking about the evil eye, for its evil is felt to be more effective when it is mentioned or even thought about. Some informants said a specialist is hired to do the rubbing, but other parents claimed to do it themselves. If an infant dies, it may be said that the therapy was not applied soon enough, before the stuff had penetrated the child's skin, for once it gets inside the body, no cure is possible. Internal organs, particularly the heart and liver, are thought to be so soft and sensitive that their being touched by any foreign object will cause death. Nyansongo parents are quick to notice adherent particles on their infants' skin, for they are most anxious to prevent the onset of the fatal disease.

The lack of strength and motor control manifested by all infants is attributed in part to their "hot blood," which makes them weak and fearful of a cold environment. The superior strength of adults and older children is thought to be caused by their experience with cold, which has made their blood firm and resistant. This belief does not lead to a determined exposure of children to the cold, but it may help to account for the relatively little concern which Nyansongo parents have about the warmth of naked infants and children on chilly days. The only medicines used to facilitate growth are herbs given to infants during the first three months of life to promote the growth of teeth.

CARETAKERS

The infant's most intensive relationship is with his mother, who nurses him. The Gusii word for breast feeding (*okogonkia*) is the same word as that which means "to give birth," and this identity conveys the importance of breast feeding to the infant in Gusii thought. A mother is expected to feel rather exclusively about her nursing infant, as expressed in the proverb, "Someone else's child is like cold mucus (i.e., disgusting)." Women do not nurse each other's children. The infant sleeps in his mother's arms at night, is carried on her back when she goes on long trips, and is not far from her when she is near the house. During much of the day, however, the mother is working in nearby fields and around the house, and the infant is carried and cared for by a child nurse (*omoreri*, from *okorera*, "to take care of").

The nurse, 6 to 10 years old, is usually an older sibling and plays an important part in the infant's life. In the cases of 24 Nyansongo children of different families whose mothers were interviewed, 19 had been cared for by child nurses, 4 were cared for exclusively by their mothers (who were unable to commandeer a child for the job), and 1 was taken care of by an old, ailing grandfather. Twelve of the child nurses were sisters of their infant charges, 2 were brothers, 2 were fathers' sisters, and there was one each of mother's sisters, father's brothers, and father's sister's daughters. The pattern of mothers using their younger sisters in the caretaking of their first and second children was observed to be more common than this sample indicates. Mothers who have no children of their own to act as nurses and who cannot find an unoccupied child of the right age in their husbands' or parents' homesteads consider themselves unfortunate, since they get little more aid from other adults than anyone else. They are forced to carry their infants around to a much greater extent. Twelve child caretakers remained with their infant charges until the latter were walking, 6 for two years or more, and 1 for only two months, since she was the preceding child and was too small to manage the growing infant. Typically, then, at least until he walks, a Nyansongo infant spends a good portion of the daytime being carried and cared for by a sister 5 to 9 years older than himself. In no case is he left alone; there is always someone nearby to attend to his needs.

FEEDING

Attending to the infant's needs is thought of primarily in terms of feeding it. There are no feeding schedules; the mother nurses whenever the infant cries and does not try to anticipate his hunger. At night the mother sleeps naked under a blanket with the child in her arms, even when her husband sleeps with her. The one-year-old infant may sleep beside the mother rather than in her arms, but no farther away than that. Ordinarily he may feed when he wants to without crying to wake her up. In the morning the mother gets up at dawn, picks up firewood outside the house, and cooks food until the infant cries, then nurses it. Shortly afterward, she turns him over to the child nurse and goes to work in the nearby fields. When the mother is hoeing, sowing, and weeding corn, the infant is often left at the house with the nurse in the following manner. He lies on a cloth beside the nurse or is carried on the latter's back in the house and yard; the nurse sometimes visits friends at adjacent homesteads with her charge on her back. During the eleusine weeding season, however, the infant is bound to the mother's back as she weeds from a kneeling position. On the mother's back, the infant's cries are heeded almost immediately, and she stands up, loosens the cloth, and nurses him. More frequently, however, the mother is doing agricultural work which requires movements too strenuous to be done with a baby on her back. If the field is as much as a mile away and the infant is not yet used to eating gruel, the nurse brings the infant along and holds him at the side of the field. If the field is nearby, the nurse stays at the house until the infant's crying cannot be silenced by other means (such as shaking and feeding gruel), then either calls the mother to come or brings him to the mother for nursing. If the mother does not have a child nurse for the infant, she may lay him on a cloth at the side of the field in which she is working.

When the infant cries, the mother may drop her hoe immediately to nurse him, or she may continue working for a while before heeding his cries. If the crying is insistent, however, no woman will let it go on as long as five minutes without attempting to nurse the infant. The observed variation within this limit was also found in the answers the 24 mothers gave when asked how quickly they generally attended to their crying infants: 7 said they take immediate steps to satisfy the infant's needs; 7 stated they would do so *unless* they were working; 7 specifically mentioned letting the infant cry for a few minutes if they were working; 2 indicated that they would not respond immediately to crying under any conditions; and 1 mentioned letting the infant cry if he refused the breast. Thus Nyansongo mothers vary in the extent to which they allow their agricultural (and household) chores to delay their response to the crying of their infants.

Since the dress of the modern Nyansongo woman is not parted in the front, the mother must pull her breast up to the neckline in order to nurse the child. With little more than the nipple protruding from the dress, she holds the child to it. The mother usually does this mechanically, without looking at the child or fondling him, and she often continues conversing with the other women and older children.

The women usually stop working in the fields before noon to avoid the midday sun and do not resume until the cool of the late afternoon. In the interim, the mother returns to her house, feeds the older children, and nurses the infant if he cries. During the time the mother is working around the house, putting out grain to dry, grinding, and so on, the nurse continues to carry the child on her back, handing him over for nursing only when he cries. The mother may have to leave the homestead to go to the power mill to have corn ground or to fetch water and collect firewood and edible leaves. Since all of these activities require her to carry heavy loads, the mother cannot take her infant, and he must remain at home with the nurse. At such times the infant may become hungry and have nothing to eat if he has not yet become used to supplementary foods. In general, however, the Nyansongo infant does not go long without being nursed by his mother once his hunger has been expressed in crying.

Traditionally Nyansongo infants were fed eleusine gruel from birth, or a few days afterward, as a supplement to mother's milk. The gruel (*erongoori*) was administered by force feeding: cupping her hand against the infant's lower lip, the mother poured gruel into it and held his nose so that he would have to suck in the gruel in order to inhale. Eventually he learned to drink it from a bowl-like calabash. Nowadays, partly because of mission teachings, early force feeding is coming into disfavor and gruel is being introduced at a later age. Middle-aged mothers in Nyansongo, used to the old system, still use force feeding and begin it within the first month of life; Christian wives of nearby schoolteachers abjure force feeding and wait until the infant is 6 months old before feeding gruel. Young but conservative Nyansongo women fall somewhere in between. If the mother dies in childbirth, the neonate is most likely to be given cow's milk, although it may be nursed for a short while by a grandmother (real or classificatory) who has milk in her breasts. After a week it is fed a mixture of gruel and cow's milk, which becomes its entire diet. This is also done in the case of a mother with completely dry breasts, although there is root medicine given to women whose breasts are not producing sufficient milk. Ordinarily cow's milk and other adult food are not given children until weaning. The early introduction of gruel is viewed as a convenience for the mother. She leaves some with the nurse, with orders that the infant is to be fed it when he cries. Under such conditions, the mother may go off for a considerable time during the day without making the infant go hungry and without being bothered every time he cries. When she is at the house, however, she is much more likely to nurse the infant than let him eat gruel. In our judgment mothers always leave more than enough gruel for their infants' needs during the day. The nurse is usually quick to feed it to the infant when he cries, and indeed she often pushes food into his mouth after he has shown that he does not want more.

There seems to be no particular problem about infants not wanting to eat their gruel or refusing the breast often. The only feeding problem mentioned by informants was that of an infant who wants the breast too often. The mother eventually becomes annoyed and refuses it, although she will relent if it keeps on crying. Some mothers are said to get angry at such a demanding child and to slap it lightly. In the main, then, the infant's needs for food are well taken care of.

OTHER RESPONSES TO CRYING

Feeding is not the only response which Nyansongo caretakers make to infantile crying, but it is by far the most nurturant of their responses. Mothers recognize a kind of crying during the first three months which cannot be satisfied by nursing, and they call it *enyancha,* which means "the lake." Some view it as a disturbing stimulation of the child's genitals caused by the wind from Lake Victoria; others think it is a kind of stomach trouble and have potions to feed the crying infant during the night. Most often at night, however, the mother puts on a light, binds the infant to her back and walks about in the house, shaking him up and down. With the side of his face pressed tightly against her back, the infant is frequently silenced by jostling in this position. In the daytime, child nurses also use shaking, either on the back or in the arms, as a means of calming a small infant who cries but refuses food. If the mother is at hand, the nurse may turn the infant over to her for breast feeding, but if he continues crying, the mother ordinarily turns him back to the nurse for shaking rather than do it herself. The shaking is not accompanied by kissing or hugging but sometimes by tapping on the child's body. Nurses train infants to get into position for going on the back when the baby-talk word *titi* is uttered. When the nurse wants to carry a one-year-old, either because of his crying or her own desire to move elsewhere, she kneels with her back to him and says, "Titi, baba" (mother) or "Titi, tata" (father), and he clutches her back and spreads his legs as she hoists him up.

A common way of quieting older infants is to frighten them. When a one-year-old on a nurse's back begins whimpering, she will say, "Aso, aso, esese," which is a way of calling a dog. There may or may not really be a dog nearby, but the calling of it (or, more rarely, a cat) is intended to make the child think that the animal will come and harm him if he does not stop crying. This often works to silence him. The infant is prepared to respond in this way by his mother, grandmother, and other caretakers, who often point out animals of any kind—cows, chickens, dogs, insects—and label them all *ekuku,* who "will bite you," a name (again in baby talk) which is supposed to inspire terror in the child. The mother and grandmother believe that this fear is good because it will safeguard the child from actual harm incurred by animals, such as being stepped on by a cow, and also explicitly because it can be used by a parent to control the child's behavior, particularly excessive crying. When we visited one homestead, one mother said to her 2-year-old, "You always trouble me by crying at night. Now Getuka (the investigator) is going to take you away. Will you agree to be taken in his car to his home?" The child screamed, "No, no!" and clutched his mother. When we were about to leave the homestead, another woman said to us for the child's benefit, "You'll come early tomorrow to pick up this child." After four months of such comments, whenever we approached the child and mother together, the little boy would run away screaming, although he had not done so originally. Nyansongo parents consider this amusing. When a toddler followed his mother and some other women who were on their way to the market, he was picked up by his mother, brought over to the ethnographers, and told, "They will eat you!" The child screamed and finally ran back home amidst the laughter of the women. These are not peculiar reactions to ethnographers or white people but represent a determined attempt on the part of Nyansongo mothers to frighten their children with animals and strangers in order to make them more subject to parental control. Such fear training begins before the child can actually speak and is one of the first kinds of verbal cues learned by the infant.

TEMPORARY CARETAKERS

Aside from the mother and child nurse, few other individuals participate in the care of an infant. It is rare, for example, to see a man holding an infant or paying much attention to it. Occasionally a young father was observed with his child in his arms when the mother was away, but this was exceptional. Of 21 children with living fathers, only 11 were reported to have been cared for by their fathers between the ages of one and six. Even many of the 11 do not represent true cases of the father as caretaker, as when a mother said, "Yes, her father also took care of her. Especially when she was sick, he would try to get medicine." Another mother who answered affirmatively stated that when she was not present, the father would tell the child nurse to cook food for the infant. Such caretaking does not involve actual contact with the child and is typical of the father's participation in child care. Women who reported that their husbands were not at all involved in child care made such statements as, "The father doesn't take care of small children." One woman said her husband claimed that as an old man he couldn't look after children; another said that if her husband heard of a beer party he would just go and leave his infant son alone. In addition to their aloofness when at home, many fathers spend a good deal of time working outside of the district.

Females in the homestead play a greater part in temporary caretaking than males. In polygynous families, co-wives sometimes take care of each other's toddlers and feed them when the mother is away for the afternoon or the whole day. If the child nurse is 8 or 9, however, she may be left in charge of the small children, especially if the co-wives are not on good terms. If the child's paternal grandmother is living, she may also act as baby sitter in the absence of the mother. When still active in agricultural work, however, the grandmother spends less time with her grandchildren than one who is blind or feeble and has nothing to do but sit with children. In Nyansongo a blind grandmother and a feeble great-grandmother helped rear the babies of their homesteads. Older siblings, aside from nurses, sometimes play a part in child care, and in families where there is more than one sister between the ages of 5 and 9 the responsibility is shared to some degree, although one of them is definitely charged with the duty by the mother and performs it more frequently. Initiated unmarried girls supervise child nurses, but rarely play the latter role themselves, since they are freed from that chore by their newfound status. The wives of brothers in an extended family may care for each other's children in much the same manner as co-wives. In most cases, however, caretakers, aside from mother and child nurse, are clearly secondary, playing that role sporadically and for short·periods. Mothers recognize that the other women in the homestead are also busy, and they do not rely on them greatly in matters of child care.

AFFECTION

The Nyansongo mother does not act very affectionately toward her infant, although other caretakers may do so. It is rare to see a mother kissing, cuddling, hugging, or cooing at her child. Individual variability among mothers on this score is considerable, but in the main it is not done. As described above, the mother nurses the child mechanically and only occasionally takes it from the nurse when unprovoked by its crying. Most mothers observed saw to it that their infants did not get into trouble and were not neglected by the nurses but intervened only when they felt the nurses or the infants were doing wrong.

When things were going smoothly, the mothers tended to remain aloof. The caretakers who were most affectionate were nurses, grandmothers, and occasionally fathers' brothers' wives. When she is alone with the infant, the child nurse frequently hugs him, kisses him, tickles him, and indulges him in other kinds of affectionate play. Sometimes, however, she does this in a rough manner which tends to alarm the infant and other times she ignores her charge in favor of interacting with her peers. There is, then, little consistency in the nurse's affectionate behavior, and it may not always be communicated to the infant as nurturance. Grandmothers exhibit overt warmth and nurturance, repeatedly kissing an infant left with them, sometimes lightly biting its feet or hands. Fathers' brothers' wives have occasionally been seen behaving this way also. Perhaps the discrepancy between the amount of nurturance displayed by the real mother and that by other caretakers is due to the mother's fear that such an exhibition on her part might provoke the ill-wishing jealousy (*okoema*) of people watching her and her child. A grandmother or other person, however, would be motivated to show that she loves the child and wishes him no harm. We have no information on the truth of this nor on whether mothers are more affectionate with their children when completely alone with them. The mothers of older children all stated that they had left flowers and leaves or tins to beat on for the nurses to distract their children when they were infants, but we rarely saw such articles in use during the observation of infants. The only observed case of a toy frequently used for distraction was that of an infant whose hand had been badly burned; he was given a gourd rattle to shake with the other hand to draw his attention from the pain.

Despite the fact that mothers do not display a great deal of affection toward their infants, it is always to his mother that the frightened toddler will run, and he typically attempts to follow her even when she wants him to remain with the other children.

CLOTHING, CLEANLINESS AND WALKING

The Nyansongo infant is loosely wrapped in a thin, store-bought, cotton cloth which is also used for binding him to the nurse when he is a bit bigger. Sometimes the cloth is laid out as a groundcloth on which the naked infant lies, and we have seen this done in the cold of morning when it must have caused some discomfort to the child. The belief that the bodies of infants are excessively warm and must become hardened through exposure to cold may account for this behavior.

In some of the wealthier and more acculturated families, infants wear cotton shirts (if male) or dresses (if female) from as early as 6 months, but it is as frequent for them to be naked until weaning. Feces and urine are wiped away with soft fuzzy leaves collected by the mother for that purpose, but the mother does not try to anticipate the child's excretion. Most mothers are very casual about it and show no sign of disturbance when their infants soil the cloth and the mother's person as well. Sometimes their response is not immediate, but eventually they wipe up the excrement with the leaves, cleaning the infant, cloth, and themselves. No attempt is made to effect sphincter control during infancy. Mothers are said to suck mucus from the infant's nose, but we have only seen them pull it away with their fingers. Nurses and grandmothers also wipe away mucus, but all caretakers are rather erratic about this. The cloth or shirt the infant wears is typically filthy and not frequently washed. Infants themselves are bathed approximately twice a week with cold water; little effort is made to keep their skin free of ashes and dirt between baths, although, as mentioned earlier, adherent articles such as feathers and wool are viewed seriously as signs of the evil eye. Masturbation is considered bad, and on one of the few occasions when we observed an infant touching his genitals, his sister-nurse (8 years old) threatened him with a large stick and told him to stop.

Both mothers and nurses encourage infants to stand at about the age of one year. The most frequently used method is to hold the child in a standing position by his hands and say "person-pole, person-pole" over and over quickly as he remains on his feet. This is done in a good-humored way and may be the focus of family attention on a particular occasion. In general, however, nurses help the children in such motor advances during the time the mother is away. This is the case with walking, for example. Although some mothers do this themselves, the usual practice is to have the nurse guide the infant in walking in the cold dew of the early morning, which by cooling the "hot blood" of the child's feet makes them firm and is supposed to reduce his fear of walking. The nurse sets the child on his feet in the grass and says "Ta, ta," encouraging him to walk toward her. Although most children are taught to walk in this fashion and are able to walk well before they are 2 years old, there is no emphasis on early walking as an accomplishment.

If a mother becomes pregnant early (i.e. before her infant is 18 months old), she will put pressure on the nurse to teach the infant to walk as quickly as possible and will devote more of her own efforts to that end as well. This is because it is strongly felt that a child should be able to walk and not need the care of a nurse by the time its "follower" is born. Attainment of motor skills is not, however, a particular source of pride for the parents or of rewards for the child. It is viewed by parents as a prerequisite for the adequate care of the subsequent child but one which is fraught with danger. The cryptically worded Gusii proverb, "Lameness is up" means that when a child gets big enough to walk by himself, he will be confronted with physical dangers and may be so badly injured as to become lame. To some extent this is a realistic fear, for children who are learning to walk sometimes stumble into the fireplace and get burned. Three toddlers in Nyansongo were severely burned in this way during our stay.

SUMMARY

The foregoing picture of Nyansongo infancy needs to be modified for children of certain status. Girls and boys are treated alike in infancy, except that a string of beads is put around the girl's abdomen, and sex-typed dress is used by some of the more Westernized families. The oldest child of a particular mother is most likely to be cared for by the mother herself rather than by a child nurse, and the last child is least likely to be pushed toward walking or other independent behavior. A child born after many have died or a boy born after only girls have survived becomes the center of attention and is treated with more care and affection.

The general picture of the Nyansongo child as he emerges from infancy is that of a dependent, fearful individual, capable of making demands on his mother and other caretakers for food and protection, but unaggressive, quiet, and timid in his approach to the physical environment and to strange things.

Chapter 13

Weaning

Weaning is the first of a series of drastic changes which take place in the second and third years of the life of a Nyansongo child. The other changes are the birth of a sibling, replacement in the mother's attentions by the new sibling, the beginnings of responsibility and aggression training, and toilet training. In this chapter we shall describe weaning from the breast and then proceed to the later changes in the order in which they occur in the child's life.

In accordance with the Nyansongo value of postponing weaning until the child can walk fairly well and take care of himself to some extent, mothers try to prevent conception during lactation. This they do by refusing to have intercourse with their husbands while they are menstruating, as this is thought to be the only time during which conception can take place. As might be expected, such a practice is not invariably effective, and some births do take place before the older child has attained the desired maturational stage, occasioning early weaning. Women who have several children so closely spaced are criticized by other women for being oversexed and inconsiderate of the infant's welfare. Such success as people in Nyansongo do have in conforming to ideal rules of child spacing is due to the polygynous setup in which a husband can spend most of his time with nonlactating wives, to the absence from the home of many employed fathers, and perhaps to psycho-physiological factors as well. The fact that monogamous families produce children more frequently than wives in polygynous families indicates that plural marriage has an effect on child spacing even in the absence of a formal post-partum taboo on sexual intercourse.

Weaning begins within two months of the time the mother discovers herself to be pregnant. Numerous reasons are given for this timing: that milk from a pregnant woman causes diarrhea in the child, that the mother fears her suckling will use up milk intended for the unborn child, that mother's breasts dry up during pregnancy. Since some mothers do not complete weaning until the eighth month of pregnancy, none of these beliefs can be accepted as universal. The feeling which is probably most common to Nyansongo mothers is that the child, now thoroughly used to cereal foods and strong enough to walk by himself, should be prepared for his replacement as the primary focus of the mother's attention.* One mother told her preweaning child that bitter substances were on her breasts (although this was not true and she shortly afterward nursed him) in order to "prepare him for weaning." Although this in itself is not typical, it indicates the kind of reasoning which mothers apply in beginning weaning as soon as

_____

* There was no indication that the resumption of parental sexual relations was experienced by the child as a deprivation or replacement by the father. Such a possibility cannot be ruled out, however.

they discover their pregnancy. The feeling is strong among Nyansongo women that there must be no competition between older child and infant for the mother's attention, and weaning during pregnancy is one step toward preventing such conflicts. Thus weaning should not begin until the child is thought capable of getting along without considerable maternal attention, and yet it should be completed before there is another child born whose demands for attention must be given priority.

Although Nyansongo people, particularly women, do not ordinarily keep track of dates and time periods taken up by events, some fairly reliable figures on age of weaning were collected. In a sample of 24 women, each of whom was questioned concerning only one of her children, the average age at which weaning was reported to have begun was 20.7 months, and the median was 19 months. The range was from 11 to 30 months. At the lower end of the range, the early weaners were wives of monogamists who became pregnant "too early," as some of them apologetically put it. The children who were weaned later than 24 months were last children whose mothers, having reached menopause, allowed them to nurse almost as long as they wanted. The last child (*omokogoti*) is considered very fortunate in that he never has to relinquish his mother's breasts nor her attention to a younger sibling.

METHODS OF WEANING

The word for weaning in the Gusii language is *ogotacha*, which literally means to stamp on or to step on. The painful aspect of the weaning process for the child is thus explicitly conceptualized, and there is the general belief that the more severe the mother is with the child she wants to wean, the quicker and more smoothly will the goal be achieved. The estimated time between onset of weaning and its completion ranged from one week to six months among the mothers questioned, but most reported that they accomplished it in one or two months. The methods in use among mothers include putting bitter substances (pepper, goat dung, juice from sour fruits) on the nipples, slapping the child, burning his arms with a caustic plant juice, ignoring his cries in the daytime and wearing a dress that prevents access to the breasts at night, sending him to live with a grandmother, giving him large amounts of solid food to make him forget the breast. Of the 24 women questioned, 16 used bitter substances regardless of what else they did, 4 others used slapping alone, 2 made few attempts to wean at all because the children in question were their last, 1 fed the child solid food to make him forget, and 1 mentioned only that she kept her dress on at all times. Eight of the 16 mothers who used bitter substances mentioned supplementary techniques: 3 slept with their dresses on, 2 slapped, 2 fed quantities of solid food, 1 turned the care of the child over to its paternal grandmother, 1 sent the child to sleep with its father at night. Although none of the mothers interviewed sent children to live with maternal grandmothers in order to effect weaning, this is a recognized practice, and there were two children from other communities living with their maternal grandmothers in Nyansongo during our stay. It is said that mothers who cannot bear to be severe enough to wean their children themselves send them away in this manner. The child who lives with his grandmother for a few months during weaning is usually fed a great deal and receives much nurturant attention from her. If he stays at home, as the majority do, nighttime during the weaning period presents the most serious problem. The child continues to sleep next to his mother and naturally tries to suck at her breast for nocturnal comfort and nourishment. Some mothers continue to sleep naked but keep their backs to the child, in contrast to the practice of moving the suckling every time the mother turns over so that he will always have access to the breast. Others, as noted above, sleep with their dresses on to prevent nursing, and attempts to ignore the child's demands seem to accompany this. Some mothers send the child to sleep in the house of a co-wife, which is considered a rather drastic measure for so young a child.

Sometimes daytime may also be painful for a child, as the following case demonstrates. A 30-year-old mother of four girls expected her husband, a policeman working outside of the district, to come home on vacation and impregnate her. She felt that her youngest child, 22 months old, was big enough to be weaned and that the process should be begun even before the husband returned. The child had been walking well for some time, and the mother wanted to have her weaned by the time she was 2 years old. On one occasion after the onset of weaning, we observed the child sitting on her mother's lap for 20 minutes, crying continuously and occasionally pulling at her mother's high-necked dress. Throughout the period of incessant crying the mother was looking at pictures we had brought and talking animatedly with a visiting neighbor. Only once did she pay any attention to the child's cries, shaking it briefly and then continuing her conversation as the child resumed crying. At one point, when the child's cries were loudest, the mother was laughing at a remark made by the other woman. Despite her almost unbelievable (to the observers) capacity for ignoring the bawling of the child being weaned, this woman was not less nurturant than other mothers in her treatment of her other children. Interestingly enough, she reported in an interview two months later that the child observed gave her no trouble during weaning. Her behavior, while perhaps not typical of Nyansongo mothers in general, at least illustrates the diminution of response to the child's demands for attention that can result when a mother is determined to wean. Many mothers did report trouble (crankiness, etc.) during the weaning period, and it is a commonplace among the older women that children being weaned are troublesome. Since virtually all of them are accustomed to solid foods long before weaning begins, it can only be concluded that the disturbance of the children during weaning is due to a certain degree of emotional abandonment by their mothers.

The only method reported of comforting a child during weaning is feeding it quantities of solid food. It is doubtful that this allays the frustration of the child's desire for the close physical, dependent relationship of nursing, especially during the night. Thus, although Nyansongo mothers vary with respect to nurturance, it is most usual for them to avoid and/or punish the child during the weaning rather than offering another kind of emotional comfort to replace the breast.

THE BIRTH OF A SIBLING

Since weaning usually begins during the mother's pregnancy, it is ordinarily followed a few months later by the birth of a sibling. The mother may inform the child that a little sister or brother is on the way, but whether she does or not, she hopes that the child will be nurturant to the new arrival. Such an attitude on the part of the newly weaned child is not always achieved without considerable training, however, as is illustrated by the following case. Nyanchoka, the younger of two wives of a middle-aged man, had her second child when her first daughter, Moraa, was 25 months old. Moraa witnessed the birth of her sister and ran off to the house of her mother's co-wife, crying, "My mother has killed a hen; I don't want to be there any more." She cried a great deal but returned toward evening to find her mother holding the neonate. Moraa said, "Take away the hen; I want to sleep next to you." When Nyanchoka refused to sleep without the infant in her arms, Moraa went back to the elderly co-wife, who had no small children, and slept with her. After six nights with the co-wife, Moraa returned to her mother voluntarily and was gently and repeatedly shown that the neonate was her sister and not a chicken. She soon wanted to hold the baby and be affectionate with it, and during the following three months, Nyanchoka taught her how to hold it and to be very cautious about sitting or stepping on it. During the same period, Moraa, who had previously been taught to chase chickens and dogs away from drying grain, showed a strong tendency to beat every dog and chicken she saw with a stick until she had to be punished for doing so. She also engaged in acrobatics and boasting to attract the mother's attention, although her efforts in this regard tended to annoy rather than amuse Nyanchoka. This sequence of behavior illustrates that the birth of a sibling and its important place in the mother's attention are disturbing to the child who has been replaced and that the Nyansongo mother trains and punishes to control the dependent and aggressive manifestations of this disturbance.

Often a child does not easily accept the diminution in maternal attention which follows the birth of his younger sibling, and severe punishment results. The feelings of both mother and replaced child are most likely to come to a head when the mother has to make a long trip or work in a field. She will take her infant or have the nurse take it but refuse the urgent demand of the older child to go along. Often the older child follows the mother, crying bitterly, and in 22 out of 24 cases, mothers reported caning their children for such behavior. The mother feels particularly strongly about the older child crying when she is holding or carrying the infant because the crying is interpreted as *okoema,* murderous jealousy. In other words, the succorant cries of the older child are held to mean that he wishes the death of his younger sibling.* Since such aggressive motivations are considered reprehensible, the child is punished for them. An observed incident will illustrate the intensity which emotions can reach in such cases. Nyaboke is the younger of two wives of a policeman; she and her co-wife are very friendly and cooperate closely in work and the caretaking of children. Nyaboke had sent her 2-year-old son, Manyara, to his maternal grandmother for weaning, and he had returned after a while. The infant developed dysentery, causing a great deal of anxiety to his mother. One morning when he was ill, she left Manyara, her 2-year-old, with the co-wife and a group of children who were helping the co-wife smear mud on the wall of her house. As Nyaboke left, infant in her arms, to visit a neighbor living higher on the hill, Manyara began to run after her, calling her name. Nyaboke chased him back to the homestead, a stick in her hands. Manyara was crying hard, but his mother threatened him with the stick and told him to sit down and wipe his nose with a leaf. He did so but continued bawling violently. Nyaboke

* No children were observed or heard of who tried to harm their newborn siblings.

struck him across the legs several times, then picked up the infant and began to walk away again. As Manyara again began to follow, the co-wife threatened to tie him up with some rope and, when this did not work, beat him on the feet with a stick. He continued screaming and trying to follow his mother. Suddenly the co-wife told him to go ahead and follow Nyaboke, who had turned around and come back again. She beckoned Manyara to come to her, and when he did, she caned him sharply on the legs. The co-wife pushed him into his mother's hut and locked the door as Nyaboke went off for good. Locked in the hut, Manyara continued screaming his mother's name, and eventually the co-wife sent her daughter to let him out. He began crying and calling for Nyaboke again, and when the girl shut him up in the hut once more, said, "I've stopped now," and did not resume crying after she let him out again. Nyaboke blamed her son's behavior on the fact that he had lived with his grandmother, who did not cane him enough. On the afternoon of the same day, Nyaboke was home and Manyara quietly approached. She said to him, "You're always crying. I'm going to tie you with a rope and then I'll buy a *kiboko* (rhinohide whip) and beat you with it." An 8-year-old female cousin on her way back from the river said to him, "I see you're quiet now, Manyara; you realize you did wrong." Although emotions ran high in this instance because the infant's illness made Manyara's "death wish" seem more dangerous, it is typical of mothers to punish a replaced child severely for crying when the mother is holding the infant.

Children who cry frequently or throw temper tantrums during the period following the birth of a sibling have to face severe punishment and threats even when the mother is not holding the new baby. Nothing annoys a Nyansongo mother more than a child who cries "for nothing," that is, a child who cries when he does not want food and has not been hurt. We observed a child of about 30 months crying loudly and long after his older brother hit or pushed him slightly. His mother, who was sitting beside him and thought his crying excessive for the amount of hurt he had suffered, hit him on the head with a piece of grass and continued doing so, saying "Quiet!" each time until he would tolerate being hit without making any sound. One mother reported that she warned her small child, "If you cry, I'll throw you out in the darkness and you'll be eaten by hyenas." Children who are threatened and beaten learn to be quiet, to refrain from crying, and to stay at home without trouble when their mothers go away with younger siblings; actual temper tantrums are infrequent. Usually the child stays at home with an older sibling whom he follows to a field or other homestead where other children are playing. When the group of children goes somewhere, the little 2-year-old is always desperately afraid of being left behind. We frequently saw children running and crying after older children who were moving a bit too fast. Despite the anxiety, however, a small child is rarely left behind, for the parents hold the older children responsible for its care.

TOILET TRAINING AND RESPONSIBILITY

Another event in the child's life which takes place shortly after the birth of a younger sibling is training in sphincter control. The primary aim of such training is to teach the child to defecate in bush or pasture some distance from the house; urination control is a secondary consideration. The approximate average age for the onset of toilet training is 26.7 months, and the median is 25 months. It is most commonly a three-stage process. First, the mother takes the child to an uncultivated field or pasture near the house several times to show him the correct procedure. (Some mothers, instead of teaching, simply tell the child to imitate what the older children do.) Secondly, when the mother feels he has had enough instruction, she will cane him for daytime defecation in the house and yard but not for nighttime infractions. At this stage the child ordinarily wakes up the mother when he wants to defecate at night, and she puts him in a corner of the house or outside, depending on her own fear of the dark. In the morning the mother sweeps out the feces. In the third stage, the child is punished for defecating in the house even at night, for he is supposed either to perform his elimination in the daytime or to wake up someone to accompany him outside at night. Infractions at this time are punished by caning and by making the child sweep out the feces himself, as the mother points out to him what he has done. The amount of time mothers reported for this training ranged from a week to a year, with the majority around a month. Some mothers who trained quickly attributed it to the fact that they were "serious" about it and punished severely for infractions. A significant minority of mothers took a year to train and seem to have been undisturbed by whatever the child did in this regard.

Proper habits concerning urination, though not stressed seriously as early as bowel control, are acquired by the child gradually as an adjunct of bowel and modesty training. Three-year-olds have learned to urinate away from the house, although boys occasionally do it within sight of adults, and not much more than that is required of them. Neither boys nor girls of this age wear any garments around the lower half of their bodies, so soiling of clothes is not a serious problem. The infrequency of observing 3-year-olds in excretory activities suggests that they learn modesty of this kind quite early.

A final change in the child's life that takes place after the birth of a sibling is his induction into the performance of tasks. If he is the oldest, he will be required to carry food to his mother from her co-wife or mother-in-law during the lying-in period. Many other little tasks are given all children during the first few months of their replacement, and the mother consciously does this to distract the child from his desire to continue as the exclusive object of her nurturance. The chasing of chickens from drying foods, carrying things from one adult to another, and even helping the older boys in herding cattle—these are the beginnings of a responsibility training that is intensified in later years.

In summary, the period between 18 months and 3 years is one of severe punishment for the child's infantile dependency behavior, and there are the beginnings of new behavior patterns in his learning simple tasks and his orientation toward other children with whom he is now forced to interact more than when he was primarily oriented toward mother. What effect on sibling attitude is produced by the neonate's place in this rough transition can only be speculated on, but our guess is that strong feelings of jealousy and hatred are engendered but prevented by parental punishment from being expressed in behavior.

❊

❊

❊

Chapter 14

Childhood: The Years from Three to Eight

This chapter covers the period in the life of the child from the year following his replacement by a younger sibling to the time when the boy begins sleeping outside of his mother's house and the girl prepares for her initiation. For both sexes this is approximately a five-year period—the years from 3 to 8—uninterrupted by schooling, for hardly any Nyansongo children attend school.

STATUS OF THE CHILD

As Nyansongans themselves view it, the training of the child in the proper patterns of behavior takes place largely in the years between weaning and initiation. Although many behavior patterns improper for adults are tolerated up to the time of initiation, the child is expected to show signs of his readiness by some adult-like behavior beforehand, and this must be taught during childhood. The period from weaning to initiation is a longer one for boys, who are initiated between 10 and 12 years of age, than for girls, who undergo it at 8 or 9. Girls are said to "grow up more quickly" and are therefore ready to be initiated into adulthood at an earlier age. Until initiation, a girl is referred to as *egesagane* and a boy as *omoisia*, usually translated by English-speaking Gusii as "uncircumcised girl" and "uncircumcised boy." Both terms are strong insults when used among adults and are even considered insulting by the children to whom they can be properly applied. They carry the connotation of inferior status. In some sense, childhood is the most inferior status position in the Nyansongo life cycle. During infancy the child is the object of maternal attention, and few demands are made on him. After weaning, however, it is not too long before the child is at the beck and call of everyone around, with no one younger or more inferior for him to order about. During this stage the child is also most subjected to physical punishment by elders attempting to curb his impulsive activities. These are some of the reasons why the words for "boy" and "girl" connote inferior status and are used as epithets. Nyansongans believe the child who can walk and talk requires punishment in order to learn correct behavior, and he has few rights or privileges that must be respected by elders.

Despite the low position of childhood in the hierarchy of age-statuses, it is not viewed as unrelated to adulthood. Indeed, adults see in the behavior of individual children foreshadowing of their adult characters: a troublesome child will become "bad," while an obedient child, who is restrained, responsible, and respectful of his parents' wishes, will turn out to be a "good person." This does not mean they are completely fatalistic about the character development of children, but they come to regard some children as responsive to parental training, and others as incorrigible.

SLEEPING AND EATING

The Nyansongo family goes to sleep early in the evening except when a beer party is in progress. Children are allowed to stay up during a beer party held in the house, but smaller ones often fall asleep in the arms of mother or grandmother or lie down to sleep on the floor despite the noise. On ordinary nights, the mother sleeps with her infant and husband (when he is home and not staying at the house of another wife). One or two of the younger children are usually huddled close to the mother, especially when the traditional, slightly raised, hide-covered, dried mud bed is used. When the more common rope-spring bed on legs is used, they may sleep on the floor beside it or in a nearby children's house (*esaiga*) outside. Nights in Nyansongo are cold, and it is customary to sleep naked under blankets not far from the cooking fire which burns all night.

In the morning the mother is usually the first one up, building up the fire for cooking, nursing the infant, and preparing to work in the fields. If she plans to work in a small garden near the house, she may do some of this while the children are still asleep and return later to dress and feed them. The family then sits down to some gruel, the children drinking it either out of a dish of their own or out of a dish which has first been used by the father and mother. During the period of intense cultivation, the mother is often in such a hurry to join her cooperative work group that she leaves leftovers for the children to eat. The leftovers may be remnants of dry corn or eleusine porridge (*obokima*), sweet potatoes, bananas, or cooked squash. Sometimes they are inadequate, and the children are hungry during the morning. If a sister 8 years old or more is home, she may cook some gruel, but sometimes she is off hoeing herself, and the smaller children get food from a co-wife or grandmother. When the mother returns at midday, the children tell her they are hungry, and she hurries to cook for them before doing any other work. If she left hastily in the morning without cooking, she may come home as early as 10:30 A.M. to feed them, particularly if she is told they are hungry. At those times of the year when she is home during the day, or on a rainy day, she will cook for the children whenever they are hungry and ask for food. The midday meal may consist of boiled sweet potatoes or the more traditional dry porridge eaten with cooked beans, spinachlike leaves, curdled milk, or meat. There is usually a good deal of food available at this time, enough to satisfy the children until late afternoon or evening. During the afternoon, especially between October and January, children often break off corn stalks in harvested fields and chew and suck the sugary pulp inside. The evening meal is ordinarily eaten just after sunset at about 7:00 P.M. and consists of dry porridge by itself or with one of the condiments mentioned above.

The predominance of starch in the diet means Nyansongo children must eat stomach-bloating quantities of porridge to obtain necessary nutriments, and such quantities are generally, though not always, available to them. Mothers usually feed children on demand except when they have recently eaten and have conspicuously bloated stomachs. One reason given for refusal under such circumstances is that the child will become so heavy and sluggish with food that he will be unable to leave the house or yard to defecate. There are instances of children who continually ask for food, but feeding problems involving reluctance to eat are extremely rare, and some mothers regard such behavior as inconceivable except when a child is momentarily angry at his mother.

Nyansongo mothers consider providing food as their primary responsibility to their offspring, and there is evidence that food constitutes an important symbolic bond between mother and child. One third of the women interviewed concerning their reactions to an obedient child spontaneously mentioned giving or promising food, and some stated they would favor the more obedient child over his siblings in the apportionment of food. Forcing a child to miss one or more meals is used as a punishment for children of 6 and over, but some mothers find it difficult to refuse to feed even a misbehaving child, and this punishment is often reserved for serious offenses. One widow, a somewhat overprotective mother, expressed the generally felt association of maternal care with feeding when she said of her 14-year-old initiated son, "I take care of him—he's a young child. I'll let him go when he is married and has a wife to cook for him."

During July and August, when grain stocks are running low and the harvest has not yet begun, the family suffers a food shortage which is experienced by children as well. Adults voluntarily limit their eating during this time, and children may go without eating from early morning to evening. Small children are fed as usual because "they will cause trouble if they are not fed" and they "do not understand." From the age of 5, however, the child "can understand when the mother says there's not much food," and she begins limiting his consumption. If he cries for more at first, he will be fed a little bit of food from time to time but not as much as he wants and is used to. If he is persistent in his demands, the mother will cane him and say, "We have no food and you're still crying for more. You'll get food later." Informants report that children at this time cry and trouble the mother a great deal. The increased cultivation of bananas may be alleviating these preharvest shortages to some extent, but most Nyansongans consider bananas suitable for small snacks rather than for meals. Once the harvest is in, cereal food becomes plentiful, and eating, visiting, and ceremonial feasts become the order of the day.

The mealtime situation provides some important lessons in the rules of family behavior for the Nyansongo child. The father's dry porridge is served in a separate basket and must not be touched by the children even if the father is not present when it is served. Any man who came home late from a beer party and found that someone had taken some of the glazed top of his porridge would be enraged and would threaten his wife with sending her back to her parents for a gift of reconciliation; a second time he might really do it. When he eats the porridge, the father may finish less than half of it and give the rest to the children, but they are not to presume on the privilege. A polygynist receives a basket of food from each wife at every meal (though not more than twice a day), and he takes at least one mouthful from each, thus breaking the glazed top with his fingers. At his signal, the wife may bring the rest of it back to be eaten by herself and the children. Sometimes, however, the mother will serve all the uninitiated children their food in a single basket or dish separate from that of the father, and they sit around it together. Eating with the hands from a basket placed on the ground poses few problems of table manners. Some children are unusually greedy and tend to deprive the others of food; they are known as "black-stomach children." The mother warns such a child not to take so much but does not beat him, and eventually she may serve him his own dish of food rather than try to reform his behavior. She also tries to compensate the others by giving them more food when the black-stomach child has taken theirs. Thus the child learns to yield precedence to his father but not to his siblings in the sharing of food.

CLEANLINESS AND CLOTHING

Nyansongo individuals, in general, bathe infrequently, and children are no exception. Mothers take little interest in their cleanliness, although they encourage them to bathe at the stream with their siblings and friends of the same sex. Boys who are herding cattle sometimes take off their shirts and splash around in the water; girls, copying their nubile sisters, are probably somewhat more systematic about washing but do not appear to be very clean until initiated. (It should be noted that before the recent introduction of soap, smearing with clarified butter rather than washing was customary cleansing practice and was performed mainly for special occasions.) Hands are invariably rinsed in water before eating, the basin of water being passed from one person to another, and food is rinsed from the hands after eating, passing the same basin around again. Mothers regularly shave the heads of both boys and girls and inspect their toes for chiggers, which they patiently remove.

Although cleanliness is not stressed, the child learns a set of attitudes about the body at an early age. By the age of 3 the child knows the names of all parts of his body, and he has also learned that his parents give different names for some of these than his siblings of the same sex. The parents call the penis a "tail" when they have to refer to it, while other children use coarser expressions. When he is 3 and 4 years old, the child's naive use of obscenity, which he has learned from older siblings, provokes mirth and embarrassment in parents, and he is punished for it and warned against it. By the age of 5, most Nyansongo children have an extensive obscene vocabulary and a euphemistic one, and they have learned that only the latter may be used in the presence of adults. Masturbation is wholeheartedly disapproved of by parents, and children are beaten for it. It is extremely rare even in young children. Both boys and girls learn to conceal their defecation and urination by doing it in the privacy of the bush, and it is rare to see even a 3-year-old eliminating.

With respect to dress, modesty is more stressed for girls than for boys. In some families girls as old as 5 may be seen early in the morning playing outside the house naked, except for a string of beads around the abdomen, while in others one never sees girls unclad from the age of one. This variation bears no apparent relationship to the wealth or cultural conservatism of the family. Girls of 6 and older are never to be seen without a dress or some garment which, no matter how tattered, covers them from knee to navel and usually to neck as well. From their fourth year onward they are taught to sit with their legs together and skirts down. Even if a girl goes naked on some mornings and is seen that way by visitors, when she is wearing a dress and sitting so as to expose her genitals, her mother or father will sharply order her to "sit well." Boys, on the other hand, may wear clothes which do not cover their genitals until initiation, that is, until ten or twelve. They usually wear pullover shirts with long tails that reach to mid-thigh. When they sit down, however, their genitals are usually exposed and they are not instructed to sit modestly, since the uncircumcised penis is considered immature and asexual. Beads are not worn by boys. For both boys and girls, dressing involves putting a garment over the head and slipping arms and head into the appropriate openings. Small children are dressed by their mothers, who eventually teach them to dress themselves at ages ranging from 2 to 5. More than half of the mothers interviewed said they began expecting their children to dress themselves without help at 3 or 4 years of age, but many of the others put it off until 5. Since small children often go naked in the cold of the morning and since their clothes are scanty and lightweight, it is possible that unhealthy exposure to the elements occurs, especially on chilly days during the rains.

RELATIONSHIP TO MOTHER

A Nyansongo mother is responsible for the care and training of all her uninitiated children. They live in her house, are fed by her, and look to her for support and protection. If they become seriously ill, she may be held accountable. If her child gets into mischief at another homestead, she must face the irate adults of that homestead. If one of her children continually misbehaves, she may be beaten by her husband for her failure in child training. The burden of this responsibility is even greater for widows and women whose husbands are working outside the district. With the formal responsibility goes a strong emotional attachment between mother and child, which is vigorously attested to by mothers and children, although it is often not a conspicious feature of their observable interaction. The worst insults used among uncircumcised boys are those which derogate another's mother, and the son's defense of his mother's reputation is paralleled by a mother's passionate and partisan attempts to protect her offspring from the ill will of others both inside and outside the homestead.

Despite the almost solitary responsibility of the mother for her children and the striking solidarity of the mother-child unit against outsiders, Nyansongo mothers are overburdened with an agricultural and domestic work load which limits the attention they can pay to their weaned children. In consequence, they delegate a good deal of caretaking and training to older children in the homestead, and they reduce their maternal role to what they consider its bare essentials. These include providing food for the child whenever he wants it, seeking cure for his illness and redress when he is harmed by others, and correcting his misbehavior when it is brought to her attention. Her responsibilities in regard to food production and infant care make it impossible for her to give continuous succor and support to the uninitiated boys and girls, and she becomes impatient with them if they repeatedly interfere with her work, make trivial or unnecessary demands of her, or are capricious and difficult to satisfy. Most Nyansongo mothers will use any device they deem effective to stop the crying of a child so that they can switch their attention to something else. On the other hand, since this lack of attention is more often dictated by necessity than by principle, the warmer mothers respond with great indulgence to the child's demands when they have time, are in a good mood, or when it is the last child and there is no infant to care for. This results in inconsistent nurturance of the child. Another important consequence of the mother's heavy work load is that she trains the children to share it with her as soon as they are able, emphasizing responsibility and obedience training. Thus the children learn to help their mothers as well as to avoid making too many demands of them. In the remainder of this section, the patterns of mother-child interaction are described in greater detail.

With the exception of the older uncircumcised boys and those who go to school, most children spend at least half of the day within shouting distance of the mother. Although she does agricultural work, some of the fields are near the homestead, and cultivation is seasonal, reaching low points during the July–August ripening time, and the November–December postharvest interval. During these times, and for parts of days in working seasons too, the mother is around the house, spreading grain to dry, grinding it, milking the cows, mending clothes, brewing beer, entertaining visitors. On the other hand, due weight must be given to her by no means infrequent absences from the homestead, absences occasioned by duties other than work in the fields: taking corn to the power mill, visiting her kin, taking crops to sell at the market, gathering firewood in the late afternoon, and fetching water from the stream at other times of the day.

When the mother is at the house, her interaction with the children is limited because of her involvement in domestic chores and the needs of the infant. Ordering the children to perform errands, reminding them of their regularly assigned tasks, and scolding or punishing them when they do something wrong or dangerous—these comprise a large proportion of the content of mother-child interaction. The child can bring himself to the mother's attention by doing something "bad" (or failing to do what he has been told) or by going to her for help. When he asks for food, the mother is more likely to comply than for any other kind of request. Of 24 mothers who were asked what they did when their child between 3 and 6 years old asked for help, 14—interpreting the "help" primarily as food—said they always give him what he wants. When they are busy doing something else, however, only 7 indicated they provide immediate help, 10 reported refusing immediate help, telling the child to wait till mother is finished, telling him to help himself, or beating him for being so demanding, and 7 said they stop work right away *only* if the request were for food. If the child is thirsty, he is told to get water himself from a pot in the house, but food must be cooked for him by his mother.

Perfunctory or punitive responses by mothers to childhood succorance are elicited by other kinds of requests. For example, some of the mothers questioned about what they do when their children fall down and hurt themselves said they blow on the wound, pat it, or hold the child and say, "Oh, I'm sorry you've hurt yourself. Don't cry; you'll be better." But half of the total sample reported saying, "Don't cry; it's your own fault. No one has hurt you," without offering any other comfort. The aim is always to stop the child's crying quickly, and when he has learned to bear small hurts stoically, the mother pays no attention to them. A child of 3 to 6 years of age who attempts to have his mother dress him when she knows he can do it himself is unlikely to be successful. Twelve of the 24 mothers said they punish for such a request, with caning the most frequent method used, while 8 reported letting the child go naked or telling him to do it himself. Of the rest, only 1 definitely stated she complies with such requests, and 3 said they vacillate between refusal and compliance according to their moods. A typical sequence begins with the mother of a child who has recently learned to dress himself yielding to his request but warning him that *he* must do it in the future. If he asks her to dress him again, she becomes angry and canes him. What angers a Nyansongo mother the most is a child who cries "for nothing" or who goes on crying after attempts have been made to comfort him. All mothers reported caning their children for such behavior. Usually the mother asks him what the matter is or if he wants food, and if he does not reply, or refuses food but continues crying, she beats him severely. Nyansongo mothers have little patience with children who make excessive demands for attention and support.

One kind of plea for help which does win the mother's attention is that of a child who has been hurt by another child. Nyansongo mothers investigate such situations and try to achieve redress for their own children if they feel it is deserved. As indicated above, the mother feels that if the child hurts himself, little can be done, but if someone attacked him, she can take action by scolding the attacker or telling his mother. The underlying notion appears to be that it is more justifiable for a child to cry when he has been injured by someone else than when the cause is accidental or his own fault. That children are affected by this value judgment is demonstrated by the fact that they were observed to cry much louder and longer when injured by another in the presence of the mother than when there were no adults present. They have apparently learned that they can achieve retaliation through the mother if they make a fuss when she is there to witness it. This connection between succorance and aggression is consistent with the maternal attitude toward early sibling rivalry. As described in the last chapter, the mother considers the cries of the replaced child as hostility to the neonate and punishes accordingly because hostility to the neonate is disapproved. In later childhood, she tends to equate his succorant cries with justifiable hostility against an unprovoked aggressor, and she is willing to help him by obtaining redress.

The Nyansongo mother discourages what she considers overdependence, but she does not put her children on their own or expect them to be intrepid and fearless. On the contrary, children spend their days under a maternal injunction against going more than a short distance from the homestead except on errands, and at night they are not allowed out of the house. In fact, mothers give instruction in the dangers of the night to instill what they consider a healthy fear of the dark. Half the mothers interviewed said they mentioned hyenas, although there are none in Nyansongo, in their warnings. One said, "I used to frighten Okemwa by saying, 'If you go out, a hyena will take you. I saw a hyena waiting for you by the fence.' I did that so he wouldn't go out at night." Another reported, concerning her daughter, "I'd warn her, 'Don't you go out at night; you'll be taken by hyenas.' I know hyenas don't take children but I said it to frighten her from going out at night." Most of the mothers who did not report warning of hyenas mentioned witches, "wild things," "something which will eat you up," "men and animals who will take you away," or unspecified dangers. Although they do not themselves believe most of the specific warnings, Nyansongo women are genuinely afraid of the dark and convinced that witches who might kill their children are outside at night.

The discouragement of daytime adventurousness serves Nyansongo mothers by keeping the children near the homestead for chores and errands; the fear of nocturnal dangers gives the mother a potent threat to use in curbing the child's misbehavior, particularly crying or crankiness at night. Thus, although she is not receptive to some of their demands for attention and support, the mother also limits her children's self-reliant behavior by restricting their freedom of movement and instilling in them fear of the external environment. Together with the importance of the mother in providing food and settling quarrels, this discouragement of self-reliance keeps the Nyansongo child dependent on his mother even when she pays relatively little attention to him.

Mothers do not play with their children, fondle them, or display affection for them openly. Even an indulgent mother, by Nyansongo standards, does not initiate nurturant interaction with her child but yields to many of his requests and demands. The child comes to his mother when he wants something, and she does not ordinarily proffer goods or emotional comfort unless she has been asked to do so. Praise is extremely rare, as mothers believe it can make even a good child "rude and disobedient." Over half the women who were asked what they do when a child is very obedient answered that they feel happy about it but neither say nor do anything to the child, though some indicated they praised him to others in his absence. Another one third of the mothers reported they give extra food or other material goods or that they promised the child such things. Only two out of 24 mothers said they praised their children for good behavior.

A child who is good can expect to have his requests for clothes and sweets complied with more than one who misbehaves, but the relationship is an indirect one in those families which have little cash to buy the articles regardless of how good the child is. In any event, even when the child is good and the family well off, he must ask or even beg for the desired thing. This is frequently successful.

The mother-child relationship is relatively informal, allowing the most relaxed interaction between persons of adjacent generations that can be found in the Nyansongo social system. This is especially so for the uninitiated children, who are allowed into the mother's cooking place, where she squats "immodestly" with her skirt pulled up onto her thighs, and who may make slightly obscene references within earshot of the mother and argue with her without being punished. She is distinctly more tolerant of childish deviations than the father. Even so, mothers expect considerable deference from their uninitiated children, and most of them do not tolerate overtly disrespectful or aggressive behavior. Nyansongo mothers overwhelmingly reported severe punishment, beating and depriving of food, as their response to being struck or insulted by a child, and some regarded it as inconceivable that their children would do such things. One woman said to her child while caning him for "abusing" her verbally, "I'm not your peer; you must respect me. If you don't respect me, you won't respect any elders." Others said they would refuse to cook for a child who had been disrespectful to them until he came back and apologized. In a few Nyansongo families, sons beat their mothers or cow them with threats of physical violence, but such boys are at least 10 years old and are recognized as behavior problems by the community at large.* More frequently, children respect the authority of their mothers and do not attempt to hurt them regardless of the provocation.

TECHNIQUES OF SOCIALIZATION

To train her children and control their behavior, the mother uses fear more frequently than reward. Although the child can no longer be frightened by domestic animals as in infancy, the mother inculcates other fears, mentioned above, of hyenas, witches, and vaguely defined creatures of the night. The small child who annoys his mother by crying at night is warned, "If you don't stop crying, I shall open the door and call a hyena to come and eat you!" or, "I'll throw you out in the dark and you'll be eaten by hyenas." Great effectiveness is claimed for this method of silencing a child. As he gets older, the child's general sensitivity to dire threats and warnings remains important as a behavior control, even though the content of the warnings becomes more realistic. The mother makes exaggerated threats about killing the child, tying him up in the house, and having his father deal unmercifully with him, resorting to actual punishment when these threats do not work.

The methods of punishment used by Nyansongo mothers are caning, i.e., beating on the legs and buttocks with a tall weed or thin branch, depriving of food, reprimanding, chasing from the house overnight without a blanket, withholding clothes, and assigning laborious chores. In terms of frequency, caning is the overwhelming choice for use with children aged 3 to 6. As one mother said, "If you want to teach a child anything, you must cane him." When a mother first sees her child doing something she disapproves of, she may curtly ask, "What are you doing?", tell him to stop, or threaten him with punishment. If this does not work or if the misdeed is one she feels strongly about, the mother canes the child and reprimands him simultaneously. In reprimanding, the mother often expresses the idea that the deviation is a foreshadowing of worse offenses and immoral character development, which only caning can prevent. One mother reported telling her 3-year-old son while beating him for masturbation, "If I don't cane you, you'll go on like this and might even do it in front of people." Disobedient

* These cases are discussed in chapter 16.

children are told, "If you don't obey me, since you are my child, you'll never obey anyone," and "You're falling into bad ways and won't be a good child." A mother beating her daughter for sex play said, "You're becoming a slut!" Another girl neglecting her chores was admonished᾿ with, "You'll probably elope * and leave your parents with nothing!" These pessimistic prognostications inform the child of the reason for the punishment; they also connect a trivial misdeed with an evil character trait or immoral type of person, tending to make the person rather than the act the primary locus of negative evaluation.

As the child becomes older, methods of punishment other than caning become more frequent. More than 85% of the mothers questioned mentioned caning as first in importance for children between 3 and 6 years old, but less than half of them said they used caning most often on children near the age of initiation. One reason for this is that the major alternative to caning—food deprivation—is considered too cruel for small children, who "lack the sense" to understand why they are being refused what their mothers always grant them. Another reason for less frequent caning of older children is that the behavior of the child himself may make it unnecessary or ineffective. If the child of 6 or older has learned to be "good," that is, obedient, then he can be corrected by the verbal warning or rebuke of his mother; she need no longer beat him to enforce compliance. If, on the other hand, his early training has not produced the desired results, the mother may give up trying to eliminate his deviations by caning. There is a widespread belief that effective training by physical punishment presupposes an appropriate response on the part of the child: "Caning is for a child who controls himself." As one mother said, "Some children are so bad that you can cane them until you are tired and they are still bad, and you leave them alone." Nyansongo parents disapprove of continuing the use of physical punishment on a child who does not respond to it: "After all, I don't want to kill him!" Furthermore, many a boy of 6 or older is able to run away from his mother when she attempts to cane him. Thus, if a mother concludes that caning does not reform her child or that she cannot catch him when he does something bad, she ordinarily resorts to excluding him from one or two meals. Should she become extremely angry, she might banish him from the house for the night. The father or adult brother will be called in to administer beatings for serious offenses. To summarize, in early childhood, caning by the mother is the most common type of punishment. As the child grows older, the mother resorts more frequently to food deprivation, banishment, and referral to father when punishment is

* That is, marry without payment of bridewealth.

required, or she uses verbal correction if the child is above-average in obedience. Except in unusual cases, however, caning is not completely eliminated from the mother-child relationship until initiation.

Several of the less common methods of punishment used in Nyansongo are quite severe. Children are sometimes chased out of the house at night, when it is chilly and frightening for them, and they must sleep without blankets in the children's house or in the house of a nearby relative. Similarly, a mother punishing her child in the early morning may withhold his clothes, forcing him to suffer the cold and shame of nakedness outside or remain in the house. A widow reported chastising her 6-year-old daughter as follows for sex play with little boys: "I snatched her dress and left her naked and chased her out of the house at night . . . letting her walk in the cold and cry behind the house. Then I let her in in the morning." A punitive measure often mentioned for an extremely delinquent child is to tie him to a post in the house for a few hours. Punishments of this sort, though not frequent in the life of any child, seem to have a strong impact, for they are vividly recalled in adulthood by the individuals who experienced them.

Nyansongo children over the age of 6 develop the capacity to turn banishment by the mother to their own advantage as a means of evading punishment, and their mothers do nothing to discourage it. For example, a girl who has failed to carry out an order may find that her mother orders her out of the house, implicitly refusing food and shelter. The girl goes to her grandmother, whose house is a few steps away in the same homestead, eats and sleeps with the old woman, and returns the next day to her mother, whose anger has abated and who forgives and forgets. When the mother has been seriously offended by the original misbehavior, that is, when it was actively disrespectful, she will require an apology, but she does not beat a child who has run away and returned, even though he has obviously not suffered. The older children sometimes anticipate this sequence by escaping to the house of a relative or friend in the neighborhood as soon as they see their mothers become angry enough to punish them, thereby managing to evade punishment altogether. The Gusii practice of extending hospitality without questions to any child of neighboring kinsman contrasts with the Kipsigis custom of refusing to feed neighbors' children at any time, on the grounds that they may be trying to escape parental food deprivation. The Gusii feeling is that the mother's desire to punish her child is a private matter between her and the child which need not be enforced by anyone else. The child learns that if he can succeed in avoiding his mother during the first flush of her anger over his deviation, he may comfortably escape punishment, particularly if he acts somewhat subdued and contrite on his return.

Children are aware that punishment is contingent on the mood of the mother. If she is irritable, she may punish for something she ignored on a different occasion. If she is in good spirits, her threats and warnings need not be taken seriously. She may tolerate a particular misdeed once or twice but not more, and her intent to punish, once aroused, can be softened by a show of remorse (some children reported pretending to cry in order to avert a beating) and dissipated over time if the child absents himself. Thus the child knows his mother's sympathies, moods, and inconsistencies and takes advantage of them to avoid punishment whenever possible. There is great variation in severity of discipline among Nyansongo mothers, but many expect their children to indulge in some defensive maneuvering—falsely denying, feigning remorse, running away—after wrongdoing, and they are willing to overlook it or be manipulated by it if the wrongdoing is not excessive.

RELATION TO SIBLINGS AND PEERS

The interaction of the Nyansongo child with other children takes place within conditions set for him by his mother. Mothers do not want their children to be social isolates; on the contrary, they see positive advantages for the learning of language and other desirable behavior in the small child's association with a group of the same or slightly older age. Nevertheless, they place numerous restrictions on the extent of this association, restrictions which are gradually relaxed as the child grows older. Two thirds of the mothers questioned did not permit their children to move outside the neighborhood of nearby homesteads before they were 6 years old. In many cases adjacent homesteads or the contiguous stream were the farthest points allowed. Others set limits which were almost as narrow. One women stated, "Once you let a child walk about freely, that means he is old enough to be circumcised." While this is an extreme statement, it does express a feeling common to Nyansongo mothers. They want the children to perform their chores and errands without distraction, and they also fear that in wandering beyond the neighbors with whom his parents are most friendly, the child may get into trouble for which the parents will be held responsible, or that he may be harmed by others. Two thirds of the women said they discouraged association with children who fight. For many it was most important to protect the child in this way from the aggression of other children, while some mothers were also concerned that their children would acquire bellicose habits. A few mentioned telling their children to avoid peers who use obscene language or steal. For various reasons, then, most mothers do restrict the movements and contacts of their small children, and this frequently results in such children associating almost exclusively with their siblings, half-siblings, and closely related patrilineal kin. Wider associations are looked upon as disruptive to the child's assigned work as well as possibly harmful to him.

Within the limits set by the mother, the place where the child spends most of his daytime depends a good deal on whether the family has cattle. When there is a herd of cattle in the family, the oldest uncircumcised boy is in charge of herding, and the younger children down to the age of 3 tag along with him in the pastures, which are contiguous to the residential area. When the family has no cattle, the children are expected to be at the mother's house unless authorized by the parents to leave it. At the house, the oldest uncircumcised girl is considered by the parents to be in charge of all the younger children and the safety of the house itself. If she is there, some of the others may wander off to adjacent homesteads and, if they are older than 6, even a mile or two to the market or stream, but the house must not be left unguarded for fear of theft, and the infant must not be left unattended by its caretaker.

The importance of cattle in determining where the children spend their time can be illustrated in the case of a family which had no herds at home before the eldest sister married. Prior to her marriage, the three youngest children were always at the mother's house under the supervision of the oldest uninitiated girl, and the son of 10 was either in the house or yard with them or off fishing with his friends. The arrival of 12 head of bridewealth cattle brought about a distinct shift in the locus of their daytime activities. The older boy, formerly footloose, was now constantly occupied with tending the herds in a nearby pasture where his younger siblings followed him, and he often had to exhort his sister to return to watch the unattended house.

The physical isolation of the homestead from others in the neighborhood is also a determinant of childhood social activity. In the above case, because the family had a large pasture of its own which bordered on unoccupied land, herding did not bring the children into contact with peers from other homesteads. Frequently, however, a pasture is shared by related families of two or three contiguous homesteads and becomes a meeting place for as many as seven children who herd their cattle together. Aside from such herding groups, in which no more than half of all the children participate, Nyansongo has no organized children's groups. Where the homestead is physically isolated from others in the community, the sibling group tends to be most important.

This narrow range of friendship and association, even for the boys who herd cattle, is reflected in their somewhat exclusive and suspicious attitude toward outsiders. Older children said they would not play with a strange child unless they knew who his father was, and some claimed they would not associate with any strange child but would tell him to go home even if he were friendly. The only uninitiated child who had friends outside the circle of nearby homesteads was also the only uncircumcised boy from Nyansongo attending school, and his friends were boys he had met in school.

At home and in the pastures, older children dominate younger ones. To some extent this is promulgated by parents, many of whom said they felt it important for one child to be in charge of the others and tell them what to do, and who select the oldest of a group of children for the position of leadership. As mentioned, the oldest uninitiated girl in the homestead is usually charged with responsibility for the children at home and the oldest uncircumcised boy for those herding cattle. Since the parents may hold the appointed leader accountable for misdemeanors by and harm befalling the younger children, he is highly motivated to keep them in line and boss them around, though he is not permitted to punish them. In herding groups consisting of children from several homesteads, the oldest dominates the others, ordering them about, occasionally beating them, taking whatever articles they own. This latter aspect is recognized in the proverb, "The small boy's stick belongs to the older (uncircumcised) boy." Whenever we gave something to a boy in a herding group, it was appropriated by the oldest one even if he did not want to use it for himself. Parents consider such behavior natural and even proper, but they do not accept the idea of the group or its leader dominating a boy so as to make him ignore or violate his parents' wishes. In fact, parents do not entirely recognize the existence of children's groups beyond those of siblings, and they try to maintain direct control over their children regardless of the amount of peer activity.

Adult supervision of children is impossible for much of the day, since adults are often too far away to keep an eye on the youngsters. Boundary hedges, corn fields, groves of trees, and various bushes act as barriers to communication between the women working in cultivated fields and the children at a homestead or between adults at the homestead and the boys herding in the pastures. These physical barriers, combined with the absence of adults from the neighborhood for at least part of the day, leave the children free of supervision for considerable amounts of time. On the other hand, this freedom may be unexpectedly terminated in several ways. Much of Nyansongo is a long hill sloping down to a stream, and standing on the hill one can inconspicuously watch activity at certain places above and below. Several fathers occasionally stand in front of their houses peering at the pastures below to observe the movements of their sons and livestock. Furthermore, winding paths to the stream traverse the pastures and connect the homesteads, and the very foliage which shields the children from the view of others can suddenly yield forth a visitor, a woman fetching water or an adult sibling returning to the homestead, who may scrutinize the child and report any mischief observed to his parents. Hence the children's freedom from adult supervision, though lengthy, is intermittent and precarious. In this respect the boys herding cattle have a distinct advantage over children restricted to the homestead, for the pasture offers more constant cover for activities of which parents disapprove.

ACTIVITIES OF CHILDREN'S GROUPS

What do Nyansongo children do when they are relatively unsupervised? This can be answered best by illustrations from two "groups" which were intensively observed for four months. The first is the largest herding group in Nyansongo, with a 10-year-old leader from one homestead, three brothers aged 3 to 7 from another, and another set of three brothers, the oldest aged 5, from a third homestead. The most permanent members of the group are the three oldest, who are responsible to their fathers for the care of the cattle, while the younger children spend much of their time at home rather than in the pasture. Herding together from about 8:30 A.M., the boys bring the cows back to their homesteads during the morning for milking and sometimes return again to have a meal at midday. Other times, mothers send food to them in the pastures, and the girl who brings it eats with them. At about 1:00 P.M. the boys take the cattle down to the stream for water, and they splash around beside the cattle, put rocks and mud together to block channels of the stream, and sometimes take off their shirts and swim. The 10-year-old leader, a boy noted for his disobedience and mischievousness, frequently directs the herding instead of participating in it himself. For example, when he is playing in the stream and sees the cattle going astray higher up on the hill, he will order one of the two other responsible boys to get them, and his order is usually obeyed. Herding is mainly a matter of moving the docile cows from place to place by beating their rumps with a stick. When they are grazing in a particular spot, there is little to do, and the boys turn their attention to other activities until someone notices that the cows are about to enter someone's garden, and then there is a rush to bring them back into place. The other activities away from the stream include climbing trees and trying to shoot birds with homemade slingshots, which all Nyansongo boys had in 1956–57, watching buses and cars on the road and discussing whose they are and what they look like, and, most commonly, fighting with each other. A fight is sometimes started when a younger boys insults an older one, saying *omoisia* (uncircumcised boy) or *ngoko* ("your mother," interpreted as meaning "your mother's vagina") when the older one pushes him or orders him to do something unnecessary. Other times the oldest boy jokingly insults a younger one in the same way or shoots a berry at him with his slingshot in order to provoke a tussle. Occasionally a younger boy cries when he is hurt in a fight but usually there is more bluffing, chasing, and grappling than exchanging of blows, and good humor prevails at the end. Fantasy play, almost nonexistent among Nyansongo children, was witnessed twice in this herding group—once when a 6-year-old boy fashioned a plow out of wood and hitched his younger brother to it and once when the 10-year-old leader built a "house" of reeds. These boys got into trouble over aggressive encounters with girls passing through the pasture. This was altogether the most lively group of children in Nyansongo and probably also the worst behaved by community standards.

A group of children which gathers in a different part of Nyansongo is much more amorphous and variable in its composition. Its core consists of the children and grandchildren of three widowed co-wives who live in a homestead cluster along with their married sons and the married sons of two other deceased co-wives. The group of children from this one homestead alone can amount to 10 or 12, with the most permanent members being 9-year-old female twins who were in charge of two head of cattle and their 6-year-old brother who eventually took over the cattle when they were initiated. They herded the cattle in a small, level pasture very near the houses of the homestead, with no obstruction between residence and pasture, and were joined at different times of day by several 5- and 6-year-old girls from the same homestead, carrying their infant charges, and some boys ranging in age from 2 to 5. Since the pasture is level and adjacent to the road, it is a gathering place for children, primarily girls, from one of the three Nyansongo neighborhoods. Few of the children who join the twins there are herding cattle themselves; they are on the way to or from the stream with pots, taking care of infants, or taking time off from agricultural work to join their friends. At times there may be no children from adjacent homesteads joining the core group; other times 15 children congregate near the road. Their interaction is much less lively and aggressive than that of the herding group described above. The girls cuddle, play with, and carry about some of the others' infant charges; they whisper secrets about one another and giggle; they watch and comment on activity on the road, particularly the buses and who is going into town; they rarely fight. The proximity of the homestead with some adults usually about, and the lack of a common group activity, seem to account for the relatively subdued behavior of this group. When many of the same girls were fetching water and washing clothes at a rather secluded spot along the stream, they were much more animated, pushing and shoving one another, criticizing and jokingly insulting each other, splashing water good-humoredly, and so on.

Among the children who rarely gather in sizable groups such as the two described above, and who associate mainly with siblings and one or two cousins, interaction tends to be even less animated. All the boys of about 6 or more had slingshots, but aggressive encounters are infrequent, and when they occur, they are taken more seriously and emotionally within the sibling group than the casual fights in the pasture in a less closely related herding group. Long periods of inactivity are interspersed between tasks ordered by parents. The amount and kind of activity, however, vary considerably from one isolated homestead group to another.

THE CONTROL OF AGGRESSION

Parental control, its implementation and evasion, is a factor of primary importance in the aggressive and sexual behavior patterns of Nyansongo children. The basic fact is that parents disapprove and discourage any display of overt aggression and sexual interest, and Nyansongo children learn, for the most part before they are 5 or 6, that they must not fight or indulge in sex play in the presence of adults. Any adult stops children he sees from doing such things, and, if a parent, he is likely to punish them. The following discussion takes up aggression first, and then sex.

Mothers play an active part in the resolution of aggressive encounters within children's groups. Over two thirds of the mothers said they take some action on discovering their children involved in a fight.

The actions reported include investigating the cause of the fight ("conducting a trial," as some of them say), telling the children not to fight, reporting to the mother of the attacker and demanding that he be punished, and beating her own child for his part in the fight. Typically the investigation comes first, with the mother questioning participants and eyewitnesses as to who provoked whom and how. Her next step depends both on her assignment of blame and on whose children are involved. When the children are all hers, she may cane an attacker who struck without being provoked, tell the victim that he got what he deserved, or cane both of them for their mutual responsibility in the matter. When her child is struck without adequate provocation by another's, she complains to his parents; if investigation reveals her child to be the unprovoked aggressor, she canes him on the spot. Mothers indicated that they have a concept of just retaliation by their virtual unanimity in stating they chastise their children, mostly by caning, for beating too severely a child whose insult was slight. The general picture is one of a mother who is willing to interfere in her child's quarrels and mete out justice *when* a fight is brought to her attention.

Nyansongo mothers want (1) to discourage aggressive habits in their children and (2) to protect them from the aggression of others. In order to achieve the first objective, they urge their children not to fight, warn them of the dangerous consequences, and cane them when they provoke fights. In reacting to an offense committed by her belligerent child, a mother makes explicit which forms of aggression she considers worse than others. The most frequent response of mothers to physical aggression against other children is caning, but to verbal abuse and insult it is reprimand, indicating that the former deviation is regarded as more serious. Attacking one's own siblings is not considered as bad as doing the same to outsiders; in fact one mother reported telling her son, "Don't beat strangers; beat your own brothers and sisters." Injuries resulting from fights between children of different homesteads can lead to litigation and payment of compensation, and parents are acutely aware of this. Often when a neighbor reports that his child has been beaten, the mother of the attacker canes her child and says, "Do you want us to have a court case?" It is worse for a child to pick on someone younger and smaller than himself than for him to pick on someone of his own age and size. Parents are often extremely angered by a beating rendered to a smaller child, and even when it is a sibling and justified as punishment, it is regarded as usurpation of a parental prerogative. Finally, a fight started by a boy against a girl is considered more serious than a same-sex encounter, partly because girls are regarded as weaker and partly because of the assumption that the boy had a sexual motive. Fights among girls, which appear to be rare, are thought to be less likely to result in injury because of the feminine lack of strength. Hence, while mothers disapprove of childhood aggression generally, they explicitly prefer verbal hostility to physical violence, fights with siblings to those with strangers, attacks on age-mates to attacks on younger children, and encounters with peers of the same sex to heterosexual conflict.

To protect their children from the attacks of others, and to prevent their participation in serious brawls, some Nyansongo mothers (though not a majority) actively encourage them to report to mother when struck by another child. Actually, most mothers in discussing such matters assume that the child will report without encouragement. Less than half as many women (one eighth of the total) encourage their children to fight back when hit, and even these were at pains to say that they tell the children to retaliate *next* time he is struck but not to go back and fight with the child who just beat him. They fear that in the latter case they would be accused by the other child's mother of inciting violence which might result in injury. This is a serious accusation between parents. It is clearly what one mother had in mind when she reported, "I never encourage Nyangau to fight back; I tell him whenever he is beaten to come to me and I'll report that child to his parents and ask them if they sent that boy to fight my son." Mothers do carry through on their promises to achieve retribution for their reporting children by complaining to the attacker's parents. On one occasion a woman from an adjacent clan came to the homestead of the mischievous herding group leader mentioned earlier; numerous relatives were visiting the boy's dying father. The woman, accompanied by her 9-year-old daughter, shouted angrily to all present that the 10-year-old boy had encouraged his younger ortho-cousin to beat her girl on the arm when she was on an errand. Several men at the homestead looked at the girl's arm, which had a small swelling. The woman shouted, "If I meet the child who did this I'll beat him even if his mother is present!" An old woman from nearby said, "It is terrible what they did. Those boys are wild and bad." Mother and daughter stormed off. The boy's father then told his adult son from his deathbed, "Don't try to beat him now because he might hide. Wait till he returns with the cattle." In this case the mother of the victim was particularly aroused because the injury, though slight, was visible and had been inflicted by boys of one clan on a girl of a different clan. Another common reaction to a child's complaint of being beaten by children outside his homestead is to advise him not to associate with those children any more.

Mothers do not try to fight every battle for their children. A child who complains to his mother of being insulted and verbally abused by peers may well be told to retaliate in kind, particularly if the children are the same age. More than one third of the mothers encourage verbal counterattack, apparently feeling that a child should return an insult but not a blow, and some of the others said they ignored the complaint or simply told the children to stop. Even apart from the differential reaction to physical and verbal aggression, there is the feeling of some mothers that the child's reporting of being attacked is itself aggressive, since it can lead to the accused attacker being punished by his parents, and should not be encouraged any more than is necessary. Such women share the more widespread attitude that if a fight is serious enough to result in a visible injury, then the victim will report to mother, while if it is not that serious, has not been witnessed by an adult, and was carried on among closely related same-sex age-mates, then it is probably not worth the difficulty of reconstructing from the contradictory fabrications of the participants. For this reason, most mothers close their eyes to the fighting that goes on in herding groups unless it is forcibly brought to their attention by accidental proximity, injury, or complaint by other parents. But they do not give their overt approval to aggressive activity.

THE CONTROL OF SEXUAL BEHAVIOR

The sex play of children elicits even greater disapproval than fighting from Nyansongo parents. More than three fourths of the mothers questioned said that they would cane their 3-year-old children on discovery of masturbation and older children on discovery of heterosexual play. The drastic punishment administered by one mother to her young daughter for sex play is described above; it is typical of the intense reactions reported by Nyansongo mothers to the manifest sexual behavior of their children. However, Nyansongo women are aware that there is secret heterosexual activity in the pastures; when they sing to the girls at their initiation, "You have been the wives of the uncircumcised boys," they are alluding to this activity. As one mother of a boy said concerning the possibility of his sexual relations with little girls, "If he does it secretly and no one knows, it doesn't matter, but if he is discovered doing it anyone may cane him and when he comes home, I scold him." Another mother stated concerning the same situation, "I would cane him very badly, thinking, 'After all, it is the natural thing to do but since I found them at it I must cane severely.' " Aside from accidental discovery, parents most frequently are informed of the heterosexual activities of their children when a girl has resisted the sexual advances of one or more herdboys who then proceeded to strike her or shoot at her with a slingshot. In such cases the girl reports to her mother and shows her marks of the scuffle, and the mother complains to the boy's parents, who scold and beat him. Nyansongans generally make the assumption that an aggressive act committed by a small boy against a girl is the result of a frustrated sexual attempt, and thus it is considered doubly bad when made public. When they are not made public—which means that no child has been hurt enough to complain to her parents—then such violations are part of the permissable private life of children which parents do not attempt to supervise.

RELATIONSHIP TO FATHER

Children do not have the intensive contact with their fathers that they do with their mothers. Of the 24 children whose mothers were interviewed, 11 have fathers who are alive and live at home all the time, 6 have widowed mothers (2 with recent leviratic husbands), and 7 have fathers who are alive but whose work takes them out of Nyansongo for extended periods of time. Thus about half of a sample of children could be characterized as having fathers absent or erratically present in the homestead. Even when the father is living at home he leaves the bulk of child care to his wife and older unmarried children. In the case of a widow, her oldest adult son tends to take on the disciplinary functions of the father with respect to younger children.

The Nyansongo father is viewed by his child as an awesome and frightening person, and with some justification. Fathers do not play with, fondle, or praise their children, and, unlike mothers, they do not feed them or comfort them when hurt. The patterns of deference to the father involved in eating and mealtime activity have been described earlier. In addition, and most importantly, fathers are more severe and inflexible disciplinarians than mothers. One of the most common of boyhood memories of Nyansongo men is being beaten by their fathers for neglecting the cattle. Fathers teach at least their oldest sons how to herd, and they later check up on their herding every now and then, telling them where to take the cattle and how. When a father hears his son has allowed the cows to eat crops in a neighbor's field, he is quick to cane and scold. For example, one father who had returned from employment to hear that his son was a neglectful herder was observed standing sternly with his son in the pasture, holding a stick with which to thrash the young boy for any signs of recalcitrance. Fathers employ physical punishment for other types of offenses as well and can also order the mother to deprive the child of food. Sometimes a mother who has been so ordered relents and lets the child have some food when he begs for it. She is often more lenient to the child secretly while the father demands punishment, and most Nyansongo children seemed to associate softheartedness and inconsistency with their mothers, punitiveness and supervision with their fathers. The mother, however, helps to build up the terrifying image of the father by warning and threatening the child that she will get his father to beat him for misbehavior. As boys get older and are less easily controlled by their mothers, paternal discipline becomes more important. Furthermore, children are warned not to injure or touch various objects around the house so as not to arouse paternal ire.

Unless he is a monagamist who remains constantly at home, the father does not always sleep with the mother of any particular child, and when he does sleep in the house, he and the wife wait until the children are asleep to have sexual relations. As children grow older, they are excluded from sleeping with the parents, and it is usually the father who takes the initiative on this score because of his sexual embarrassment. He excludes girls at an earlier age, mostly 5 to 6, then boys, who are told to sleep outside at 7 or 8. The girl goes to sleep with the mother's co-wife or, even more frequently, a grandmother. Boys are sometimes sent to the grandmother's also, but it is more customary for a children's house (*esaiga*) to be erected for them, where they can sleep with older brothers. Although the children's house is near that of the mother and there are older siblings present, many Nyansongo boys find sleeping there a very frightening experience at first. This is their initial experience sleeping apart from their mothers, and they are sometimes so overwhelmed by fear of animals and witches in the dark that they run crying back to the mother's house. It is notable that this initial period of sleeping out is required only when the father comes to sleep with the mother and is ordered by the father. One can guess that, especially for boys, who when they sleep out do not have mother surrogates, the shock and terror of the nighttime separation from the mother is associated with the father's coming there to sleep and may be viewed by them as a replacement of themselves by the father.

RELATIONSHIP TO OTHER ADULTS

The relation of the Nyansongo child to adults other than parents is for the most part explicitly patterned after the mother-child and father-child relationships, although less intense in form. Children are taught to respect all persons of the parental generation, and they may be chastised by such adults who catch them misbehaving. Adults are said to be more cautious nowadays about beating misbehaving children who are not their own because they fear litigation if the child is thought to be injured. The likelihood of a particular person administering a punishment any more severe than scolding is dependent on the friendliness of his relations with the child's parents. If two brothers are on extremely good terms, one will think nothing of punishing the other's children, but if they are distant and hostile, they are afraid that punishment of a child will be misconstrued and lead to legal action. So it is with co-wives, who discipline each other's children if they have a close relationship but keep hands off if they are not speaking, for fear of being accused of witchcraft should a beaten child fall ill. In any case, adults feel a minimal responsibility of reporting a child's observed misbehavior if serious to his parents. They nevertheless extend hospitality to children who are escaping parental discipline, as mentioned previously.

A major exception to the above picture of respect and parentlike relations with adults is the case of grandparents. They are much warmer and more jovial toward their grandchildren than other adults are, and children learn that they need not respect them in the ordinary sense. Grandparents initiate sexual joking with young children, and insults, including sexual abuse, flow back and forth between them in a manner which is almost as relaxed as that of agemates. A child must never strike his grandparent, however, and he tends to obey the older person's imperious commands despite the surface egalitarianism. The house of a resident grandmother within the homestead is a useful refuge for a child being disciplined and for girls whose fathers are sleeping in their mother's houses. Although grandparents rarely play a part in the punishment of children for important offenses, they were observed curtly ordering a grandchild to stop mischievous acts and even caning slightly once or twice.

RELATIONSHIP TO ANIMALS

Nyansongo children view animals more in terms of fear and aggression than as objects of nurturance and warmth. The fear of hyenas and wild animals inculcated by mothers has already been mentioned. In herding, boys sometimes beat the rump of a cow more than is necessary to make her move, and they also throw stones at cows to herd them from a distance. No particularly close relationship between children and cattle, sheep, goats, or even dogs and cats, was observed. Boys of about 4 and 5 occasionally beat dogs, particularly puppies, with sticks, much as they would an animal in herding, and the cries of the puppies elicit no negative reaction from adults, some of whom find it amusing.

TRAINING IN OBEDIENCE, RESPONSIBILITY AND SKILLS

The "good child" as viewed by Nyansongo parents is the obedient child who does what his parents tell him invariably and without question. Obedience rather than enterprise or initiative is considered to be the key to success in the contemporary setting, and parents state that the child selected to attend school (in those families which send any children to school) is the obedient one who will do what the teachers tell him and thereby make progress in school. Smartness or brightness by itself is not a highly valued characteristic, and the Nyansongo concept of intelligence includes respect for elders and filial piety as vital ingredients. An obedient child, according to Nyansongo thought, is also responsible, that is, he performs the tasks and chores regularly assigned to him by his parents with a minimum of supervision. Parents begin obedience and responsibility training very early, often as soon as a sibling is born. The child begins by carrying dishes of food from one house to another within the homestead. As time goes on, more and more errands of this kind are demanded of him. When the father wants to smoke a cigarette or the mother her pipe while sitting in the yard, any nearby child will be sent for a coal from the fireplace to ignite the tobacco. When visitors come, a small child is sent into the house for a stool. When a beer party is planned, children are sent to notify neighbors, and once it is underway they may be sent to other houses to borrow pots, kettles, and cups. An adult will never get something for himself if he can order a child to do it, even if the child is farther from the object than he himself is. Older siblings can also command the labor of the smaller children for their own purposes, and we have seen boys who were herding remain sheltered by a tree, building a fire to warm themselves, as they sent their little brothers shivering into the rain to collect twigs for the fire. Disobedient or dawdling children are very likely to be caned by their parents or older siblings.

The training of boys in herding by their fathers and older siblings has been described; it begins at an early age. Three-year-old girls are taught to carry small pans of water from the river to the house on their heads, and as they get older, they carry increasingly large pots on their heads with grass-ring supports. The female equivalent of the boy's punishment for neglecting cattle is the chastisement of the girl for dropping and breaking a pot. The mother is angered by such an occurrence and will cane a girl of 6 or older very severely for the carelessness which has cost the family a fairly expensive object. Girls of 7 and 8 are usually so apprehensive of maternal punishment that they cry after dropping a pot. One 9-year-old girl in Nyansongo broke a pot on her way to the river and sat down gazing into space with tear-filled eyes for 15 minutes before summoning the courage to inform her mother. Mothers claim they do not cane for such an offense if the girl is weeping on her return. The emotional reaction of the Nyansongo girl to her breaking a pot is much stronger than that of the boy who allows the cattle to damage crops, even though the latter is a worse offense. Girls are, in general, considered more responsible than boys, and informants offer as proof of this the observation that in families which have no young boys, girls herd cattle in a very conscientious manner, while boys are noted for recklessly running off to snare birds and fish. As mentioned, girls 5 and older often serve as baby tenders. If a girl were to leave the infant for any reason, she would face very harsh punishment by the mother; a beating for this offense was witnessed on one occasion. Chores are not so sex-typed for uncircumcised children that boys cannot be used to act as nurses for infants, and it is often done in families lacking small girls. When boys are nurses, they are required to be as responsible as girls in their care of the infant.

Both boys and girls as young as 3 years old have been observed helping their mothers hoe a field for a short period of time. Usually they spontaneously ask to be allowed to do it and appear to enjoy it very much. Girls show more initiative in this regard than boys, and two 6-year-old girls in Nyansongo cultivated their own plot of corn from hoeing to harvest without any prompting from parents. By the time they are 6 or 7 both boys and girls do a considerable amount of hoeing in previously cultivated fields. Girls go on to learn the weeding of eleusine, harvesting, and other of the painstaking agricultural chores which men rarely participate in. Girls are also taught to shuck corn, grind eleusine, and cook porridge by their mothers.

❦
❦
❦

Chapter 15

The Initiation of Girls

The initiation ceremonies for both sexes are among the most important events occurring in Nyansongo. They are organized on the basis of *risaga*, that is, by local community rather than by lineage. Mayer (1953a: 9–10), in his detailed ethnographic account of the ceremonies, states:

. . . the initiation cycle is woven into the life of the neighborhood in such a way that nobody remains altogether unconcerned. Children too young to be initiated themselves are occupied in carrying food or running errands; they are awakened at night to hear the bull-roarers and to listen to the dramatic dialogue which is shouted loudly for their especial benefit. The older boys and girls, who have already been initiated but are not yet married, play a very important part; indeed, apart from the actual operation and the adults' beer-parties, they organize and carry out most of the rites and celebrations themselves. Some are formally engaged as sponsors or as circumcision-leaders, and many others volunteer to escort the novices to and from circumcision and to assist at the performance of the mysteries. All young people, as long as they are not married, are free to attend the parties which take place . . . at the home of one novice after another. All of them may, if they wish, take advantage of the special sexual license associated with the seclusion both of boys and girls. The young married people are less closely involved, but maturity brings the right to be entertained at the beer-drinks with which all parents celebrate their respective children's entry into and emergence from seclusion. Among the old people, some will be needed to take part in the ritual, for instance, in blessing the novices at the end of seclusion and burning their bedding.

Both male and female initiations involve genital operations and both occur annually, just after the harvest, lasting from October to December. They are performed earlier in western Gusiiland, where the harvest is earlier, and generally sweep through Gusii country in a west-to-east direction. Female initiation precedes male initiation by a few weeks in each community and is more elaborate ceremonially. The words for the genital operation (*ogoroka*) and the seclusion or novitiate (*obware*) are identical for boys and girls, and they are similar in format, although the content of the ceremonies and their consequences are quite distinct.

It is the girl herself who decides when she will undergo initiation. Unless she is at the maximum age for it, her parents will not press her to have it done in any particular year; they wait for her to show a desire for it spontaneously and without prompting. Most girls want to be initiated, not because the ceremonies themselves are attractive, but because they desire to leave the status of "little girl" (*egesagane*) and enter that of *enyaroka* (literally "a circumcised thing") or *omoiseke* (an unmarried girl). There are three components to the girl's conscious desire for initiation. The first is that she wants to put behind her the tasks and chores of childhood and assume those of an adult female. Acting as nurse for infants is almost always a responsibility of uninitiated girls, as few of the older ones want to be so house-bound, and their wishes in this regard are respected by their parents. In families lacking boys, girls often must herd cattle until their initiation, but are not allowed to do so afterward on the grounds that "it is for boys to do." The tasks they look forward to as initiated girls are proper women's work: hoeing, weeding, and harvesting of crops, grinding corn, cooking food, carrying water in large pots and pans on the head. None of these jobs is as confining as caring for infants and cattle, but, in addition, they are valued for their own sake as enjoyable and (relative to childhood chores) prestigeful feminine occupations. The second component involves the girl's wanting to avoid the aggressive encounters peculiar to childhood. Many girls state that they find being called "little girl" (*egesagane*) offensive, and they object to being fought and insulted by the younger children. Taking into account the Nyansongo equation of heterosexual aggression with sexuality, it is clear that implicit in such statements is a rejection of childhood sexuality. The girl wants to be the object of attention by circumcised boys, not by the lower-status rowdies of the pasture. As her aspirations for initiation increase, she rebuffs her former playmates' sexual advances, and they begin insulting her, shooting at her with slingshots, and so on. She assumes that initiation will terminate this annoyance, for she knows that parents have little tolerance for aggression directed against initiated girls by uncircumcised boys.

The third aspect of her desire for higher status is her fear of being left behind by her agemates. If she knows that the girls of her age in the neighborhood or community are planning to be initiated, she will ordinarily want to go with them, partly because their willingness allays her individual fears of the genital operation, partly because she wants to remain on an egalitarian basis with her friends. If they are all initiated in a particular year, and she is left behind, she will be excluded from social relations with them. Several girls said they did not want to be called "little girl" by their old friends, and they felt very strongly about it. One of them, an 8-year-old named Nyanchama whose mother refused to have her initiated because of the expense and disruption of the inadequately housed leviratic * homestead, experienced the abandonment which other girls fear. When her agemates from adjacent homesteads were being jubilantly led back to their houses from the clitoridectomy operation, she began crying. An unmarried girl involved in conducting the initiation took pity on her and said, "We'll take you tomorrow; we'll convince Mogaka (Nyanchama's leviratic father) that you ought to go." An older woman shouted, "Why aren't you circumcised when all your peers are?" The mother of one of the girls who had just had the operation performed, said, "If you come to abuse the other girls, you'll see what will happen!" Nyanchama sobbed bitterly at these unkind remarks, and during the next days starved herself in protest against the refusal by her parents.

In summary, three factors lie behind the Nyansongo girl's wish to be initiated: (1) her desire to graduate from childish and boyish chores to adult female ones, (2) her desire to avoid the sexual and aggressive molestations of uncircumcised boys, (3) her fear of being ostracized by her female agemates when they are initiated.

Regardless of whether or not they favor her initiation, the parents, particularly the mother, try to give the aspiring girl the impression that they consider her too young for it, that they cannot afford it, and that it would be too much trouble. In some families this attitude is sincere, but most frequently the parents want their discouragement to spur the girl on to proving herself ready for the important step. As the parents put it, they want to see evidence of *okongainia*, a verb which is variously translated "to be intelligent" and "to have sense." In the case of a girl, "having sense" means primarily being willing and able to do the work of an adult woman around the house and, to a lesser extent, in the fields. She should be able to grind a fine flour with the grinding stones and should perform these duties without having to be ordered

---

* A marital relationship between a widow and her deceased husband's brother or other kinsman. In this case the widow had moved to a small house at the brother's homestead, and there was no hut which could be used for seclusion.

and reminded by the mother. There is an assumption on the part of Nyansongo parents that any girl who has enough "sense" and serious-ness of purpose to do these things well will be able to undergo the painful operation of clitoridectomy without screaming or running away. A girl who runs away from the operation is terribly stigmatized as a coward (*enkuri*), and her social disgrace is compounded by the offense to the spirits which demands sacrificial propitiation. These consequences of her possible cowardice are what parents fear most, and their discouraging attitude is intended as a safeguard against her go-ing to initiation without the mature determination to carry her suc-cessfully through the painful experience. Observation and interviews of 8- and 9-year-old girls proved that the parents' ruse has considerable effect. A few weeks before initiation many of them said they wanted desperately to be initiated but were afraid their mothers would pre-vent them. In consequence, each girl began demonstrating her womanly competence. Some harvested whole fields by themselves; others spon-taneously ground flour, kept the house stocked with firewood, and carried water from the stream in the largest-size pans.

There was considerable variation in the motivation and performance of Nyansongo girls during the preinitiation period in 1956. Some of them had assumed adult domestic duties as much as a year before and made no special effort to prove themselves in the few weeks before initiation. A few were more afraid than desirous of initiation and did not accelerate their usually below-average attempts to perform woman's work. The majority wanted initiation badly, though they had some fears, and made heroic efforts to prove themselves capable. Right up to the day that initiation began, they had no idea whether or not they had convinced their parents that they had "sense," but they had become determined to join their agemates even in the face of parental op-position.

When communities to the west have begun female initiation, the mothers of the oldest of the uninitiated girls in the community let it be known on what day they are taking their girls to the home of the specialist who performs the clitoridectomy. It is not necessary for all girls who want to be initiated that year to have the operation per-formed on that day, but most will want to go along, with the oldest of their group leading the way. In Nyansongo, the girls of one of the three neighborhoods within the community did not undergo the oper-ation until more than a week after the others. Each girl whose close agemates are going will wake her mother at 5:00 A.M. and ask for the one or two shillings needed to pay the operator.* The mother typ-

---

* The operator charges according to the size of the girl; "bigger" girls are charged two shillings instead of one.

ically pinches the girl and tells her she is too small; this is to test her determination and courage. If the girl still insists on going, she leaves the house naked except for a cloth on her shoulders and accompanied by her mother. In the chilly dawn they meet the other girls with their mothers and proceed to the home of the operator, the women singing songs along the way. The operator is usually a middle-aged woman with a reputation for skill in clitoridectomy who lives within 2 or 3 miles of the community, though not necessarily in it.

In Nyansongo, the first and largest clitoridectomy ceremony took place not at the operator's home but at the homestead of twin girls who were being initiated. The initiation of twins was considered a rare and lucky event, and all the other girls wanted to have the operation at the home of the twins on the same day. The attraction of this event was so strong that even a girl not more than 7 years old managed to have it performed, and girls came from an adjacent clan. All in all, 13 girls had the operation that day at the home of the twins, with more than 50 women watching. Some of the girls ran ahead of their mothers and were gruffly greeted by middle-aged women who pulled the cloths off their shoulders and pushed them back, telling them they were too young: "Go herd cattle! Go home!" This was again testing to make sure the girls wanted to go through with it, and they did, demonstrating their determination by trying to push their way into the open place by the side of the homestead where the operation was being performed. A crowd of women surrounded a stone on which the girl to be operated on was seated. A woman squatting behind the girl supported her back on her knees and, with her arms thrust under the girl's arms, firmly held the girl's hands over her eyes. This grip served to prevent the girl from seeing what was going on and from moving her arms or the upper part of her body during the operation. The operator spread the girl's legs, put white flour on the genital area, and cut off the head of the clitoris with a sawing motion of her small knife. As soon as the piece of flesh had dropped to the ground, the crowd of women began trilling loudly, gaily screaming and shouting and, in some cases, dancing individually. The girl was then led over to the side of the house to squat, shivering under the eaves at the sides of the girls who had gone before her.

Most of the girls underwent the operation without mishap, but two of them gave more trouble than the rest. A girl from Nyansango refused to spread her legs and was subsequently slapped and cajoled into doing so by her mother and other women. She got up and ran away once before the operation was begun but was finally subdued and went through with it. The other girl, from a different clan and community, tried to get away before the operation, eventually escaping after it had been half performed. Although a sheep of redemption was not required of her, the stone was changed after her escape, indicating that her act had brought ritual impurity to the stone, which might have contaminated others. Both girls had histories of overdependence on their mothers and of crying easily when injured by playmates. In the case of the girl from Nyansongo, the rumor went around that her mother had been a coward at clitoridectomy and so naturally the daughter was too.

When all the girls have had the operation and the operator has been paid, they are led, walking stiffly with pain and covered only by cloth on their shoulders, back to the homes of their respective mothers. The women who lead them, including their mothers, begin the joyous obscenity and rowdiness which is expected of them on this day. In Nyansongo, the mother of the twin girls took off most of her clothing and danced and sang in front of her house. The 30 others from the community danced in a nearby pasture, arranging themselves in a circle and moving their hips to and fro. The words of all the songs were concerned with some aspect of coitus.

A week later, in a different Nyansongo neighborhood, the mood was even less restrained after the clitoridectomy ceremony. Bosibori, a middle-aged widow whose last daughter had just undergone the operation, led the expressive activity when the girls were being taken home. During the singing she and another woman of the same age put their arms around each other's waists and simulated sexual intercourse. In the atmosphere of hilarity, two young married women beat each other with sticks that are used to represent phalluses in the dancing. Jerking her abdomen against a road bank and shouting the obscene word for coitus each time, Bosibori noticed that the women were giving in to fatigue and cried, "I'll not give you food because I saw no one dancing with her skirt up like this." She hoisted her skirt up around her thighs and three other women followed her example. A young man from Nyansongo hurried by on the road as the women continued, and they intensified their hip movements for the benefit of a truckload of men going to the tea plantations. When her daughter collapsed momentarily by the road, Bosibori put her in the shade and resumed dancing. Some women told her to wipe the girl's blood from her hands but she jubilantly answered, "No, this is my own child," and smeared it on her own face. As the procession reached her house, Bosibori picked up a hide mat for her daughter to sit on in seclusion, but the mother first ran about with it in front of her as if it were a shield. Several women poised their sticks like spears and jabbed at the mat in mock combat. The songs included ones with the following words:

My brother-in-law (i.e., husband's brother), my brother-in-law,
Don't put me on the ground, don't put me on the ground.
You'd better have a mattress to put me on if you have sense.
Catch me at the waist and leave me before the cock crows.

A young man married a girl,
He put her on the bed,
Found she had no pubic hair,
He was very surprised, saying what kind of girl have I?
She may not bear children.

The use of obscene language, expressions of desire for prohibited sexual relationships, public mention of the sex act and its mechanics, immodest exposure and hip movements—all of these ordinarily shocking acts are expected and performed by women leading the novices back from the clitoridectomy operation. Although the performance is public, men try to avoid it so as not to suffer the inevitable embarrassment. Another notable aspect of the women's behavior is the playing of the male sex role: holding sticks which represent phalluses, singing songs of sex from the man's point of view, engaging in mock military combat, and even singing as one woman did:

I want to be a man, not a woman
I don't know what's happening at my (parents') home,
If I were a son I'd be at home and not here,
And I'd not have so much trouble.

Although the atmosphere is one of almost frantic hilarity, the women indulge in insulting, fighting, and destructive behavior which would ordinarily be taboo. For example, one middle-aged woman said to another, "You uncircumcised girl, what keeps you in the house when we take girls for circumcision? Is it your husband who keeps you?" The epithet and joking reference to marital coitus would be insulting in everyday social intercourse. Mention has been made of the young women beating each other with sticks; friendly tussling was also observed. Most striking is the wanton theft and destruction of crops. When the women accompanying her daughter arrived at Bosibori's house, they pulled up more than half of her potato garden, gorging themselves on raw potatoes and taking others with them. She became furious and tried to stop them, but they said, "This is a happy occasion; we can do anything, even annoy you." Three older women tied all the potato shoots into bundles and carried them away to plant in their own gardens. The group also trampled all the unripe maize in a small field near the house. At the houses of other women whose daughters had just been operated on, accompanying neighbors grabbed numerous ears of ripe corn from their fields. This license is expected, and even when carried to excess, as at Bosibori's, it is not recognized as ground for legal action or any other kind of retribution.

Each girl is left squatting behind a granary or some bushes near her mother's house, where she is hidden from sight until afternoon. The mother cooks food, and then, in midafternoon, the initiated women of the community gather to lead each girl into a month-long seclusion in her mother's house.

In bare outline,* the leading-in ceremony requires that several men, one of them the father or classificatory father of the novice, be present and sitting in the cattle pen, that the novice be led from her hiding place to the mother's house so surrounded by women that the men cannot see her, and that a ritual, in which a very old woman dances with a basket of flour while archaic songs are sung, be performed at the entrance as the girl is brought in. The theme song of female initiation, the *esimbore,* is sung, including the words:

> She is going to pass through the cattle-pen,
> She was a wife for uninitiated boys,
> Now she is a wife for initiated youths.

Informal behavior in the afternoon is at least as raucous and unrestrained as it was in the morning. If the girl's real father is present, the women jeer at him, emphasizing his exclusion from the house during his daughter's seclusion: "Where will you find a place for coitus now? Tonight you'll have to go behind the house, like chickens!" Sometimes they insult him with, "You're too old for coitus!" The men react with embarrassment and (sometimes mock) annoyance at this behavior, and occasionally they are goaded into returning an insult; in which case the women may saucily lift their skirts to embarrass them further. On one occasion a respected polygynist became so angered by the immodest conduct of a husky widow that he tried to whip her with a branch, but she tussled with him and threw him to the ground. Younger men were also observed wrestling good-humoredly with the insulting women. Many obscene songs are sung, some of them mentioning the name of the novice's father, as the women jerk their hips suggestively and move the phallic sticks, which most of them now hold, up and down or punch the fist into the palm of the other hand in a coital rhythm. At one leading-in the women staged a skit in which one of them played the father of the novice trying to enter the house and another took the part of his wife keeping him out during the seclusion

---

* Ceremonial details omitted in this account can be found in Mayer (1953: 27–29), although there is some subcultural variation between Nyansongo and the area he describes.

period. A moralistic song heard at one ceremony was, "A slut shouldn't sing and be happy about other women's children, lest the newly circumcised child follow the character of that slut."

When the girl has been led in and the dancing has subsided, her mother brings out food for the women to eat. They scold the hostess in abusive terms for the insufficiency of her food; at one house the women danced around holding the vegetables in their fingers and singing a demand for meat. They also pull grass out of the roof and steal corn from the fields. Among themselves, the women continue the insulting and aggressive behavior of the morning; two usually dignified matrons were observed in a rough-and-tumble wrestling bout which bordered on open hostility but ended in the humorous spirit in which it had begun. The leading-in ceremony and associated festivities are repeated at the house of each novice, in the order in which they had the clitoridectomy operation performed.

It is obvious from the above description that the girl herself recedes into the background while the women leading her use the joyous ceremonial occasion as an outlet for their usually concealed sexual interests and their antagonism toward men. The novice, preoccupied with her pain, dazed from several hours' hiding outside in the midday heat of the dry season, and overwhelmed by the noise and confusion of the female crowd, may be only dimly aware of what the women are singing and doing. In subsequent years, however, she will participate more consciously in the festivities which follow clitoridectomy and attain an awareness of its meaning for women which was not possible for her as a novice.

While the female novice is in seclusion in her mother's house, life goes on as usual in the house except that her father (or any circumcised male) may not enter and she herself may not leave (except for elimination). The exclusion of the father is mandatory even when it causes hardship, as was the case for one man both of whose wives had daughters initiated at the same time. Having just returned from employment and not realizing that both would be initiated, he did not begin to build a separate house in which he could sleep during the seclusion until it was rather late. Although the initiation of the daughters was postponed as long as it could be, when they went into seclusion, his new house had no roof on it. Nonetheless, he slept there throughout the month, being occasionally rained on during the night. The mother is not limited in her activities except that she must feed the novice a great deal of food, which is believed to aid in the healing of the clitoridectomy wound. The girl receives visitors, including her "instructor," and seems to have an enjoyable time. On several nights she is introduced by initiated girls to the "mysteries" (*chinyangi*) of female initiation. There is a ritual with obscure meaning (Mayer, 1953: 29–36), a great deal of singing (some of it involving archaic words not understood by contemporary Gusii), and provocatively sexual dancing in the nude at which it is said that boys sometimes peek. Any male caught watching might be severely beaten, however. A phallic object is constructed, which the novices are shown but which men cannot see without payment of a fee. On some nights when the older girls are sleeping with her, boys come and try to have intercourse with them (not with the novice) with varying degrees of success.* The theme of the nocturnal seclusion activities, ceremonial and otherwise, is primarily sexual and involves no direct instruction or hazing of the novice. At the end of the month a further ritual takes the girl out of seclusion, and she is smeared with butterfat and decorated with beads given by all the women of the neighborhood. She is said to be a "bride" (*omoriakari*), and she promenades around the marketplace and even in Kisii Town with other newly initiated girls similarly decorated. Both her parents and the newly initiated girl exult and rejoice in her new status.

After initiation, the life and behavior of the girl, although she is only about 9 years old, are conditioned by the prospect of her marriage. First of all, in contemporary circumstances, it is considered necessary for an initiated girl to be well dressed and neatly groomed. She may no longer wear the rags and tatters of childhood and is presented with one or more new store-bought dresses on her emergence from seclusion. At this time she begins to wear a head scarf and to spend long hours every day washing herself and her clothes. This emphasis on cleanliness is peculiar to girls between circumcision and marriage, for little girls and married women are not so attentive to their appearance. It is typical of girls of 9 and 10 years to go to the stream, ostensibly to fetch water, and to remain for several hours washing legs, arms, head, and garments with soap. Mothers fume at this behavior, especially when it delays cooking, but they appear to do little about it. In their concern about appearance, girls of the early postinitiation years, look for signs of physical maturity in themselves and each other; they can be overheard remarking on the first development of breasts in their friends. When they reach adolescence, they go to the market in groups, to be seen and eventually approached by boys and young men.

Another major consequence of initiation for a girl is the establishment of close relationships with the girls of the neighborhood or community who were initiated in the same year. After initiation, these girls tend to work together and to go to the market in a group. In the plant-

* This is "taking by stealth," described in Chapter 5.

ing season following their initiation, the girls of one of the neighborhoods in Nyansongo worked cooperatively in the fields every morning.
In fact, the name of the rotating women's cooperative work arrangement, *egesangio*, is closely related to the word which designates an age-
mate, *omogesangio*. The social ties based on the initiation experience
are relatively short-lived for girls, however, for the girls are too dispersed after marriage to continue them. Nevertheless, this initiation
work group, which lasts five or six years, is the basis for the sociability
of women when they are married and work in similar groups.

The problem of controlling the behavior of contemporary adolescent
girls is a difficult one for Nyansongo parents. The basis of the difficulty
is that the girl is oriented toward young men who give her gifts and
flatter her, expecting in return that she will yield sexually or even elope
with one of them. Parents, on the other hand, view an adolescent girl
as a family member who must of necessity leave home for marriage
and who can at least reimburse the parents who took the trouble to
raise her with a handsome bridewealth in cattle. What they fear most
is her running off with a reckless young man who has no cattle and,
secondly, her becoming pregnant or gaining a reputation as a "slut,"
both of which tend to make her undesirable as a wife. In the contemporary situation, the fear of a girl's eloping and leaving her parents
without the bridewealth cattle which are their traditional due is a real
one, for scarcity of cattle and high brideprice have made elopement
more frequent. But parents fear it so greatly that it colors all parent-
daughter relations. In an extreme case, a recently initiated 9-year-old
who failed to carry out an order of her mother was told by a neighbor
woman at the stream, "So you disobey your mother! You'll probably
run off and leave them without cattle!" Since the average marriage age
is approximately 15, the problem of elopement does not usually loom
very large until the girl is 12 or 13. At that time, the parents, especially
the father, experience ambivalent feelings toward the daughter. The
daughter is beginning to misbehave, showing a disregard of her
mother's orders, and staying away from home more than her parents
think she should. They want to punish her to arrest the kind of behavior which they believe will lead to wantonness and elopement, but
they fear the punishment itself will give her an added incentive to
leave home and injure her parents economically. This conflict is illustrated by the case of a Nyansongo father who proudly showed us a
phonograph and records he bought to entertain his 15-year-old daughter
at home so she would not have to go out to wild parties for such
amusements. When, several months later, she came home from market
after dark, the father became enraged, beat her severely (which fathers

are not supposed to do to initiated girls), and threatened to kill her. This is a common situation and often ends, as in the case cited, with the father hastily arranging her marriage to a man who is able and willing to pay cattle. The girl desires the romance and attention offered by young men but is afraid to commit herself sexually and emotionally because of the strong pressures and punishments of her father. In the most typical situation, the girl engages in sexual intercourse with different boys in great fear of discovery and pregnancy. All girls have sexual relations before marriage, although it is impossible to estimate the average frequency of such relations. If the father does not act fast enough in arranging a proper marriage to someone she will agree to live with, she may resolve the conflict by eloping with a man of her choice who pays no cattle to her father. Thus the Nyansongo girl, destined to leave home on marriage and never return to live there, becomes increasingly difficult for parents to control after initiation has brought her into the status of unmarried womanhood.

⚹
⚹
⚹

Chapter 16

The Initiation of Boys *

At the age of 8 or 9, when Nyansongo girls are being initiated into womanhood, the boys are still mere children who have not yet begun to aspire to adult status. Many of them are still timidly experimenting with the frightening prospect of sleeping outside the mother's house, and neither they nor their fathers and brothers will consider them even slightly ready to graduate from being "little boys" (*abaisia*, sing. *omoisia*) to "circumcised men" or "warriors" (*abamura*, sing. *omomura*).

The uncircumcised boy of 8 to 12 is usually the chief herder of cattle in the family and sometimes one of the major behavior problems as well. Unlike the girl, in the preinitiation period, he is not

* Many ceremonial details omitted in this account can be found in Mayer (1953a: 10–25).

being progressively introduced to the kind of life and tasks which he will have as an adult; rather, he has a distinct way of life that does not prepare him for the future. Three problems can develop during this period, involving (1) dependency on the mother, (2) irresponsibility, and (3) aggressive and sexual offenses.

Although he has begun sleeping outside his mother's house, the uncircumcised boy does not ordinarily do so every night but only when his father sleeps with his mother. For the sons of monogamists this may be every night, while for sons of polygymists, widows, and men who are working outside of the district, it may be less frequent. Even so, if there are circumcised brothers sleeping in their separate hut, the boy may be persuaded to sleep out with them rather than with his mother at every opportunity. Of the children studied, sons of widows were found sleeping outside the mother's house at·the latest age, 9 to 10, and one of them was reported to be so terrified by noises when he first tried it that he ran back crying to his mother during the night. Even when the boy is accustomed to sleeping away from the mother regularly, he is comforted by the knowledge that he can return to sleep occasionally if he wants to, and he may sit near the mother in her cooking place in the daytime and beg food, money, and permission to go places. Ordinarily the mother does little to discourage this; indeed, the boy of this age is clever at so manipulating his mother's behavior as to be rewarded for his dependence. It should be noted that this close relationship with the mother, particularly in the case of boys who do not have cattle to herd, may involve the boy's learning and practicing the most typically feminine chores, namely, grinding and cooking. All of this may be disturbing to the father, older brother, or whatever adult male is closest to the family. Even the possible sexual connotations of the boy's closeness to his mother are explicitly thought of. Nyansongo men claimed that in days of old when all of a boy's circumcised brothers were living away in cattle-villages, boys remained sexually innocent until a later age. The abolition of the cattle-villages and the presence of older boys at home are the cause, they claim, of the lowering of the age of circumcision because boys gain sexual sophistication at a younger age and have to be moved away from their mothers earlier. Whether or not this historical explanation is true, there can be no doubt that a father feels it is improper for a boy of 10, whom he knows to have some sexual knowledge, to be in such a close relationship with his mother, especially sleeping near her and sitting with her while she squats to cook in the house. In the context of the customary avoidance between mother and adult son, such dependency is viewed as fraught with sexual overtones. This is one reason why the father feels it would be good for the boy to be circumcised and initiated into adult status.

Another aspect of the boy's behavior which presents a problem to his parents is his irresponsibility. Although he is in charge of herding cattle, sheep, and goats, the boy's adventurous spirit takes him off hunting birds, fishing, and climbing trees with the other boys of the same age. Sometimes he leaves the cattle in the care of a younger brother who may not be capable of handling them; sometimes he goes off without making any provision for their care. Eventually, the cows do some damage; there is a law suit, and the boy is punished by his father, but usually he continues to find ways of evading his duty to the herds. Mothers find that boys of 10 to 12 disobey them, refuse to do assigned tasks, disappear when called for, go long distances from home and return erratically. In some of the most extreme cases, the boys take to stealing and become serious threats to neighborhood property. Some mothers say they will not beat boys of this age for fear of retaliation; food deprivation is typically used by mothers under such circumstances. But the father, if he is present, may be increasingly called on to discipline the boy, and this may be another reason for his wanting his son to be circumcised.

A third problem presented by an uncircumcised boy to his parents is his aggressive and sexual behavior. As the oldest sibling in his herding group, he is liable to bully and terrorize the younger ones to a point which parents consider reprehensible. An even more certain source of trouble is in his relations with younger girls who are already initiated. An initiated girl expects to be treated like a woman, and especially by uninitiated boys. But a 10-year-old boy is not prepared to accept a 9-year-old girl as worthy of respect. If the younger initiated girl is his sister, he may continue to order her about and to insult her as he did before. She will report this to the parents, who scold him for insulting his initiated sister. If the girl is not a sister, the boy may wish to engage in sex play with her as he did sporadically in the bush before her initiation. Now, however, she spurns him as a little boy, and he is so infuriated that he beats her or shoots at her with a slingshot. Girls invariably report such attacks, and their mothers come raging to the parents of the boy about it. The boy is often beaten and scolded by the father for such behavior, but it is considered more effective to get him circumcised so that he will not continue in an inferior status to younger girls. The boys who postponed their circumcision for several years were the greatest behavior problems for their parents; they were noticeably more disobedient, disrespectful, and overdependent on their mothers than other boys of the same age, and one of them was frequently accused by adults of sexual and aggressive offenses as well as theft of small articles.

The majority of boys are eager to be initiated and to become big men who can go away to work on the tea plantations or begin school. Like girls, they do not want to be left behind by their agemates when the latter are circumcised. Boys are more impressed by the awesome kinship duties of adulthood than girls; they seem to realize initiation means giving up dependence on mother and the relatively reckless, mischievous life of the pastures, and they are somewhat frightened. Furthermore, they know that male initiates are subjected to painful hazing as well as the circumcision operation, and this adds to their apprehensiveness. In spite of these fears, the average boy comes to want to be initiated spontaneously. He proves that he "has sense" not only by continuous sleeping in the children's house but also by wearing shorts to show he is developing a proper sense of modesty, and sometimes by doing agricultural work to indicate seriousness of purpose. The extent to which the father pretends to be skeptical about the boy's fitness in order to spur him on, or coaxes him toward initiation, depends on whether the boy is eager for it; in which case the father would be skeptical, or reluctant, requiring coaxing.

Before the day when the other boys in the community are going to the circumciser, a boy who wants to be initiated must choose his sponsor from among the initiated but unmarried boys who are of the same generation but who are not actual brothers. The sponsor is in charge of one or several novices during their seclusion and is assisted by a second boy whom he appoints. The novices shave their heads the day before and sleep at the hut of an initiated boy, not necessarily the sponsor or his assistant, who will escort them to the circumciser. Several escorts of the same age sleep there.

They rise in the middle of the night, for it is customary to reach the circumciser before dawn. The older boys may treat the novice roughly and, as a final test, try to frighten him with stories of the pain and how bad it is to be a coward. If the boy persists without crying, he bathes in the cold water of a stream and proceeds naked toward the house of the circumciser, about 2 miles from Nyansongo. The older boys buffet and shout at the novices along the way. Parents and classificatory fathers may not attend a boy's initiation, but brothers, classificatory brothers, and unrelated women who happen to be nearby may witness it. The boy is led to a special tree, and he stands back to the tree and arms above his head against the tree in readiness for the operation. In contrast to the girls, who are held tightly for their clitoridectomy, boys have to face circumcision on their feet and unsupported by another person. The circumciser kneels before the boy to perform the operation, and the older boys and men, standing behind the circumciser, aim spears and clubs at the boy's head, shouting continuously throughout the operation that he will be killed if he moves or shows signs of pain. A number of boys interviewed before circumcision expressed the conviction that they would be killed if they cried or tried to escape. The boys who were observed did not move during the operation; they looked up into space or at the men threatening them with spears with expressionless faces. After the quick operation, the boy is led away with his newly circumcised agemates, holding the penis (to prevent bleeding) with one hand and carrying a branch of a bush (*ekerundu*) used in many rituals as a fertility symbol.

In the afternoon the novices are led into seclusion by classificatory brothers who sing the *esimbore* for male initiation, with the words:

> Uncircumcised little boys have had pain!
> The circumciser has taken our penis;
> He has made you a spear and a hard shield.
> Fight the Kipsigis, fight the Kipsigis!
> Fight the Abatende,* fight the Abatende!
> Uncircumcised little boys have had pain!
> Mother's clitoris, mother's clitoris;
> Mother's pubic hair, mother's pubic hair.
> Uncircumcised little boys copulate with mother!
> Uncircumcised little boys have had pain.

The next to last line is interpreted as referring to the fact that before circumcision a boy's mother could touch his penis and sleep in the same house. The men singing this song are much more sedate than their counterparts in female initiation; they simply march slowly. Furthermore, unlike their female counterparts, the men affected by Christianity are embarrassed by the obscene lyrics and even sing bowdlerized versions on some occasions.

Mothers and other related women are unable to see the novices, for the latter are shielded by blankets and the crowd of singing men. The women express their jubilation by trilling and running about lifting their skirts immodestly. The whole affair is much less elaborate and lively than the girls' leading-in ceremony. Unlike girls, who are secluded in their mothers' houses, male novices are led into a newly built house which two or three of them will share during seclusion. There is considerable ritual paraphernalia associated with seclusion and the postcircumcision rites of initiation; bull-roarers, a fire that must not be allowed to go out, a particular kind of grass (*esuguta*)

* The Gusii word for the Kuria, the linguistically related people to the south of them.

stuck into the floor of the hut, which must not be allowed to wither. The mothers of the novices prepare food and send it to them, but no one else may eat the leftovers. Much food is needed for the novices "to heal their wounds." Boys of different seclusion huts meet each other outside, primarily for hunting. Until about 10 years ago, they would steal chickens from homesteads in the neighborhood without reproach, but now the fathers of novices who do so are faced with lawsuits and the practice has virtually died out. Married persons are barred from entering the seclusion hut, although others may come and go freely. In or out of the hut, however, the novice must not be seen by classificatory parents. He carries ashes with him outside to throw up as a warning when persons of the parents' generation inadvertently approach. There must be no fighting among the novices in the seclusion; a sacrifice would have to be performed if an outbreak occurred. The boy's life in seclusion is generally an enjoyable one, although he must carefully follow ritual prohibitions on dressing, bathing, and licking his lips as well as rules limiting social intercourse.

Hazing by other boys is an essential feature of the seclusion period, although it is not so severe as that found in many other East and South African societies. On the third night after circumcision, an indoor event known as *esubo* is conducted by the older boys. The novices are forced to eat a number of caustic and nauseating substances which the older boys tell them are delicious foods. Refusal to eat brings a beating. They are threatened with being eaten by an animal called *enyabububu* and are then shown that the noises attributed to the animal are made by a bull-roarer. Another bull-roarer is used outside the hut, with an announcement for the benefit of women and children that a great beast is swallowing the novices. Soon after, the older boys announce that the beast has vomited them up again. Toward the end of the night, the novices are beaten with nettles, made to pull up pegs near a fire with their teeth, and have their fingers twisted in long bows. Although formalized hazing occurs on this one night only, older boys can come and torment the novices throughout the initiation period. They may tell a novice to call for his mother, then beat him when he does so, telling him he's a man now and shouldn't need to call her. Sometimes they explicitly warn him against further familiarity with mother and stress the keeping of initiation rituals secret from women. Direct instruction rarely goes further than this, but there can be no doubt that the novice understands the moral lessons presented to him in this manner. All boys are aware of the respect and avoidance rules of adult status long before their initiation, and hazing helps to make them realize that the rules now apply to them.

Traditional ceremonies of emergence from seclusion involve several cycles of cleansing, blessing, anointing, and feasting. Most significant is the anointing of the boy's forehead with white earth by the father, who promises to "respect" the boy (i.e., to refrain from beating him) and commands the initiate to respect him in turn. Underlying this ritual is the assumption that, morally, the boy is now a finished product. Having learned the correct rules of behavior through the instruction and chastisement of his parents, he is thought to have no further need of the physical punishment used as a teaching method for children. In our opinion, the majority of Nyansongo boys accept the moral trust of their fathers with great solemnity. Fathers whose sons were particularly delinquent in their preinitiation behavior entertain the hope that initiation will have made them "sensible" enough to behave properly when put on their own, although there is some cynicism about this under contemporary circumstances.

The difference between boys' and girls' initiation sheds some light on the meaning and function of the male rite. The girl is accompanied to the genital operation by her mother and secluded in her mother's house; the boy is kept apart from his parents from the time of his leaving the house to be circumcised to his emergence several weeks later. The girl is held down during the genital operation, while the boy must stand to face the knife alone. The girl is confined to her mother's house during seclusion; the boy's seclusion in a special house involves going out to meet others for adventures in hunting and theft. In short, initiation encourages boys to be self-reliant, to do without parental support, to endure hardship unflinchingly, to cooperate with related agemates, and to venture forth with weapons. There is no such encouragement for girls, and this is congruent with the fact that the girl leaves her mother's house, not at initiation but at marriage, five or six years later, when she will be transformed from *enyaroka,* "a circumcised thing," to *omosubaati,* a young married woman. Initiation, however, is the only formal change of residence and status for the young male, who moves permanently from his mother's house to his own hut nearby and becomes *omomura,* "young man," which he continues to be after marriage, until his son is circumcised and he becomes *omogaka,* "elder." The emphasis in female initiation is on sexual stimulation, while in male initiation, sexual avoidance and respect for parents are stressed. In augmenting and manipulating her sexual attractiveness in postinitiation years, the girl becomes increasingly inconsiderate of her parents' wishes and commands. The initiated boy, however, is more respectful and obedient than he was as the footloose roughneck of the pastures. While they are not pleased with the girl's misbehavior during adolescence, parents do not consider it unnatural nor try to correct it more than is necessary to assure a legitimate marriage. "If she is bad, let her husband beat her," Nyansongo adults say of the unmarried girl, adding that once she is initiated it is not the place of the parents to punish her. The boy's behavior continues to be the concern of his parents, for he never moves away from their homestead, and physical punishment by the father is replaced by economic and supernatural sanctions after his initiation. The parental concept of initiation as a moral finishing school for boys and the lack of such a concept for girls thus appears to be related to the patrilocality of Nyansongo marriage.

After initiation, the boy assumes adult responsibilities. In the past he joined other warriors in the cattle-villages for defense of the herds and raiding other groups. Nowadays, after a few years he usually goes off to work on the tea plantations or in the city. When he is home he helps his father build houses and mend fences, and occasionally he supervises the herding of his uncircumcised brothers. Living in a separate hut within the homestead, he eats food cooked by his mother and brought to him by younger children. His relations with his mother become more distant although still affectionate. In the past it was mandatory for a boy to give his mother a goat before entering her house after initiation, but this custom is rarely practiced nowadays. In any event, he may not enter the cooking and sleeping area of her house and must avoid obscene language or any mention of sex in her presence. His sex life is now private as far as his parents are concerned. They make no mention of the girls he brings to his house, and no longer punish him for participation in sexual relations. His father expects great deference and obedience from him when he is home and financial contributions when he is working away from home.

While young initiated boys usually have stiff, formal relations with their parents, they tend to spend a good deal of their time with boys of the same age, usually from the same neighborhood or community. If they were circumcised in the same year, regardless of whether or not they shared a seclusion hut, such boys are *abakiare* (sing. *omokiare*), "pals," and this means they can hurl obscene insults at each other and deride each other without offense being taken. In a sense, the pal relationship is the mirror image of the father-son relationship; all conditions are reversed. Whereas the son is bound to his father by kinship and economic obligations, nothing ties him to his pal except shared ephemeral interests. While he must respect his father, he can jokingly but sharply insult his pal. Sex is a forbidden topic for discussion with the father but is foremost with the pal. Pals cooperate in seducing girls together in their youth, but the permanence of their relationship depends on their actual kin and residential relationships to each other. Regardless of whether the specific relationship is continued, the pattern of contrast between intergenerational relations and peer relations becomes solidified in the postinitiation period and perpetuated throughout the life of the Nyansongo male.

✻

✻

✻

Chapter 17

Child Rearing and Cultural Behavior in Nyansongo

Several general patterns of behavior which may be abstracted from the ethnographic study of Nyansongo are characteristic of its residents as a group, compared to cultural groups elsewhere in the world. The patterns that receive primary attention in this section are (1) authoritarianism, (2) emotional restraint, (3) interpersonal hostility, and (4) sex antagonism.

Authoritarianism

Apart from its use in the analysis of Western political movements, the concept of authoritarianism denotes a general tendency to structure relationships in terms of dominance and submission, unquestioning obedience to a strong leader, and dependence on powerful individuals for the attainment of goals such as law enforcement and social mobility. It is in this sense that Nyansongo can be characterized as authoritarian, for its people explicitly prefer social arrangements in which the aged, the wealthy, and the domineering exert a controlling influence over others. Other arrangements are viewed as potentially anarchic, for strong leaders are thought to be needed to keep in check the hostilities of social equals. This general tendency can be seen at several social levels: within the domestic group, it is evident in the relationship of the homestead head to his wives and sons; within the local community, in the orientation of its residents to the local elders; and at the level of the wider community, in the uses which Nyansongans make of the chief and the courts. Politically and spatially, Nyansongo is not a separate autonomous entity but a small segment of an area ruled by an extremely autocratic chief.

The authoritarianism of the Gusii of Nyansongo exhibits itself in three aspects of social behavior, dependence, aggression, and social control. Under dependence, we may include the feeling of Nyansongans that they need a strong leader; thus, they criticized the subheadman appointed by the chief for being weak and compared him unfavorably with his more forceful predecessor. They similarly criticized homestead heads who "let themselves be ruled by their wives and sons," men who were not able to exact obedience from homestead members. Until he dies, a homestead head is owed obedience, deference, and loyalty by his adult sons, regardless of how arbitrary he is. For the community as a whole, this is parallel to the respect and deference the younger generation must give its elders. Nyansongo does not contain any men of great enough wealth and influence to command obedience as well as respect from their neighbors, but the chief, who lives nearby, plays this role in their affairs.

The community is partly dependent on the chief for subsistence since he employs several of the men and allows a number of Nyansongo families to use his land. Over and above this economic relationship, however, Nyansongans go to him for help in dealing with the outside world, in deciding what to do about witchcraft substances they find, and in propping up paternal authority when it is flagging. There is no community mechanism for reaching decisions other than minor judicial ones; the standard procedure is to see the chief and ask him what to do. His advice is usually taken, and when it involves recourse to the organs of government outside the community, his influence with government officials is sought. Thus Nyansongans depend on the chief for making decisions that affect their lives in many ways.

This dependence on authority figures is evident in the achievement behavior of the people. The school situation is seen as an exercise in obedience to the teacher which may lead to academic success. Similarly, men with political aspirations deem it appropriate to become domestic servants to the chief. The emphasis in status mobility is on gaining the favor of important people by demonstrations of loyalty and obedience, rather than on perfecting skills or working hard by oneself.

Those individuals who are deferred to and obeyed tend to dominate their followers. Older men in the family demand benefits from their employed sons and grandsons. Teachers use their students as servants. The chief or his sons can order about men anywhere in his domain, regardless of whether they are employed by him. It is expected that powerful individuals will make use of their power over others for personal advantage, and this is not seen as undue exploitation.

A second major aspect of Nyansongo authoritarianism is evidenced in the resolution of interpersonal conflict. When an open dispute develops between neighbors within the community, they tend to go to the chief or the tribunal court to accuse one another of wrongdoing rather than settle the matter between themselves. This is the culturally approved way of handling aggression between persons of different homesteads, but the tendency to use it is so strong that litigation for assault is much more frequent than the actual occurrence of interpersonal violence.

The third aspect of authoritarianism in Nyansongo concerns social control. As noted before, it is considered right and proper to resort to constituted authority for the settling of open disputes, but the tendency to involve powerful individuals in the maintenance of law, order, and morality is more general than that. Persons of higher status and authority regard themselves and are regarded as the custodians of the moral lives of those beneath them; they have the responsibility to take firm action against offenders. The great amount of litigation over land, cattle, marriage, sex offenses, and assault can be seen as one demonstration of the pervasive tendency to bring matters of moral concern to constituted authorities for adjudication. Nyansongans are sensitive to the disapproval of powerful persons and tend to vary their behavior according to whether or not they are being supervised. This adjustment of behavior can be seen in the intergenerational taboos, which enjoin greater propriety in sexual talk when persons of the parental generation are present, and in the tendency to inhibit beer-party aggression in the presence of respected individuals. The clandestine nature of much sexual behavior is also indicative of this desire to keep immoral acts secret from elders.

The ancestor spirits are the only set of authority figures who cannot be evaded, although their concerns are limited. Consequently, persons in judicial authority, when faced with the usual denial of guilt by the accused, find it helpful to use ancestor-enforced oaths to obtain confessions and settle cases whose facts have been obscured by perjured testimony. In similar fashion, closely related elders of a dying man attempt to persuade him that his own misbehavior is to blame for his misfortune and that he must confess and make restitution to save himself from ancestor punishment or legitimate sorcery. In sum, the conformity of Nyansongans to their own moral ideals is contingent on the felt presence of supervision and threatened punishment by authority figures. They cannot be said to be unequivocally a peaceful, law-abiding people, for they do violate cultural rules in situations less subject to control by powerful persons.

Each powerful person is thus called on to act as a sanctioning agent, and it is essential for him to administer severe punishments to correct offenders' behavior and deter others from committing the same offenses. Husbands beat and humiliate their disobedient and quarreling wives. Fathers whose sons have appropriated cattle without permission have the sons incarcerated by the chief's police and burn down their huts. A father also has the power to curse, but this is used as a threat more than an actual practice. The chief takes strenuous measures with offenders, ranging from incarceration with forced labor, through beating, to exile from the district with a threat of being killed for noncompliance. Many of these severe sanctions are used only when the authority of the person in power is actually threatened; when someone under him commits an offense without threatening his authority, his verbal reprimand may suffice to induce feelings of shame and remorse. In the supernatural realm the ancestor spirits visit death, disease, and sterility on wrongdoers and on those who fail to pay them the proper respects. The severely enforced authority of homestead head, chief, and ancestor spirits is considered the morally correct alternative to an anticipated war of all against all.

Emotional Restraint

This term covers a number of related behavior patterns of Nyansongans, for example, their low degree of nurturance, sociability, and display of affection in situations that might, cross-culturally, seem to call for them. In part this is a function of their explicit system of prohibitions of physical and verbal intimacy with individuals of adjacent generations and, to a large extent, with individuals of the opposite sex. Shaking hands, which might be thought of as a greeting of slight intimacy, is allowed only between generational equals; greetings between members of adjacent generations involve no physical contact whatsoever. Similar restrictions apply to sleeping in the same house, bodily exposure and bodily functions, and discussion of topics related to sex and reproduction. A father may not even enter his son's house; an adult son may not go farther than the entrance foyer in his mother's house. In what appears to be a system of rules controlling sexual transgression, severe limits are put on opportunities for informal and intimate contact among persons, including members of the same family.

Even when social equals are in public contact, their interaction displays ambivalence or lack of interest. Boys circumcised in the same year, who regard each other as "pals," consider the joking abuse which they hurl at one another as the most important indication of intimacy. The interaction between grandparents and grandchildren can also be described as playfully abusive. Young men courting girls jokingly threaten them with forceful violation, and the girls roundly insult them in return. One never sees a boy and girl or a man and woman walking together or touching one another in a gentle way. Marital contacts, sexual and otherwise, are not expected to involve tenderness or physical demonstration of affection. Men and women spend their time apart and do not accompany one another even when they are going to the same place; a man does not discuss important matters with his wives. Among persons of the same age, generation, and sex, friendships and cooperative activities exist in a context of polite restraint.

Perhaps the most striking illustration of this lack of positive emotional display is in the extended family homestead, to which great loyalty is expected. The rules separating the generations and sexes in the family have already been mentioned. Members of the same generation often develop bitter hostilities, as discussed later. The emphasis within the family is on instrumental rather than expressive forms of nurturance. First and foremost is the preparation and serving of food by women to their husbands, children, and aged and infirm kinsmen. The financial aid and store-bought items that the men give to family members are also important nowadays. Other than this giving of material objects, to which great symbolic value is attached, there is little nurturance of a purely affectionate variety. The family atmosphere is not one of easygoing solidarity and mutual dependence. As the generational taboos divide the group horizontally, so polygyny divides it vertically into potentially or actually hostile mother-son units. Each unit has its own allotted fields, granaries and food supplies, dwellings, debts, and credits. Cooperation and sharing between these units can never be assumed, for their relationship may be formal or openly uncooperative. Spatial separation emphasizes their independence of one another. Altogether, the lines of cleavage and formal relationship within the extended family are so numerous that mutuality and emotional warmth are exceptional rather than expected.

In the community, members of the various dispersed homesteads interact with mixed feelings. Excessive sociability is thought to be dangerous because of witchcraft and sorcery, but people also talk of the dangers of ordinary beer-party sociability. The community as a whole never gathers, since it has no corporate function, and large gatherings are generally frowned upon and rarely occur. Nyansongans do not appear to have a great need to congregate and converse. They cherish the privacy of their secluded residences and prefer to meet others individually and in small groups. In this sense their dispersed settlement pattern, lacking a spatial focus for group activity, is consistent with their attitudes and values. Cooperation is carried on, but expressions of community solidarity are rare. In fact, disputes between homesteads tend to result in the blockage of paths, erection of fences, and the cessation of social intercourse—all legitimate means of avoiding overt conflict—that reduce further the solidarity of the community.

Each of these aspects of emotional restraint is more characteristic of men than women. Men are quieter and more withdrawn, less nurturant, and less sociable. Nyansongo men view their women as more emotionally volatile and expressive than themselves; this difference in behavior coincides with ethnographic observation and can be seen in the raucous initiation of girls (conducted by women) as compared to the sedate public ceremonials of boys' initiation (conducted by men), as well as in funerals at which women wail loudly and dance while men stand quietly by and exhibit few visible signs of grief. These are only the more obvious and institutionalized forms of sex-differentiated expressive behavior in Nyansongo.

Interpersonal Hostility

The people of Nyansongo cannot be described as violent or short-tempered, but they are preoccupied with the aggressive potentialities of their fellowmen, and they often indulge in verbal forms of hostility against neighbors and kinsmen. Three aspects of their interpersonal hostility stand out as distinct behavior patterns: suppression of overt aggression, paranoid tendencies, and the choice of peers as objects of hostility.

Nyansongans are rarely belligerent or conspicuously irritable when sober; especially among the men, it is unusual to hear a raised voice or see a breach of superficial good manners. Persons involved in a dispute avoid meeting to prevent a direct confrontation. Nevertheless, it is explicitly recognized that polite interaction frequently conceals bitter grudges, and these feelings come to the surface when men are intoxicated. Such concealment suggests a conscious inhibition of overtly aggressive or violent tendencies; in psychoanalytic terms, there is *suppression* rather than *repression* of aggression.

The paranoid tendencies of Nyansongans are manifest in many facets of their cultural behavior. The most frequent reaction to death, disease, sterility, or other misfortune is for the person afflicted to accuse someone else of witchcraft or sorcery. There is a general fear of being poisoned or bewitched while visiting one's neighbors and a fear of going out in the dark because of witches. People do not praise one another's property, prowess, or progeny for fear of being thought jealous and likely to bewitch the more fortunate person. They use protective "medicines" to vitiate the alleged witchcraft of their enemies, and hire professional sorcerers to kill the enemies by black magic. Backbiting is pervasive, and much of the gossip concerns the witchcraft or other nefarious practices of persons in the community. Land disputes give rise to litigations in which the first disputant to reach the chief or court lodges a complaint for an imaginary or slight assault. All these practices are frequent, so that the ethnographer has the impression of continual suspicion, gossip, accusation, counteraccusation, magical or legal retaliation, etc. The Nyansongan is distinctively paranoid in that he views his close interpersonal environment (including the family) as full of malevolent enemies, and he reacts to his own anger or frustration by accusing others of hostility and ill will.

It has already been indicated that Nyansongans choose as their objects of hostility persons within the community; this is especially true in allegations of witchcraft. However, it is more common for persons of the same generational and social status to accuse each other of hostility than for them to vent their spleen on persons of higher or lower rank. But intergenerational conflict is not entirely absent; in fact, between 1955 and 1957 one man assaulted his mother and another accused his of bewitching him. These events, however, are seen as deviant and unusual, whereas it is expected that peers will develop mutual hostility. For example, co-wives are expected to hate one another and to acquire suspicions of witchcraft if one is favored over the other. Disputes and accusations between brothers (and half-brothers) after the death of their father are also expected.

Both of these types of hostility develop in the polygynous family and are starting points for the normal process of lineage segmentation. The division of land and other property on dissolution of an extended family homestead can leave a neighborhood full of litigation and witchcraft suspicions for decades afterward. Aside from these fraternal quarrels, other neighborhood disputes usually involve approximate peers, partly because persons of higher status have power to hurt and are feared and partly because peers are inevitably viewed as competitors for scarce resources.

In sum, the people of Nyansongo suppress their desires to injure or kill their fellowmen in physical combat, but express hostile impulses by attributing malevolence to others, for which the witchcraft-sorcery complex and litigation are cultural media. Their preoccupation with the malevolence of others, especially persons of equivalent social status, acts as a divisive influence in community life.

Sex Antagonism

A striking feature of Nyansongo social life is that all its married women have come from outside the community to live with husbands already residing there. The women must come from clans other than those of their husbands; in the past these clans were intermittent enemies with whom feuds were carried on.

This pattern of marriage with its politico-military implications had several consequences in traditional Gusii society that are present in contemporary Nyansongo. One result is that it puts women at a disadvantage, since they are "enemies" living among their husbands' kin without the direct protection of their own families. Each bride is a newcomer to an unfamiliar community. This is one aspect of the subordinate female status against which Nyansongo women rebel ceremonially each year during the initiation of girls (see Chapter 15). Another apparent consequence of compulsory intermarriage between hostile clan groups is the expression of hostility in the marital relationship. The traditional marriage ceremony contains many conventional expressions of antagonism between the kin of bride and groom. This antagonism is carried into the sex act on the wedding night, with the bride refusing to cooperate to test her mate's potency and the husband attempting to break her will and force her to submit to a painful experience. Sexual intercourse under any circumstances is viewed as a contest in which the male gains satisfaction through coercion.

Nyansongo women are in general more inhibited sexually than their husbands, and this coincides with the double standard of sexual morality that they value. Over and above their marital fidelity, however, Nyansongo females exhibit a reluctance in sexual intercourse that gratifies their husbands and premarital lovers, who enjoy the idea of inflicting pain on a woman during coitus. This pattern of heterosexual behavior is legitimate and considered desirable but is difficult to distinguish behaviorally from criminal rape. Under modern conditions, when warriors no longer protect their sisters from violation, there are many opportunities for sexual contact; some of these lead to rape indictments. The Gusii as a whole have a high rate of rape, which can be seen as the consequence of interaction between the sadomasochistic pattern of normal heterosexuality and the sexual frustrations of unmarried men. Thus the people of Nyansongo, who pride themselves on the strength of their sexual morality, as indicated by the fidelity of their wives, their regulations concerning physical modesty, and their low rate of venereal disease, are troubled by sex crimes resulting from female inhibition and from the antagonism of the sexes.

THE CHILD-REARING ANTECEDENTS OF
CULTURAL BEHAVIOR IN NYANSONGO

What relation is there between the childhood experience of Nyansongans and their cultural behavior? We have summarized some distinctive features of Nyansongo cultural behavior under four headings: authoritarianism, emotional restraint, interpersonal hostility, and sex antagonism. It cannot be assumed that these patterns are caused simply by childhood experience, for to do so would be to overlook powerful economic and structural determinants of social behavior. Many behavior patterns of Nyansongans have obvious roots in aspects of their social structure such as dispersed settlement, polygyny, and interclan marriage. These and other demographic, economic, and political factors have a profound influence on individual motivation. As the previous chapters indicate, however, this influence is not postponed until adulthood; it shapes the behavior of the child through the conscious and unconscious impact of his immediate interpersonal environment. This chapter attempts to suggest which aspects of that immediate environment mold the motives, values, and habits of the Nyansongo child into the cultural forms described.

Authoritarianism

Certain aspects of childhood experience in Nyansongo favor the acquisition of the prevalent authoritarian orientations. One is the frequent use of physical punishment and fear control in discipline, which is exercised almost exclusively by parents rather than by siblings and peers. The child becomes fearful of persons in authority whose severe punishments are anticipated by him. Another relevant antecedent of authoritarianism is the emphasis on obedience and dominance training. From their earliest years Nyansongo children are expected to be obedient servants of their parents who take the view that one child should be in charge of the others when adults are not present. Thus there is early training in taking and giving commands, although the former is stressed. The inculcation of obedience to elders and authority figures is the primary aim of Nyansongo parents.

In the authoritarian resolution of interpersonal conflict there is continuity of training and behavior from early childhood to adult cultural behavior. Mothers respond readily to small children who claim their siblings have attacked them, and later on they encourage reporting of fights rather than direct retaliation by the child. Parents conduct hearings and punish offenders or complain to the parents of the offending children. As the child grows older, he is warned that if he fights with children of other families he may bring litigation on his own, and that if he is injured by another child he may actually be the subject of a legal complaint brought by his own family. All these early experiences lead directly to the tendency of Nyansongo adults to respond to interpersonal conflict by immediately lodging complaints of assault with constituted authorities.

The final aspect of training in authoritarian behavior that Nyansongo children receive involves the extended family homestead as a unit of social control and a model of interpersonal relations for the developing child. The father, who is often homestead head as well, has relatively little direct contact with the child and is presented by the mother and older siblings as a severe and frightening disciplinarian. Occasionally, he lives up to his reputation which makes the child eager to avoid further punishment by him. Good behavior, including obedience, task performance, and restraint of aggressive and sexual impulses (both physical and verbal) are required by parents and directly enforced by them when they are present. Parents are nonetheless tolerant of behavior that does not meet these standards when they are not present and when it has no serious repercussions in the community. Children acquire a relativistic attitude toward moral conduct: restrained and respectful behavior in the presence of elders, uninhibited behavior, especially in regard to sex and aggression, when only peers are present. This relativism is reinforced because other adults in the community, to whom the child may run when evading parental punishment, do not cooperate with parents in disciplining the child.

If the family can be viewed as providing role models from which the child acquires behavioral orientations toward authority, it is easy to see that the Nyansongo family favors a generation and sex hierarchy. The parent-child relationship, universally hierarchical, is emphatically so in Nyansongo. The interaction of the homestead head with his adult sons follows the same pattern, and the child usually has the opportunity to observe male adults of the younger generation responding deferentially to paternal dominance. The husband-wife relationship is also unequivocally ranked, with wives subordinate to their domineering and sometimes severely punitive husbands. Every child has many chances to learn the prerogatives of the older generation and of males simply by observation in his own family. Not every relationship in the family is ranked, however; co-wives and brothers are viewed as competitors of roughly equivalent status (with the partial exception of the oldest brother) whose relations are not governed by mutual recognition of seniority and submission. It seems likely that the child learns to distinguish these relatively uncontrolled peer relationships from the hierarchical relations ordained by generation and sex. In his own direct experience, it is notable that he is not urged to share food or other goods with his siblings; it is each for himself, with a dominant one emerging with the larger share. Thus the family authority system teaches by example that dominance-submission relations obtain between the generations and sexes but that peer relations within generations are governed not by the peers themselves but by other persons of superordinate status. The child's observational and imitative role-learning supplements the training in authoritarianism effected by instruction and discipline for obedience, dominance, aggression, and moral behavior.

Emotional Restraint

The Nyansongo child's training in emotional restraint begins in infancy when his mother is not demonstratively affectionate in handling him and does little to stimulate his positive response to other persons. Throughout childhood little overt affection is shown for the child apart from giving him food on demand, which may account for the great symbolic value adults place on food in dependent relationships.* In later childhood the most prominent aspect of this child-rearing pattern is the lack of praise for good behavior. Praise is thought to make children conceited and disobedient and is avoided; thus, the Nyansongo child is at no time conditioned to expect generally positive and rewarding responses from his most significant agents of socialization, even when conforming to their demands.

Children from the age of 5 on may have to care for their infant siblings or other relatives, and a certain amount of training in nurturance is deemed necessary at this time. The extent of this training should not be exaggerated, for child nurses often treat their infant charges with a good-humored roughness that goes beyond the bounds of considerate care for their well-being. Furthermore, that parents do not expect their children to be generally affectionate and considerate toward weaker creatures is shown by their toleration of and amusement at the beating of puppies and house cats by young children. Neverthe-

---

* The withholding of food by mothers as a disciplinary technique for older children is probably also an important antecedent of the adult emphasis on food.

less, the experience of caring for an infant may be a significantly formative one for a Nyansongo child, and may help to account for the greater warmth and expressiveness developed by females who have this experience so much more often than males. The weaning period and its immediate aftermath are critical for the development of emotional restraint. Once a new baby is born, the mother is completely intolerant of crying and displays of temper by her recently weaned child, since she interprets his pleas for maternal nurturance as a desire to kill his infant sibling. The severe punishment administered for crying at this stage has a general effect on the child's emotional expressiveness. He becomes much more quiet and passive and to a large extent remains so. The extraordinary lack of animation among Nyansongo children may be partly caused by maternal punishment for emotional display beginning at this point and continuing into later childhood. In this early period the child is also punished for verbal immodesty or other disruptive behavior in the presence of elders, which adds to the total inhibition of expressiveness.

The relatively low degree of sociability of adult Nyansongans has obvious roots in the parental treatment of sociable behavior in children. The movements of most children are restricted to their own homesteads or the immediately surrounding area, which makes it difficult for them to form wide-ranging peer relationships. The exclusive feelings fostered by this pattern of experience are reflected in statements in the child interviews to the effect that the respondent would play with a new child under no circumstances or only if he knew the father or was of the same clan. Furthermore, the prior claims of chores assigned by parents discourage the formation of stable, cohesive children's groups with their own activities. Mothers foster the brittleness of peer relations by urging their offspring to avoid those children with whom they have had quarrels. Thus, Nyansongo children do not usually have opportunities for extensive sociability behavior, nor are they taught that such behavior is valued. In this respect, however, girls differ somewhat from boys; those girls initiated together at about the age of 9 form a group for work and sociability which lasts until they marry in adolescence. This variation coincides with the variation in sociability between Nyansongo women and men.

In all the child-rearing patterns we have described the people of Nyansongo either fail to encourage or actively discourage the expression of positive, affectionate, or sociable impulses in their children. For many parents, this training is part of a larger pattern in which anything resembling aggression or disobedience, or thought to lead to these disvalued behaviors, is discouraged. Regardless of the conscious intent of parents, this type of child training prepares children for participation in a social system in which avoidance relationships are highly valued. It seems also to have the incidental effect of producing individuals who do not eagerly participate in solidary groups or actively seek aesthetic expression, but this conclusion is less certain. That adult women are more expressive and sociable than their male counterparts may be attributable to the apparently less severe punishment of females for aggression, their greater childhood experience as infant caretakers, and their greater participation in organized peer groups as children.

Interpersonal Hostility

The suppression of overt hostility among sober Nyansongo adults is a continuous outgrowth of their childhood experience, for parents strongly discourage fighting and punish it severely. On the other hand, it is possible for children to get away with a good deal of fighting and boisterousness when out of parental sight, which may account for the development of superficial inhibition of aggressive tendencies rather than a deep and generalized repression of them. In childhood, boys fight more and are punished for it more frequently; in adulthood, females are less restrained in their verbal hostility but are also less frequently involved in serious acts of violence, even when drunk. Thus it appears that the physical punishment Nyansongo males suffer for fighting in their early life makes them slow to exhibit their anger but does not eliminate and may even aggravate their deep-seated tendencies toward aggression. The relatively high homicide rate, the incidence of assault litigations, and the preoccupation with malevolent magic all support this conclusion.

Three different aspects of Nyansongo child rearing can be seen as contributing to the child's development of paranoid tendencies. One is the direct and explicit inculcation of fear of others, beginning in infancy with domestic animals labeled *"ekuku"* and extended to the father, imaginary hyenas, and witches, all of whom are presented as waiting to devour or injure the child for misbehavior or even for simply approaching them. In this connection it is important that parents never disillusion children about many of these malevolent beings, since they themselves are afraid of witches and the dark; thus their instruction has the persuasiveness that only a sincere believer can impart. To appreciate fully the impact of this training in fear of others, one must bear in mind their lack of training in positive response to others; fear and suspicion thus come to outweigh sociability, nurturance, and other dependent patterns of behavior.

Another contributory factor in the development of paranoid tendencies is parental encouragement of reporting attacks to adults. The child finds he can gain the nurturant attention of his mother (as well as retribution against the playmate with whom he may be quarreling) by accusing another child of assault. Thus the attribution of aggression to others is rewarded in childhood. The third child-rearing pattern that fosters paranoid behavior is the relatively indulgent treatment by parents of verbal hostility among children. It is as if parents were saying, "Don't fight, but say nasty things to one another if you like." This encourages the expression of aggression in verbal or symbolic form, as by blaming and gossiping about others.

The diverting of aggressive tendencies into relationships among peers rather than in superior-subordinate relations has antecedents in many aspects of childhood experience. One of these is the sternly enforced parental prohibition of disrespectful behavior toward adults, which is considered much worse than fighting among the children themselves. The child has many more opportunities to be openly angry and belligerent toward his peers than he does toward his elders, who are themselves enforcement agents for the taboo on aggression. Another factor is that the mother believes fighting between children of roughly the same age to be more excusable than either disrespect toward elders or taking advantage of smaller children, and she communicates this to her child. Finally, the patterns of competition and suppressed hostility among brothers, half-brothers, and co-wives are transmitted directly to the child by his participation in the homestead. Specifically, a mother who hates her co-wife is likely to train her offspring to share this feeling and extend it to the children of the co-wife. A male child is likely to grow up with profound suspicions about his half-brothers whose mother was hated by his own mother. Thus the social atmosphere of the homestead fosters a certain amount of hostility among peers.

Sex Antagonism

Sexual activity of any kind is actively discouraged by Nyansongo parents, who do not educate their children in matters of sex except to punish them for any signs of sexual interest. Nevertheless, children develop their own surreptitious sexual practices, especially the use of obscene vocabulary, when they can be assured of privacy. For many Nyansongo youngsters sex is like fighting, an illicit but sometimes possible form of activity.

The sex training of girls is earlier and more severe than that to which boys are subjected, mainly because of the emphasis on female modesty. Girls wear dresses covering the pubic region from a much earlier age, and they are instructed to sit with their thighs together and to pull their dresses down over their knees, so that by the time they are 6 years old most of them automatically conform. Boys, on the other hand, do not take measures to cover their genitals until they are at least 10, and they are not even casually told to be modest. Furthermore, girls are expelled from the room in which parents are sleeping at an earlier age than boys. If we couple this differential treatment with the fact that Nyansongo girls are more conscientious than pre-initiation boys about conforming to parental expectations (see later), we can see that by the prepubertal period females are likely to be much more inhibited sexually than their somewhat reckless male counterparts. Nevertheless, the herd boys of the pastures are determined to try out heterosexual play, and this brings them into conflict with the inhibited girls of the same age.

Nyansongo parents treat the heterosexual misdemeanors of boys as though sex is mainly a matter of fighting. To some extent this attitude is justified because the boy has usually taken the initiative and may have become aggressive when rebuffed by the girl, but their attitude appears also to result from the reluctance of adults to talk publicly about sexual matters. Thus, adults would rather pretend to be beating the boy for his aggression than for his sexual activity. This seems to have two consequences: it creates an association between sex and aggression for the boy, encouraging him to think of his sexual impulses as having aggressive concomitants, and it gives the girl a sense of power; she can retaliate against an annoying boy by complaining of his sexual attempts and thus subjecting him to severe punishment. In a sense both males and females never seem to outgrow this latency attitude in which sexual activity is not only illicit but aggressive. It is in light of this childhood background that one must view the battle of the sexes among Nyansongo adults.

Nyansongo children may also acquire the attitude of sex antagonism by imitation of parents and through their own relations with the parent of the opposite sex. Husband-wife relations lack tenderness and affection, and a young child is likely to hear his mother's cries and protests at least once during marital coitus. Some women pinch their small children to awaken them when they want to avoid coitus with their husbands; in such situations the child is likely to awaken to see his mother actively refusing the sexual advances of his father. It is likely that each child has the opportunity to observe the aggressive idiom of sexual intercourse between his parents; this exposure may make a deep impression on his own concept of what sexual behavior is and should be.

The tendency of girls to avoid sexual encounters may be reinforced by their experience with stern, aloof fathers with whom they must be modest and respectful. The experience of boys with their mothers is much warmer and more rewarding, which may help account for their tendency to approach rather than avoid persons of the opposite sex. Thus, if a child's orientation toward sexual behavior is influenced by his observations of relations between his mother and father and by the warmth of his relations with the cross-sex parent, he should acquire at an early age the attitudes of sex antagonism characteristic of Nyansongo. However, the early experience of the individuals is only one factor in the maintenance of sex antagonism and a high rate of rape; the adult role of women and the nature of intergroup marriage are also involved.

Sex Differences in Development

In this discussion of childhood experience and cultural behavior in Nyansongo, differences between males and females in emotional restraint, aggression, and sexual inhibition have often been mentioned. There is, indeed, in Nyansongo a general belief that girls develop differently and at a different rate than boys. In the years between weaning and initiation, girls are thought to develop more rapidly into mature and responsible individuals; they are more likely to be conscientious about the performance of important tasks, even when unsupervised. Boys are viewed as somewhat irresponsible and pleasure-seeking, more difficult for the mother to control. This view coincides to a large extent with ethnographic observation. The most important institutionalized form of recognition of the girl's quicker moral development is the earlier age of initiation for girls, currently at about 9 years old, whereas the age for boys can be as late as 12. Initiation for either sex is supposed to be contingent on demonstrated "sense," which conveys the idea of emotional and moral maturity. Girls show this maturity earlier than boys by performing a wide range of adult, womanly tasks by the age of 8, whereas boys may continue to be conspicuously juvenile until they are well past 10 years old.

Why do girls acquire the adult role behavior appropriate to their sex at an earlier age than boys? One reason seems to be the greater role of the mother in child rearing and the opportunities for girls to imitate the sex-appropriate behavior of their female parents throughout childhood. Boys do not have such extensive opportunities to observe and imitate their fathers, first because fathers play a very small role in child rearing and second because they are often working outside the district and come home only when on vacation. Furthermore, the work done by men at home consists of occasional strenuous tasks which small boys cannot do and of participation in community decision-making which is a prerogative of mature adulthood. Like girls, boys help their mothers in the fields and perform chores around the house; some of them even cook. But they know that they are not destined to do these things, that they will eventually become men and avoid the low-status work of women. Thus they evade responsible performance of tasks in general but are unable to do anything distinctively masculine. Since the girls eagerly imitate the domestic and agricultural work of their mothers at an early age, they are initiated early. However, the unavailability of adequate models for masculine role performance, the less routine nature of the male work role, and the close contact between the boy and his mother make it more difficult for a boy to become a man in his behavior and thus delay his initiation. The identification of girls with their mothers occurs early, is strongly reinforced, and continues into their adult life, but boys undergo a partial identification with their mothers which must be terminated at initiation to prepare them for the roles of adult males.

BIBLIOGRAPHY

LeVine, Robert A. Omoriori: smeller of witches. *Natural History,* 1958, **67**, 142–147.
————. An attempt to change the Gusii initiation cycle. *Man,* 1959a, **59**, 117–120.
————. Gusii sex offenses: a study in social control. *American Anthropologist,* 1959b, **61**, 965–990.
————. The internalization of political values in stateless societies. *Human Organization,* 1960a, **19**, 51–58.
————. The role of the family in authority systems: a cross-cultural application of stimulus-generalization theory. *Behavioral Science,* 1960b, **5**, 291–296.
————. Wealth and power in Gusiiland. In P. J. Bohannon (Ed.), *Markets in Africa.* Evanston, Ill.: Northwestern University Press, 1962a.
————. Witchcraft and co-wife proximity in southwestern Kenya. *Ethnology,* 1962b, **1**, 39–45.
————. Witchcraft and sorcery in a Gusii community. In J. Middleton and E. Winter (Eds.), *Witchcraft and Sorcery in East Africa.* London: Routledge, Kegan, Paul, in press.
————, and LeVine, Barbara B. Studying child rearing and personality development in an East African community. In *Anthropology in Africa Today,* Annals of the New York Academy of Sciences, 1962.
————, and Sangree, Walter H. The diffusion of age-group organization in East Africa: a controlled comparison. *Africa,* 1962, **32**, 97–110.

Mayer, Philip. The lineage principle in Gusii society. *International African Institute Memorandum 24*. London: Oxford University Press, 1949.

————. Privileged obstruction of marriage rites among the Gusii. *Africa*, 1950a, **20**, 113–125.

————. Gusii bridewealth, law and custom. *The Rhodes-Livingstone Papers Number 18*. London: Oxford University Press, 1950b.

————. The joking of pals in Gusii age-sets. *African Studies*, 1951a, **10**, 27–41.

————. Two studies in applied anthropology in Kenya. *Colonial Research Studies, No. 3*. London: His Majesty's Stationery Office, 1951b.

————. Gusii initiation ceremonies. *Journal of the Royal Anthropological Institute*, 1953a, **83**, 9–36.

————. Ekeigoroigoro: a Gusii rite of passage. *Man*, 1953b, **53**, 3–6.

————. Witches. Inaugural Lecture, Rhodes University, Grahamstown, South Africa, 1954.

Wagner, G. *The Bantu of North Kavirondo*. London: Oxford University Press, 1949.

Index